Male Idols and Branding in Chinese Luxury

Male Idols and Branding in Chinese Luxury

Fashion, Cosmetics, and Popular Culture

Amanda Sikarskie, with Peng Liu and Lan Lan

BLOOMSBURY VISUAL ARTS
LONDON • NEW YORK • OXFORD • NEW DELHI • SYDNEY

BLOOMSBURY VISUAL ARTS
Bloomsbury Publishing Plc
50 Bedford Square, London, WC1B 3DP, UK
1385 Broadway, New York, NY 10018, USA
29 Earlsfort Terrace, Dublin 2, Ireland

BLOOMSBURY, BLOOMSBURY VISUAL ARTS and the Diana logo are trademarks of Bloomsbury Publishing Plc

First published in Great Britain 2023

Cover design by Adriana Brioso
Cover image: Lian Jun, modeling clothing and accessories designed by Wang Jingwei, graduation show 2020, Beijing Institute of Fashion Technology. Photographed by 0204.

A catalogue record for this book is available from the British Library.

A catalog record for this book is available from the Library of Congress.

ISBN: HB: 978-1-3502-8331-2
ePDF: 978-1-3502-8333-6
eBook: 978-1-3502-8332-9

Typeset by RefineCatch Limited, Bungay, Suffolk
Printed and bound in Great Britain

Contents

Illustrations

Figures

Tables

Contributors

Lan Lan (兰岚) is Senior Lecturer at Beijing Institute of Fashion Technology (BIFT). She received her M.A. in womenswear design at London College of Fashion (LCF). Her research and writing are devoted to fashion study and visual study.

Peng Liu (刘鹏) is Assistant Professor at Macau University of Science and Technology (M.U.S.T.). He received his Ph.D. in visual art at Curtin University, Australia. His artworks have been exhibited internationally working within a wide range of mediums. Peng writes academic journals and book chapters in the fields of cultural studies, fashion studies, museum studies, and heritage architecture.

Amanda Sikarskie (宋漫漫) is a fashion scholar whose work explores the intersections of dress with popular culture and the digital. Since receiving her Ph.D. in 2011, she has published four books—*The Duprees of Spitalfields* (2015), *Textile Collections* (2016), *Digital Research Methods for Fashion Studies* (2020), and *Storytelling in Luxury Fashion* (2020)—and taught courses in fashion, art and art history, and Asian studies. Along with her colleagues Peng Liu and Lan Lan, she is in the beginning stages of a new book project on *yaoguai* and fashion, and she has been a frequent contributor to *Bloomsbury Fashion Business Cases*. She has also studied both Mandarin and Japanese (the latter as a FLAS Fellow). In her spare time, she loves music—everything from the Rolling Stones to C-Pop and K-Pop—thrifting, cats, squirrels, and flowers. Follow her on Instagram @ sikarska.

Some Notes on Pronunciation

Mandarin-language pronunciation is fairly intuitive for English speakers from the Pinyin, with perhaps the following exceptions:

- "A" is pronounced more like "ah" than a hard, short "a" sound. The surname "Wang" (王) should never be pronounced like the name of the 1980s New Wave band Wang Chung.
- When followed by a vowel, "c" is pronounced "ts." Many Chinese American families changed their spelling of the common surname "Cai" to "Tsai," such as celebrity chef Ming Tsai.
- "E" is often pronounced close to "uh," as in "feng shui" or the name "Jiang Cheng. (江澄)."
- "Q" is pronounced "ch."
- Using the example of "feng shui" again, "ui" is pronounced close to "way."
- "X" is pronounced "sh."
- The pronunciation of "Y" is quiet but not absent when followed by "i." For example, in the name Wang Yibo, the pronunciation is closer to "ee-bo" than "yee-bo."
- "Zh" is pronounced "j." For example, in the name Zhou Yixuan, "Zhou" sounds close to the Western given name "Joe."

Acknowledgments

First and foremost, thanks very much to Peng Liu and Lan Lan, contributing authors to this project, without whom this book most certainly could not have been written. Your Chinese perspective and survey-driven qualitative methods complimented so well my outsider perspective and popular cultural studies-driven research methods. You're both so generous, patient, polite, professional, and I cannot wait to work with you again on our next project.

A huge thank you to Wang Jingwei (王菁伟), designer of menswear appearing on this book's cover, for allowing us to use the image as the cover of our book. Thanks very much also to our cover model, Lian Jun (连骏), and photographer 0204, for their kind permission.

A big thank you also to YouTuber China Star News, who webcasts English-language news programs covering celebrities in China. Thanks also to the many netizens who post English subtitles for shows like *Day Day Up*, *Produce 101*, *Street Dance of China 3*, and *Happy Camp*. This book could not have been written without your work.

Thanks very much also to Getty Images for working with Bloomsbury to provide many of the illustrations in this book and to the Los Angeles County Museum of Art for donating the image of a peacock *buzi*, or civil service badge, to the public domain.

Finally, many thanks to Publisher Frances Arnold, who kindly told us that Bloomsbury doesn't just publish books, they publish authors, and to Assistant Editor Rebecca Hamilton, and everyone at Bloomsbury.

Amanda Sikarskie

Preface: "Are you that Unicorn?"

"Are you that unicorn?" asks the first chapter of *K-Pop Confidential*, a young adult novel by Stephan Lee. The story follows Candace Park, a fifteen-year-old Korean-American New Jersey native who "becomes the unicorn," that is, she is recruited by a Korean management company. Most of the novel focuses on the brutally rigorous nature of idol school training, the physical, mental, and aesthetic transformation the idol trainee must undergo prior to debuting with a K-Pop group. Lee is quick to point out to young readers that management companies do not groom idols for the love of the music, nor even for the money, but rather, for capital groups that "own hundreds of other companies: TV networks, grocery chains, film studies, home appliance lines, and all sorts of random industries, even missiles and tanks for the Korean military"; idols "are the image of the company, facing not just Korea, but the entire globe."[1] Brands are also searching for their own unicorn, a squeaky clean idol who will boost sales and never tarnish the image of the brand. To ensure that idols will never be threats to corporate or national interests, China has, effective March 1, 2021, imposed an industry-wide ban—the "Management Method of Professional Self-disciplining for Performers in the Performing Arts Industry"—on any performer in the entertainment industry writ large (including not only idols, but also acrobats and operatic singers) who engages in "obscene" activities, drunk driving, glorification of drug use, the promotion of national disunity, or the promotion of negativity generally, or even attempting to fool fans through lip-synching.[2]

Idols not only must dance and sing for multiple hours daily, flash their standard smile no matter what the conditions or the idol's emotional state, and hock their brand sponsors' products effectively, but they must also be pure. Pure in refraining from those activities mentioned in the "Management Method of Professional Self-disciplining for Performers in the Performing Arts Industry," but also sexually pure, at least in the public imagination. As a manager puts it to a trainee in Lee's novel, "In Korea, K-pop idols belong to the fans, to the country. Think of it as [if] you're in a serious, committed relationship with your fans. It's not like Hollywood, where dating around and bad behavior are celebrated. Imagine how ruinous it would be to your own reputation, to your group, and to the entire company, if you're caught cheating on the Korean people. You must always maintain a pure image."[3] "Unicorn" was not chosen by Lee haphazardly; the animal, with its radiant white coat—pure as the cold driven snow—and its shy, benign demeanor, perfectly represents this theme of idol purity. Unicorns are also imaginary, a fiction. Idol culture is its own mythology, operating as a fictional aspirational utopian reflection of what countries want their citizens to aspire towards. Even in a sexually-charged atmosphere as fans ogle them in revealing performance clothing, expect them to perform skinship with each other, and call male idols *xiao xian rou* (little fresh meats), the illusion of idol purity is paramount in this system. In Western folklore, unicorns are also exceedingly rare. "Are you that unicorn?" means "are you that one in a hundred million who has the beauty, stamina, and fortitude to become an idol?" Lee likely had another reason for his use of the word "unicorn"; it already exists in the K-Pop lexicon as the official name of the fan base of the real life K-Pop group UNIQ, the members of which will be introduced in the course of this book.

Could you be that unicorn, reader? Not becoming an idol, of course (that would be exceedingly foolish, not to mention impossible), but rather becoming a *fan*. I hope that in the course of gleaning from this book an understanding of the complex relationship of idols, fan-consumers, and luxury brands in China, readers will also develop a sense of empathy with these idols, visit a music streaming service platform, and actually listen to one of the songs or artists mentioned in this book. See what all the fuss is about, and perhaps even become a fan.

1

Introductions—Peacocks: Male Idols and Marketing in China[1]

Amanda Sikarskie[2]

In the 2019 esports/online gaming drama *The King's Avatar*, Ye Qui (played by popular actor Yang Yang) asks, "I've always wanted to know what an idol is. Is it a person, or a word, or a power?"[3] Idols are people, to be sure, and this book reads almost as a litany of names of Chinese male celebrities. But an idol is much more than a person. Using the traditional Western, Christian meaning of the word, an idol is an object of extreme devotion—such as a saint—or the tangible artistic representation of the object of worship. In the more modern, Pan-Asian sense of the word, an idol is an object of social devotion, worshipped by the adoring masses, and in China and Korea, is expected to be an object of social and moral uplift. Because of our worshipful devotion to these people, the contemporary idol is also a power . . . the power to influence taste and to sell. Fashion. Shoes. Cosmetics. Jewelry. Phones. Cars. Food and beverages. Any consumer good or service, really. This book is chiefly concerned with male idols for the power they possess to arouse the consumer appetite to buy.

Peacocks

Having purchased this book, you may be wondering, "Why the focus on male idols? What about female idols as brand ambassadors?" Using men to sell lipstick and eyeshadow palettes and eyebrow pencils is only just starting to become a regular practice in the West, but it is such a huge business in China, where makeup-loving men are somewhat affectionately known as *jingzhunan* or "luxury pig men" (see Figure 1.1). As Laurie Chen wrote in an article for the *South China Morning Post*, "Skincare-savvy jingzhunan, as they are known in Chinese, have gathered widespread attention for their intricate and time-consuming beauty regimes in a stark contrast to the traditional macho ideal. But the trend may be driven not just by fashion but by greater female empowerment and the increased attention to what women want."[4] The objectification of male idols under the female gaze (as *xiao xian rou*, or "little fresh meat") is also totally different in East and Southeast Asia compared to the West. Objectifying beautiful male youth in East Asia has a long history going back to homosocial courtly ideals in medieval China and Heian Japan,[5] and later the *wakashu* (a sort of third gender, teenage and early twenty-something boys dressed as women and available for relationships with adult men and women) of Edo period[6] Japan. The wakashu manner of dress was ended during the Meiji era, but eventually gave rise to the *bishounen*—or beautiful boys (who are nonetheless athletic or good at martial arts)—phenomenon in twentieth- and twenty-first-century manga and anime, which in turn inspired the androgynous look of male K-Pop idols in South Korea and *xiao xian rou* in China. And in the United Kingdom or United States, there has not been a controversy involving two male brand ambassadors anything like the AO3 incident, which will be discussed at length in this book. In short, the theoretical meat of this book is located around male idols. This focus on male idols is warranted as it is here that fashion and fashion marketing and retailing is most divergent from the West, even as these trends are emerging worldwide.

Male idols also uniquely play a more dominant role in fashion magazine storytelling and advertising, compared to their male celebrity counterparts in the West. Parsons Paris M.A. candidate Wang Jingxin, who interned at *L'Officiel China* in 2020, attributes this to the gendered nature of the idols' fanbase in relation to the typical fashion magazine consumer. During the question-and-answer portion of her master's thesis defense on "The Future of Fashion Magazines in China: From Print to Douyin," Wang replied to my question about *L'Officiel Homme* and working with male idols versus female idols at the magazine by revealing that, "When we had a male idol on the cover, like Wang Yibo, it sells out so quickly, like in twenty-four hours or forty-eight hours, but when we had female celebrities [like Angelababy, the *L'Officiel* cover model about whom she spoke in her defense presentation] not as much. I think it's because the male idol fanbase tends to be female [and thus more likely to buy fashion magazines] while the female idol fanbase is more male and does not want to buy, just wants to look [at the digital Douyin version] for free."[7] In China, male idols often simply sell more magazines faster than female idols, and this is fundamentally a matter of fandom.

"Peacock" in the West can take on a pejorative connotation, meaning a man who is vain and haughty. In China, however, the peacock is more serene in its

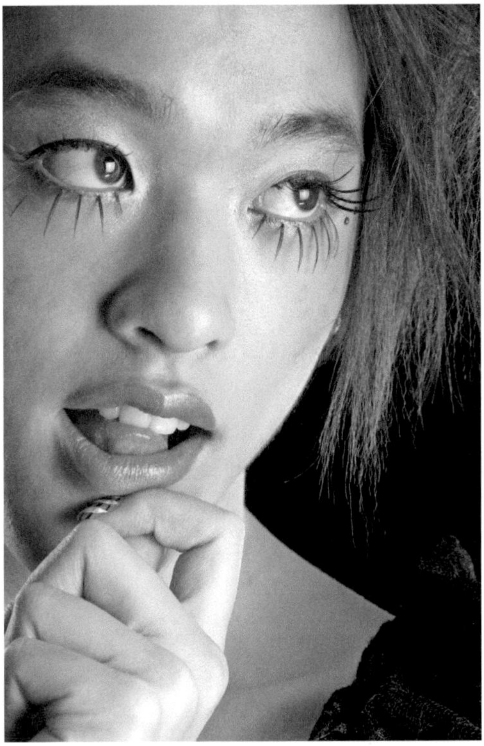

Figure 1.1 A Canadian teenager models the peacock makeup trend. Photo by Vala Grenier. IStockPhoto.com.

nobility. "One of China's oldest and most influential texts, the *I Ching*, or *Book of Changes*, describes the peacock as a cultured bird with nine virtues. It had a dignified appearance and a clear voice, walked with grace, and was punctual. Content and loyal to its fellows, the peacock was also restrained in its appetite, and capable of learning from its mistakes."[8] Idols, or pop stars, and peacocks (in Chinese folklore) have quite a bit in common. They must be physically beautiful, talented singers, and graceful dancers. Often getting their starts in boy bands before going on to solo projects, idols often display great loyalty to their former bandmates, as displayed by Wang Yibo to his UNIQ bandmates, inviting them on his variety show *Day Day Up* from time to time. And for career longevity, an idol must absolutely be able to learn from his mistakes, as Xiao Zhan (the subject of the case study by Peng Liu and Lan Lan) did when his career was threatened by online anti-fans in early 2020. This book considers male idols in China—such as Wang Yibo of UNIQ (b. 1997), Xiao Zhan of X-Nine (b. 1991), Lay Zhang of EXO (Zhang Yixing, b. 1991), Z.Tao of EXO (Huang Zitao, b. 1993), Jackson

Wang of Got7 (Wang Jiaer, b. 1994), Han Geng of Super Junior (b. 1984), Henry Lau of Super Junior (b. 1989), Ding Zeren of NEXT (b. 1999), Zhou Yixuan of UNIQ (b. 1990), and Li Wenhan of UNIQ (b. 1994)—particularly in their capacity as brand ambassadors for fashion and cosmetics, as well as a few South Korean K-Pop artists with broad appeal in China—Korean idols such as G-Dragon of Big Bang (Kwon Jiyong, b. 1988), Taeyang of Big Bang (Dong Youngbae, b. 1988), Cho Seungyoun of UNIQ ("Woodz," b. 1996), and Kim Sungjoo of UNIQ (b. 1994). Beauty, grace, loyalty to the brand, and an ability to adapt and learn from faux pas are essential characteristics of the successful brand ambassador. Unlike their feathered counterparts, these peacocks must also learn to adapt to the lack of privacy and intrusive photography and interviews, the female gaze and being branded "*xiao xian rou*" (little fresh meat), scrutiny, haters, and anti-fans. Even under these sometimes unsettling circumstances, idols contribute to the success of some of the world's most iconic brands, such as Chanel and Gucci, in China.

I arrived at peacocks after looking back at research I did on peacocks as quilt motifs back in 2014 at the International Quilt Study Centre and Museum at the University of Nebraska, Lincoln. Before arriving at "Peacocks," I had initially toyed with titling the book "*Didis*" (Little Brothers.) (In China, one often refers to older males as *gege* and younger males as *didi*, even though they are not actually relatives.) But I thought this was too presumptuous as to the age of the reader and might be too confusing for English-language audiences. Adding to the confusion would be the fact that one of the idols discussed at length in this book is the brand ambassador for Didi—a popular taxi service in China. I also considered naming the book "*Xiao Xian Rou*," but quickly dismissed that idea, not wishing to perpetuate a negative stereotype. "*Gong Cai*" (*Lettuce Stems*), which I propose in this book as an alternative term to "xiao xian rou," had also been on the shortlist, but again, I thought this might confuse English-language readers.

About this Book

During the Ming (1368–1644) and Qing (1644–1911) Dynasties, there were nine ranks in the imperial civil service system, each rank identified by a *buzi*, or embroidered badge, depicting a different bird. Rank three was denoted by a peacock, as seen in the *buzi* from the Los Angeles County Museum of Art collection (see Figure 1.2). The peacock represented "beauty, protection, and holiness."[9] In today's China, beautiful and highly venerated popular culture idols

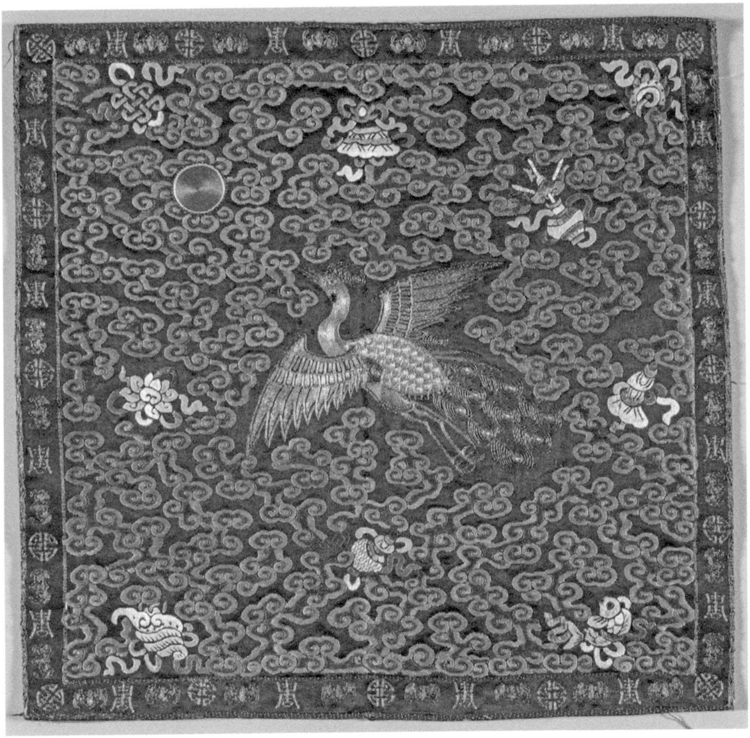

Figure 1.2 Badge (Buzi) of the Third Civil Rank with Peacock, China, probably Canton, late Qing Dynasty (1644–1912), late nineteenth century. Gift of Martha Rannells Partin in memory of Doris Wilson Rannells. Los Angeles County Museum of Art.

play a vital role in the luxury fashion and cosmetics industries as brand ambassadors—this volume hopes to fill a critical gap in the English-language literature on this subject, bringing together authors from the United States and China, and featuring case studies on idols Wang Yibo and Xiao Zhan. Ultimately, this book should help readers to:

- Understand the role that male idols play in fashion and cosmetics brand marketing in mainland China, Hong Kong, and Macau, learning from case studies featuring specific idols and brands, including the role of the female gaze and male idols as "xiao xian rou" ("little fresh meats").
- Understand subtleties of branding and marketing in China, Korea, and Japan, and the relationship of Chinese idols to fans and consumers in other Asian countries, as well as the potential for Post-95 Generation (the Chinese term roughly equivalent to Gen Z) idols breaking into luxury markets outside Asia-Pacific.

- Gain insight into what works—and what doesn't—in brand-idol collaborations and some major pitfalls that can be avoided when a brand works with an idol as an ambassador, including how brands can continue to work with idols while protecting their brand image from toxic fan culture and inappropriate reactions by fans online.

Most crucially, this book gives readers a sense of the scope of the importance of idols, who contribute to the success of some of the world's most iconic brands in China.

The introduction to this volume provides background on the subjects of idols and luxury in China, including the spaces of luxury capitalism in China—including perspectives from the fine art market, the concept of celebrity styling, fandom and idolatry, idols and the #MeToo movement, *zhai nan* and *zhai nü*[10] (the Chinese equivalent of the Japanese hikikomori), idols and body bleaching, and idols and BL (boy's love),[11] as well as the research methods used in the book. This introduction also foregrounds the case study chapters by Chinese co-authors Peng Liu and Lan Lan, which deal with Xiao Zhan and the AO3 incident (though through a different lens and using a qualitative survey approach, rather than the cultural studies approach used in this introduction).

Roadmap to this Book

In Chapter 2, "Exploring the Relationship Between Fashion Brands, Culture Idols, and Fans: The Power of Naming as Market Strategy," Peng Liu and Lan Lan note that having culture idols as luxury fashion brand ambassadors has been seen as a successful achievement in the China fashion market in terms of brand improving, sales/profit boosting, and potential customer attraction. Rather than being simply called a generic ambassador, idols are categorized by brands via various collaborations differentiated by their "hierarchical-like" names given in the Chinese market, namely from high to low, brand ambassadors or muse (Dai Yan Ren/代言人), brand face (Da Shi/大使), and brand friends (Zhi You/摯友).[12 13] However, the classification of the sets of names are not strictly allied with all brands across industry, so that idols may be named the brand face as the top role at one brand for example, while their name is only considered secondary at another brand. These rather confusing and complex names have caused ambiguities among fans. Acknowledging the approach of fashion brands in marketing certain products requires various levels of collaboration with culture idols in China: the relationship between brands, idols and fans reflects the exercise of the power to name in terms of sociological studies. Giving people a name is the "bestowal of status honours" (Anagost: 133) in sociological terms, demonstrating the power of the authority to define discursive positions in its political culture in which the names given shall be precise and indisputable. However, Peng Liu and Lan Lan's chapter shows that the relationship between brands and idols is more than a classificatory strategy by brands (which do the naming) and sorting idols (who are named) into hierarchically-arranged categories. Because fans who tend to talk up the names in favor of their own idols on social media for example plays an important role in the relationship. The chapter, therefore, focuses on male idols in marketing cosmetic products as a case study[14] to explore the interactive relationship between brands, culture idols, and fans, and particularly on the effectiveness of naming as a market strategy of luxury brands in targeting fans in high-context cultural environments.

In Chapter 3, "Idol Case Study—Wang Yibo, Aloof White Peony of Luoyang: Subverting Celebrity Styling," I use the case study of super idol Wang Yibo, particularly his work with Chanel and Shu Uemura. This chapter looks at how male idols, as brand ambassadors, appeal both to female customers and the female gaze as *xiao xian rou*, "little fresh meats," but also maintain a sense of control over their bodies and identities through subverting celebrity styling in arenas such as interviews, airport style, and awards shows, fashion shows, and other red-carpet public appearances. The importance of male idols in the marketing of womens' cosmetics in Asia is also analyzed.

In Chapter 4, "Capitalizing Yaoi/Danmei Fans: Fashion Brands and Male Popular Culture Idols as Brand Ambassadors in the Chinese Fashion Market," Peng Liu and Lan Lan examine the relationship between luxury fashion brands, male popular culture idols as brand ambassadors, and yaoi[15] (danmei in Chinese) fans in the Chinese fashion market. The controversial event involving Xiao Zhan on social fanfiction platform Archive of Our Own (AO3) reflects the interaction between culture idols and their yaoi fans in the fictional world, and the implications for the fashion brands in selecting ambassadors and marketing products in reality. Originally developed in Japan, yaoi fans are mostly female, self-called fujoshi, which literally means rotten girls who fantasize male boys' love (BL) characters in various genres such as manga, animation, game, and so on. Acknowledging the extensive discussions of BL studies in contemporary literature, the chapter is particularly interested in the application of the subjective gaze of females initially applied on flat and two-dimensional bodies of fantasized male BL manga characters, which is now applied to Chinese culture idols in reality. In other words, Chinese culture idols have increasingly appeared in BL fandom as a romantic pairing, male to male, through recasting and recharacterizing in texts and genres. The consumption of culture idols as BL characters, which is rather prohibited within the yaoi/BL community, has taken place in recent years in China. The chapter, therefore, investigates the consumption of culture idols in terms of BL studies and the impact upon the idols as brand ambassadors in terms of fashion studies. The research analyzes Xian Zhan as a case study that reflects the engagement of fashion brands capitalizing danmei/yaoi fans in marketing cosmetics and skincare, and illustrates the life of their own that these idols have in the imaginations of their fanbases beyond the heavily curated lives created by their managers.

Big Bang, BTS, EXO, GD x Taeyang, Got7, Holland, Infinite, JYJ, Kim Sungjoo, Super Junior, SHINee, UNIQ, WOODZ—these are some of the biggest male K-Pop (and K-Pop/C-Pop hybrid) groups and solo artists of the 2010s and early 2020s, in South Korea (hereafter simply, Korea) and throughout East Asia—including China, and globally. There are several terms for the influence of Korean idol culture in China—Korea Craze, Korean Wave, *hallyu, ha han*—and Korea's influence on China's youth culture and fashion in the twenty-first century is undeniable. Korea's consumption of idols as brand ambassadors leads the world, and this influence on marketing in China is palpable as well. Advertising data supports the far-reaching impact of Korean idols on Chinese consumers. According to an article in *SeoulBeats* from 2012, commercials featuring celebrities occur (out of the percentage of total TV and web commercials) at rates of 15% across all Western countries (except Brazil—in which celebrities appear in 25% of commercials), 25% for China and Hong Kong, 25% for Malaysia, and a whopping 65% for South Korea.[16] Thus, in South Korea, more than one in two products promoted in a commercial is promoted by a celebrity, and this is most often a K-Pop idol. This book concludes, by way of comparison, with Chapter 5, "A Comparative Perspective: The Culture of Korean K-Pop Idols as Brand Ambassadors," considering the influence of the Korean Wave, which historically has as its precedent Korean-language radio programming in China, on the idol economy in China, including the alleged "feminization" of Korea-crazed Chinese youth and the role of mandatory military enlistment in Korean idol brand ambassadorial agreements.

The Epilogue on "Xinjiang Cotton" looks at the human rights controversy surrounding cotton produced in China's Xinjiang region, and the subsequent moves by brand ambassadors such as Wang Yibo to leave Western fast-fashion and athletic brands such as Nike, who began boycotting Xinjiang cotton in 2021, for Chinese domestic brands, such as Anta Sports. The Epilogue also explores how many luxury labels escaped the controversy and boycotts entirely, having circumvented the problem by sourcing cotton from places like Australia, California, Egypt, and Texas long before the reported plight of the Uyghur people in Xinjiang.

Places and Spaces of Luxury Capitalism in China

In a discussion of place and space, it is useful to begin with a map. Pictured is a map of Chinese locations pertinent to this book, including super idol-turned-actor Wang Yibo's hometown of Luoyang, Henan Province, as well as Chongqing, home of idol-turned-actor Xiao Zhan (and the city which is positioning itself as a new luxury center by offerings brands incentives of up to 1 million yuan to open their first brick and mortar store there)[17], and Hong Kong and Shanghai—the locations of most Western luxury retailers' Asia-Pacific corporate headquarters (see Figure 1.3). McNeil and Riello note that, "The spaces of luxury are multiple. As an example, let us contrast two emerging Asian economies, China and South Korea. In 2014, while in China two-thirds of all luxury products were sold in shops located in shopping malls, in Korea 75 percent of luxury goods were sold in department stores."[18] And in 2014, "In none of the major Asian luxury consumer economies (India, China, Japan, South Korea, Hong Kong, and Singapore) did the street-level retailing of luxury goods account for more than 6 percent of sales. In the case of Hong Kong this is remarkable, as the metropolis has more big brands than any capital city in the West: eight Gucci stores compared to six in London and Paris, seven Hermès stores compared to just five in London, three in Paris, and two in New York."[19] It remains to be seen what effect Coronavirus will have on this shopping-related travel trend in the long term.

> Travellers do not just purchase luxury goods at airports when they happen to be travelling; increasingly, they actually travel around the world *in order* to purchase luxury goods. This is especially the case with Chinese consumers. A 2014 report reveals that, of Chinese travellers abroad, 100 per cent admitted to going shopping, compared to 90 per cent who said they had been sightseeing, 85 per cent who had sampled the local cuisine, and just over 20 per cent who had been to bars, nightclubs, or pubs while on holiday. In 2014 the most popular destinations for the rising Chinese middle classes were Hong Kong, Macau, South Korea, Thailand, Japan, Taiwan, and Singapore, all relatively local destinations and with excellent European and North American branded goods shopping.[20]

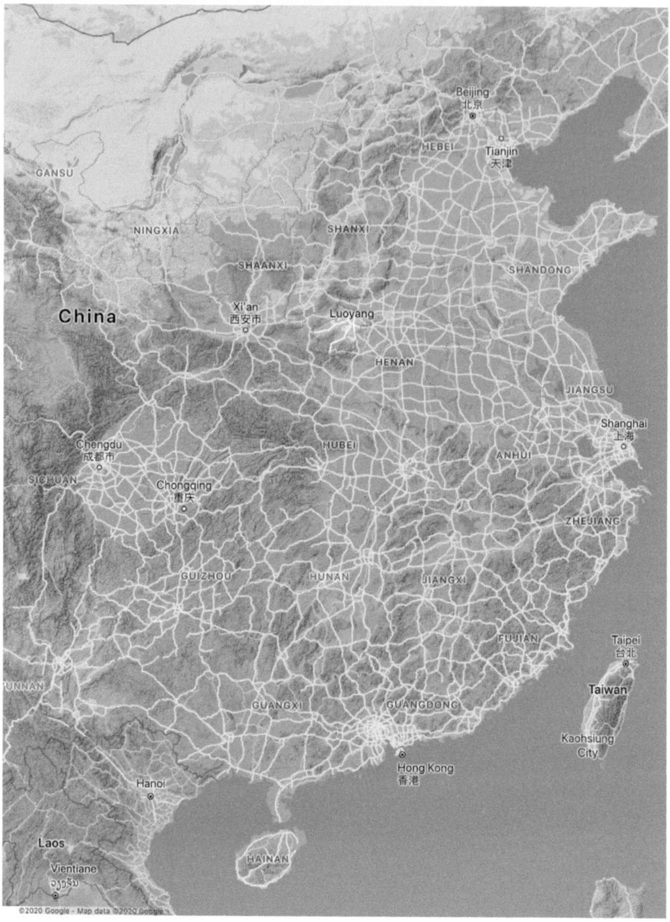

Figure 1.3 Map of Chinese locations pertinent to this book. Created by Amanda Sikarskie using Google Maps.

Regarding the problem of Hong Kong, because of China's contested geographies, it behooves idols, particularly as brand ambassadors, to remain largely apolitical in their public lives. There are times, however, when this proves an impossibility. Lay Zhang of the globally popular K-Pop/C-Pop group EXO, and former ambassador for the Samsung Galaxy mobile phone, for example, was obliged to cancel his agreement with Samsung after the company listed Hong Kong as a country (apart from the PRC) on its website:

> Lay Zhang, Jackson Wang, Lai Kuan-lin and Victoria Song were among the K-pop singers who recently uploaded a Chinese flag and declared themselves as "one of 1.4 billion guardians of the Chinese flag" on their official Weibo social

> media accounts. Wang is from Hong Kong and Lai is from Taiwan . . . Song and Zhang, a member of popular group EXO, have shown their Chinese pride on Instagram, in Song's case by uploading an image of the Chinese flag last week with the caption "Hong Kong is part of China forever." Such posts would only be seen by their international fans because Instagram, like most Western social media sites, is blocked by the ruling Chinese Communist Party's censors. For over a decade, South Korean entertainment agencies have been grooming Chinese singers to be part of their Korean pop, or K-pop, bands in an attempt to win over the massive mainland Chinese market. Only a few made it to a much-coveted debut. But a number of Chinese K-pop stars—citing unfair treatment—left their K-pop groups to pursue lucrative solo careers in mainland China.[21]

Hong Kong-born Jackson Wang has faced death threats from irate citizens in Hong Kong for allegedly turning his back on his roots and siding with the PRC over Hong Kong. Many brands are also betting on Mainland China over Hong Kong, with luxury houses such as Bulgari, Givenchy, and Versace relocating Hong Kong-based personnel to Shanghai as of May 2021, or eyeing growing markets in Southeast Asia and moving even further afield to Singapore. As Zoe Suen reports for *Business of Fashion*, these moves are not so much a move away from growing political tensions in Hong Kong as a move toward the lion's share of the consumers.[22] Brands want to set up headquarters as close to the clientele as possible. Other luxury brands, like Salvatore Ferragamo, intend to keep their Asia-Pacific headquarters in Hong Kong for now, however. It remains to be seen whether a move to Shanghai or Southeast Asia or remaining based in Hong Kong is the best Asia strategy for luxury houses long-term.

Chinese Shops (that Look Like French Ones)

Chinese shoppers also like to travel in their own imaginations. The setting of the music video for "Ice Cream (My Girlfriend)" by idol Zhou Yixuan, a cotton candy-colored, vaguely French high street, lined with charming little boutiques with "mode" (French for "fashion") in their names, reflects this impulse for the shopping holiday. The color palette in particular suggests a European shopping fantasy of the past, recalling the heyday or Parisian haute couture, and reclaiming that past for the Chinese shopper. Pastels were a hallmark of European and American fabrics in the years 1910–35, and especially the 1920s.[23] According to Eileen Jahnke Trestain, author of *Dating Fabrics: A Color Guide*, this shift to pastels reflected a new youthful optimism in fashion: "Historians theorize that fabric colors may have lightened because of the passing of Queen Victoria, who had been in deep mourning for many years after the death of her husband and her mother. The Queen had made it fashionable to be a widow. Many Civil War widows were also passing away. In addition, it may have been an economic move on the part of manufacturers, because pastels could be manufactured with the same dyes used in smaller quantities."[24] This youthful optimism and buoyancy bears similarity to the current climate in Chinese youth culture and fashion.[25] These colors hearken back to the days of the most celebrated generation of Parsian couturiers: Coco Chanel, Jean Lanvin, Mainbocher, and Madeleine Vionnet, as well as the fashion house of Callot Seurs.[26] Ultimately, the set of "Ice Cream" is a liminal fantasy space, existing somewhere between the streets of France and China. This saccharine atmosphere is also a kind of metaverse for the spaces inhabited by idols: pastel and sugar-coated, globally-situated, expensive but seemingly attainable, sexy but never sexual.

China's Consumers Shake the World

Crazy Rich Asians, the Hollywood film about a wealthy Sino-Singaporean son returning home for a wedding, begins with a quotation from Napoleon Bonaparte: "Let China sleep, for when she wakes, she will shake the world."[27] For much of human history, the largest city in the world was located in modern-day China. Luoyang, Xi'an (Chang'an), and Beijing were all the largest cities in the world at one point in the pre-modern era. Ancient, medieval, and early modern China was also notable globally for its inventions—paper and paper currency, printmaking, gunpowder, the compass, a system of civil service—and its wide-reaching and extremely lucrative trade along the Silk Road and by sea.

At the hands of the West, China certainly did sleep in the eighteenth and nineteenth centuries, falling prey to the opium that Great Britain was peddling in China to reduce its global trade deficit. Sara Liao explains the historical context for the rebuilding of China as a world power following the Opium Wars: "The discourse about technology advancing the nation has always been part of the development of modern China. Historical accounts associated the declining power of the nation with a strong sense of humiliation and loss of pride associated with the Middle Kingdom at the hands of the technologically advanced nations in the period since the Opium War, a sense that has served as the starting point for Chinese leaders' efforts to restore the country's technical supremacy and its status as a great world power (Qiu, 2004.)"[28] Today, Chinese consumers certainly aren't sleeping on the luxury fashion market, even in the age of Covid-19.

Shopping in a Time of Coronavirus

As I began to write this introduction during the spring and summer of 2020, Debenham's in the UK, Nieman Marcus in the United States, and other department stores around the world all filed for some form of bankruptcy protection. Is the Covid-19 era the end of the shopping experience as we know it? This is certainly the end of the "try me" experience at the beauty counter. Probably never again will we use nail polishes, foundation, moisturizers, and (eek!) lipsticks that have been used by other shoppers. Friends on Instagram posted that they were dressing up at home, putting on nice dresses—or at the very least, jeans instead of yoga pants. I commented to an acquaintance that I was starting my mornings by putting on Revlon's blackest black eyeliner and a kawaii cat ear headband, though staying in my pajamas. Still others, like Colleen Hill, Curator at the Museum at FIT, found inspiration in pajama-wearing, posting several examples from the FIT collection. And the Instagram account @historicpajama, which posts vintage photographs of chic beach pajamas, has gained popularity during the Coronavirus crisis. Watching the death of the department store in real time from the safety of my quarantined abode made me quite nostalgic as I researched and wrote this essay. I am left wondering what strategies for the curation and management of space, technology, and time retailers will adopt in the future as they navigate this forever-altered retail landscape.

Even during the pandemic, however, L'Oréal Finance observed that during the first quarter of 2020, "E-commerce continues to grow at more than 60%, especially in China, Japan, Australia, Thailand and Indonesia,"[29] and,

> L'Oréal was able to rebound quickly to achieve growth in March and a positive first quarter, gaining market share and reinforcing its leadership position on the beauty market. This rebound was due to the early restoration of operational capabilities in February, strict application of safety measures to ensure a safe working environment, as well as the rapid adjustment of activation plans in favour of Online and O+O (Online + Offline) activities. A strong bet on the Women's Day Festival triggered the recovery. During this online festival, L'Oréal China gained significant market shares with a strong contribution from *L'Oréal Paris, Lancôme, SkinCeuticals, Helena Rubenstein, 3CE Stylenanda* and *Kérastase*.[30]

According to the *Business of Fashion*'s "The State of Fashion 2021 Scenarios" report,[31] while fashion sales will be down in the European Union, United States, and globally in 2021 from their 2019 numbers, sales in China will actually be up in 2021 over 2019. And fashion sales in China took much less of a hit in 2020 compared to the rest of the world. By the numbers, in the fourth quarter of 2020 fashion spending in China was down 7–12% and in 2021 is projected to be back up 5–10% over Q4 of 2019. Globally, fashion spending is down 15–20% in late 2020 and is projected to be down 0–5% in 2021, bolstered by Asia. In the United States and Europe, the picture is considerably more grim. The US and Europe, respectively, are down 17–22% and 22–27% in Q4 2020 compared to Q4 2019, and in 2021, US fashion sales are still projected to be down 7–12% over 2019, whereas Europe is still projected to be down 2–7%.

A Fine Arts Perspective

A cowboy hat-clad Deng Xiaoping visited the United States in 1979 and went to a rodeo (see Figure 1.4). This "cowboy hat diplomacy" goodwill tour unofficially marked the opening of China's economy to the West—socialism with Chinese characteristics. At home, Deng Xiaoping "progressively shifted economic policy so as to expand domestic demands and promote consumerism (Gerth, 2010)."[32] With the creation of the corporate-friendly Special Economic Zones (SEZs) across China and the 1990 reopening of the Shanghai Stock Exchange, the transition to a market economy was complete. The idol economy of the 2020s shares much in common with the contemporary fine art economy of the 1990s and early 2000s in China:

> Indeed, internationally successful artists like Zhang Xiaogang, Yue Minjun, and Zeng Fanzhi, whose works have sold regularly for more than a million dollars each and who are represented by prestigious Western art dealers, hardly feel ashamed of their financial and artistic success. Unlike their Western peers, they ostentatiously show off their wealth by driving in luxury cars made by Lexus and Mercedes Benz and buying opulent houses … The long-term focus of Western art dealers and their artists on building a solid career also contrasts with the short-term focus of Chinese artists. "There's an instinctive urge to capitalize immediately on any fleeting opportunity before it disappears … Everything in their experience has taught them that it's foolish to be on the long run."[33]

Although my own research has dealt with fashion and textiles throughout my career, my undergraduate training was in art history, and I have been teaching art history since 2004. In those days, according to Olav Velthuis, "In China, these auctions are embedded in a wider speculative culture, which has been developing

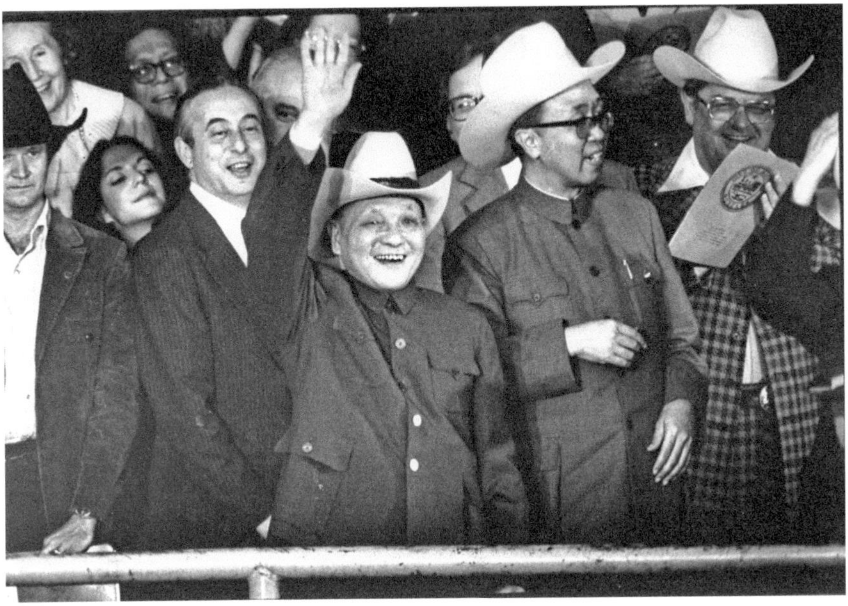

Figure 1.4 Deng Xiaoping's "cowboy hat diplomacy." China's paramount leader Deng Xiaoping waving, wearing a cowboy hat presented to him by his hosts, attending a rodeo, with entourage-in-tow, during a stop on his state visit after normalizing ties with the United States. Photo by Dirck Halstead/The LIFE Images Collection via Getty Images/Getty Images.

ever since the country liberalized its economy and integrated into the global financial and commodity markets ... a new class of Chinese collectors buy contemporary art to make a quick profit ... Auctions in China also enjoy legitimacy by default, just like those of the impressionists in nineteenth century France: at least in the 1990s—the early days of the Chinese market for contemporary art—they were one of the few official art institutions. Hardly any museums or other cultural institutions existed that could establish the reputations of artists."[34] In an interview with Norah O'Donnell on the CBS Evening News on June 23, 2020, John Bolton acknowledged that while American political and business leaders tend to think of the economy in terms of quarterly reports, Chinese leaders tend to think in decades.

Team Wang x Monet

Jackson Wang, of the K-Pop/C-Pop group Got7, takes being a brand ambassador seriously (see Figure 1.5). In the If Fashion interview at the 2020 Shanghai Cartier

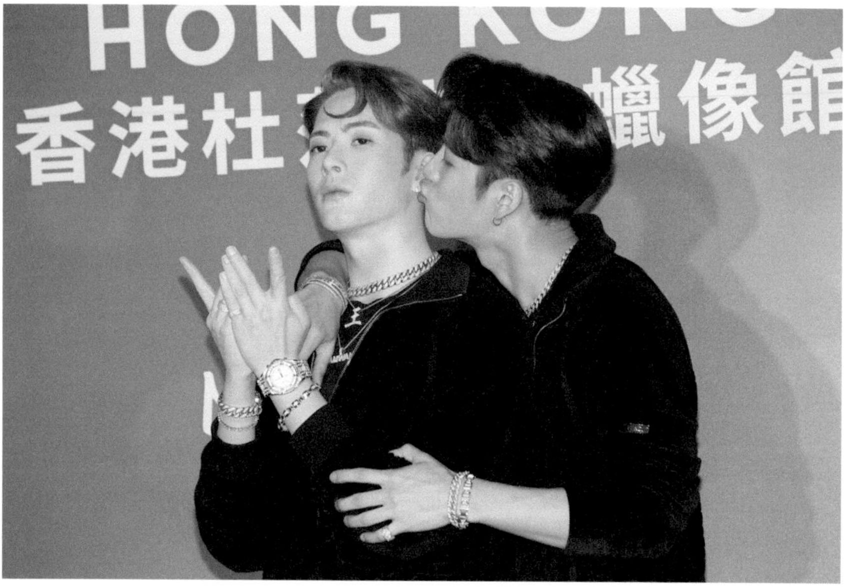

Figure 1.5 Jackson Wang kisses a waxwork of himself. Singer Jackson Wang attends his wax figure unveiling ceremony at Madame Tussauds on July 29, 2019 in Hong Kong, China. Photo by Visual China Group via Getty Images/Visual China Group via Getty Images.

exhibition, Wang made sure to point out that every piece in the clash de cartier collection is handmade and takes at least ten hours to produce. He also pointed out that he was wearing four Cartier pieces at the time, and while growing up, Cartier was for his family one of those almost unattainable brands in which owning one signified that one had "made it" financially. Jackson Wang also has his own clothing label, Team Wang, and is global spokesperson for L'Oréal. In multiple promotional videos and interviews in 2020, Wang has sung the praises of L'Oréal Men Expert hydra boost toner: "A functional drink for your skin" that "boosts hydration in three seconds." Jackson Wang has also used his platform as a celebrity to advocate for the #StopAsianHate[35] movement in the wake of the shootings of women of Asian descent at Altanta-area massage parlors in March 2021.

Wang is keenly interested in the cultural exchange between China and the West. In conjunction with the nineteenth-century French Impressionist Claude Monet's exhibition in Shanghai in 2020, Team Wang created shirts featuring an image of Monet's 1874 painting *Impression, Sunrise*, the painting after which the art movement takes its name. Neither the setting nor the subjects are important—what matters is the mood evoked by the color choices and the misty, atmospheric quality, literally a painting of a sunrise. But the painting, which is highly regarded today, was not so in its own time. The story goes that art critic Louis Leroy, upon seeing the painting, despaired that it was not even a painting of a sunrise, but rather merely an impression of a sunrise, and the pejorative name amused the artist and stuck. The anecdote seems to have metaphorical significance for idols, who are often described in the Chinese press as not really being actors when appearing in film and television roles.

Many American Impressionists wished to show purity, not idealized beauty. This is quite particular to American Impressionism—in European Impressionism, female beauty was typically classicized and sexualized. Cecilia Beaux, American Impressionist and friend of John Singer Sargent, studied in France. Her painting *Sita and Sarita* is a portrait of her cousin. Fully clothed in white, the sitter suggests purity, but the little black cat perched atop her shoulder suggests sexuality. Compare this to Edouard Manet's *Olympia*, a painting of a courtesan, which Beaux saw in Europe. One could also compare *Sita and Sarita* to the portrait of her brother-in-law, Henry Sturgis Drinker, a railroad lawyer. Men usually wore dark colors, while he wears a white suit and is depicted with a kitten, which suggests innocent and playful feminine sexuality. Male idols in East and Southeast Asia are often attributed with a similarly "soft masculinity," though as Joseph Bazil Manietta explains, "the feminine aspects associated with South Korean soft masculinity allow idol group members who are associated with this variety of masculinity to perform aegyo [a specific kind of cuteness popular throughout East Asia] more successfully than those who present other kinds of masculinity (i.e. global 'cool' masculinity or 'tough' masculinity … What is special about this soft masculinity is that it has been reconstructed with some feminine aspects, but it has not been feminized (Jung 2011: 48). Though soft South Korean masculinity has certain features that are often associated with femininity, such as tenderness, politeness, and gentleness, the overall impression is that of masculinity. This is not unlike 'metrosexual' masculinity, which includes features such as interest in fashion and grooming—features often associated with women—yet it is still ideologically a construct of 'masculinity.'"[36] This nineteenth-century Western Impressionist treatment of male sexuality is interesting when understood in the larger context of idols and fine art in today's China and Korea.

Shopping and Tears

The idea that haute clothing stores are fundamentally committed to their shoppers' affective experience is not a new one, and the emotional experience of the guest or visitor is also of great interest to the museum professional, a theme manifested in James Elkins' book *Pictures and Tears: A History of People Who*

Have Cried in Front of Paintings. Here, Elkins, an art historian, is not concerned with the works of art themselves, but with the reactions of visitors to works of art, specifically crying in front of paintings. One theory, no doubt descended in part from Martin Heidegger's *Being and Time*, is that people cry at various aesthetic experiences—films, paintings, picturesque views, and so on—because we are made keenly aware in those moments of the passage of time. Elkins writes:

> It's amazing that even a hopelessly clichéd, underacted, overplayed, underfunded, overwritten movie like *Cool Runnings* might yank a tear from a few viewers [it did from me]. Hollywood movies are romantic, and like Pavlov's dogs we respond to them even when we don't want to. Any theory that links crying to the passage of time has to come to terms with these exceptions and perplexities. I'm going to sidestep the equation of tears and time arts because it has too many problems. I'm content to say that paintings are time arts [and for the purposes of this essay, so, too, are visual merchandizing displays in shops], and their ways of capturing time are very specific. *The angel's cry*. Unlike opera, theater, novels, poems, movies, and orchestral music, pictures give us what appears to be one instant of time, dilated and fixed until it lasts far longer than a lifetime. If there is something peculiar to tears shed in front of paintings, it should be related to that distinctive distortion of time.[37]

It is obviously a bit of a stretch to compare the visitor experience of the Shanghai Cartier exhibition with watching the film *Cool Runnings*. The point, however, is that, as Heidegger described it, "Curiosity is 'activated' not by the endless immensity of what we have not yet seen, but rather by the falling kind of temporalizing which belongs to the Present as it leaps away. Even if one has seen everything, this is precisely when curiosity *fabricates* something new. As a mode of temporalizing, the 'leaping-away' of the Present is grounded in the essence of temporality, which is *finite*."[38] Monet's *Impression, Sunrise*, a painting that captures the misty, atmospheric, and, importantly, ephemeral qualities of a sunrise is precisely the sort of painting that Elkins considers as a potential tearjerker. Idols, retailers, and art museums all trade in playing with the public's affective state, to one extent or another.

Some Notes About Language and Methodology

Since many Mandarin Chinese words appear in this book, it is worth making a few notes about language before we begin in earnest. First, Chinese (and Korean) names appear in the traditional way, Family Name then Given Name, as in "Wang Yibo." When searching for Chinese names in the index of this volume, search for the family name (the name that appears first). Chinese figures who use a Western given name, however, appear with their names styled in the Western way, such as Jackson Wang or Lay Zhang or Sean Xiao. Second, Chinese characters that appear in this book may be either simplified characters (which are used in mainland China) or traditional characters (which are used in Hong Kong and Macau—where Peng Liu, one of this book's authors, lives.) On a related note, because of his extensive international scholarship, Peng Liu is the one exception to the "Family Name then Given Name" rule in this book. Finally, Romanizations of Chinese words are done exclusively in the Hanyu Pinyin, and are referred to simply as "pinyin," for short, rather than in the older, colonial Wade Giles system.

The research methods used in this volume include both a fashion business approach grounded in quantitative economic data, as well as qualitative approaches from popular culture studies, gender studies, art and visual culture studies, and anthropology. Cultural theories and theorists utilized in this book include (but are not limited to) writings on semiotics by Jacques Lacan and Jacques Derrida in unpacking the idol as image-sign and the brand event as simulacrum, Susan Sontag's *On Photography* in the analysis of image and visual culture, and in thinking about jewelry, Roland Barthes's "From Gemstones to Jewellery."

As a fashion historian who is also a Unicorn, or fan of UNIQ, I am both scholar of and participant in this world of idol culture. In *Coming of Age in Second Life*, Tom Boellstorff notes of participant ethnography that, "There is no illusion of detached objectivity to shatter in participant observation because it is not a methodology that views the researcher as a contaminant."[39] That is, my status as Unicorn does not detract from my ability to research the group, and if anything, enhances it. For readers who may still be skeptical, Boellstorff constructs a lineage of participant ethnography, differing from nineteenth-century anthropology that relied, and indeed was predicated upon, a colonial chasm between the research and the Othered subject of study:

> [Matti] Bunzl notes that "in a Malinowskian framework, the production of anthropological knowledge was a function of mere observation, as long as it occurred across—and, thereby, reproduced—a cultural chasm between ethnographic Self and native Other" (Bunzl 2004: 438). This supposed cultural chasm has led many to mistakenly conclude that ethnography will not be objective if researchers are similar to (or personally involved with) those they study, with the result that persons conducting ethnographic research in communities to which they somehow belong may see themselves as "virtual anthropologists" (Weston 1997). In contrast, "in [Franz] Boas's fieldwork, a constitutive epistemological separation between

> ethnographer and native was absent" (Bunzl 2004: 438). Thus, "Boasian anthropology did not produce 'native' anthropology as the virtual Other of 'real anthropology.'"
>
> Bunzl 2004: 439[40]

As an interesting historical aside, "Franz Boas was Margaret Mead's teacher at Columbia and wrote the foreword to Coming of Age in Samoa."[41] Of course, published ethnographic research has the potential to have both great positive and negative impacts upon the subjects of that research.[42] I have taken the utmost care that the idols' images, including that of their patriotic loyalty, are not harmed in the pages that follow.

Fans and Idols: Situating Idol Studies

Celebrity endorsement is a long-standing and reasonably effective practice in the marketing of goods. In the past twenty years or so, a period of time corresponding to the rise of social media, fandom increasingly approaches idolatry. For these fans, who love their idol with a religious fervor, endorsement of a product becomes akin to a new religious doctrine. According to Singh and Banerjee's 2019 paper on celebrity worship and brand attitudes, companies must consider not only traditional positive associations with celebrities but also this new and pervasive idolatry when choosing brand ambassadors for their products:

> With the ascent of mass media, a misguided feeling of closeness with celebrity is conceived, as open and private existences of celebrities became interchangeable (Leff Leonard, 1999). This misguided feeling of closeness has risen significantly to facilitate the appearance of web-based social networking and unscripted reality show, which empower consumers to interface with the day to day life of the celebrity. Regardless of the truth of not really knowing superstars, individuals feel as though they do know them personally, regularly framing exceptional enthusiastic and mental associations with them (Schnickel, 2000). This phenomenon leads to adoration and worship of celebrity rather than mere appreciation for their achievements. Individuals having a parasocial association with celebrity are more persuasive and it is similar to that of trusting a true friend's advice (Forrester, 2012). It is an important question to the Marketers and advertiser practitioners, whether to reformulate their approach from traditional celebrity endorsement to celebrity worship which is now becoming a cult in the majority of consumers especially among youngsters.
>
> Ang & Chan, 2016[43]

While some idols only enter the profession as young adults, discovered on talent boot camp TV shows, many idols in Asia enter the profession around the ages of twelve to fourteen (or even younger).

Idols, #MeToo, and Sexualized Childhood

Idols entering the profession as youths are typically trained for four to five years in intensive residential idol schools, often in South Korea, whose globally-reaching K-Pop culture has built a reputation for being more rigorous than domestic Chinese idol training, but also for being more effective. Life in these schools is strictly controlled, with ten-hour minimum days (and often quite longer),[44] restrictions against dating, and limited access to mobile phones and even contact with parents. In such an atmosphere, it is important to recognize the potential for abuse of trainees and idols. In an article in the *Guardian*, entitled "Spycams, sex abuse and scandal: #MeToo reaches Korean pop," Justin McCurry detailed abuses committed against idols as well as abuses allegedly perpetrated by a former idol. In particular, McCurry discussed the suicide of Korean idol Jang Jayeon, who left behind a suicide note detailing her sexual exploitation, having been beaten and "forced to have sex with 31 influential men, including politicians, business and newspaper executives and entertainment industry figures" over the course of her career.[45]

Young male idols are not immune to (what would be considered in the West, at least) sexual harassment in the workplace. On the December 14 Christmas episode of the Korean TV music chat show *Idol School*, Cho Seung-youn of UNIQ detailed how he and his bandmates (not all of whom were over 18 at the time) were forced by their dance instructor to kiss each other as well as the teacher himself as a team-building exercise (see Figure 1.6).[46] The admission drew giggles from the other idols who were guests on the show that day, and seemed remarkably unremarkable to the hosts of the show. The next year, the group appeared on television in Thailand to promote their March 2015 fan meeting in Bangkok. The maknae of the group, seventeen-year-old Wang Yibo, who was then sporting a chin-length blond bob as a *luo li*, or Lolita, wore a sweatshirt that read 'Escort Boys' in English across the chest.[47]

Toward the end of her book *Fashionable Childhood: Children in Advertising*, Annamari Vänskä urges fashion academics to advocate for minors in the fashion and related industries: "Another task is to widen research from fashion magazines and their featured advertising to the internet and to the different platforms of social media that are mainly constructed around visual images, whether still or

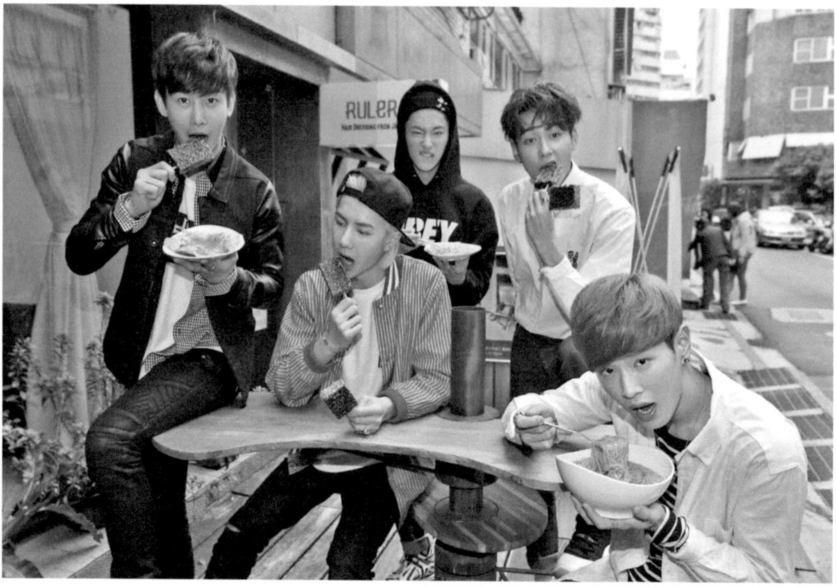

Figure 1.6 UNIQ eating ice cream for a press photo. The group take photos together during an exclusive interview on December 2, 2014 in Taipei, Taiwan of China. Photo by Visual China Group via Getty Images/Visual China Group via Getty Images.

moving. Academics researching children's fashions should also be more vocal in public debates. They should add critical questions to the debate on sexualization, including that of why we consider innocence so important when it comes to clothing and visual representations of children."[48] Certainly, what Vänskä notes about child labor in the aesthetic economy of fashion modeling has a bearing on children who train—often from a young age—to be idols. Vänskä writes, "In this frame of reference, the sassy styling does not represent the child as victim, but as the neoliberal ideal [ironic in a communist country such as the PRC]: a free agent for whom self-fashioning and a sexualizing appearance are the best way of improving their personal situation."[49] In this light, one can read Wang's "Escort Boys" shirt as a transactional means to an end, the promise of popularity and its associated wealth through the fans' gaze. As Annamari Vänskä opines, "The sexual child has the job of arresting the restless gaze, to cause affects, and to channel attention. This is the central reason for the contemporary popularity of the child model."[50] Chapter 3 of this book on idols as brand ambassadors features a discussion of the term *xiao xian rou*—literally "little fresh meat"—one liberally applied to male idols in both their teens and twenties (see Figure 1.7).

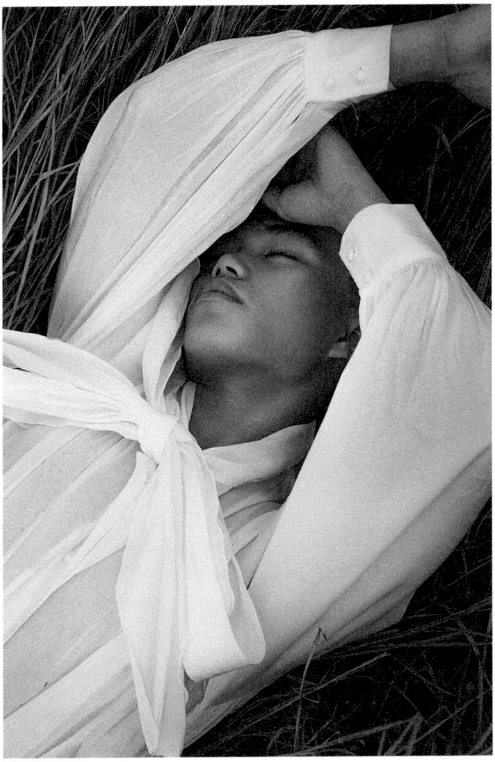

Figure 1.7 An illustration of the *xiao xian rou* concept. Photographed by Gabb Tapic. Pexels.com.

Rice Rabbit: What the Chinese #MeToo Movement Means for Brands and their Ambassadors

In July 2021, Chinese-Canadian idol Kris Wu (Wu Yifan, b. 1990), formerly of the K-Pop group EXO, was detained by Beijing police, accused of date-raping a minor, KOL (influencer) Du Meizhu, and then paying her hush money. Wu has also allegedly made inappropriate overtures to at least twenty-four women. Besides his work with EXO, Wu is known for his appearance on *The Rap of China*, for his (arguably sexually-objectifying) solo song "Big Bowl, Thick Noodle," as well as starring opposite Yang Zi in the romantic costume drama *The Golden Hairpin* (2021). The arrest and detainment of Kris Wu and surrounding media hullabaloo will almost certainly give the #MeToo/#MiTu movement in China more traction (see Figure 1.8). MiTu is written using the characters for rice (mi 米) and rabbit (tu 兔), and hints at the homegrown, grassroots nature of the contemporary Chinese feminist movement. Kris Wu, who walked for Louis

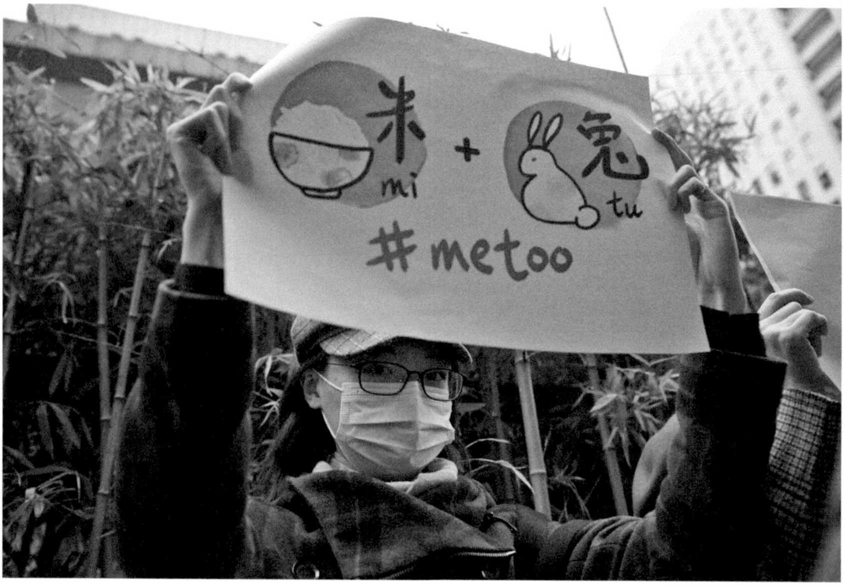

Figure 1.8 A MiTu protester in China. Supporters of Zhou Xiaoxuan, a feminist figure who rose to prominence during China's #MeToo movement, display posters outside the Haidian District People's Court in Beijing on December 2, 2020, in a sexual harassment case against one of China's best-known television hosts. Photo by Noel Celis / AFP via Getty Images.

Vuitton SS/21 Menswear in Shanghai and appeared on the cover of Chinese *Cosmo* in July 2021, faces as much as ten years to life in prison in China, according to the *Global Times*.[51] As of August 2021, Wu had already been dropped from several endorsement contracts, based on violation of immorality clauses in those contracts, including with Louis Vuitton, Bvlgari, Lancôme, and Porsche. Such invalidation of endorsements underscored not only the social, but also the economic importance of respectful, unblemished personal conduct for brand ambassadors in China.[52]

Hikikomori: Home Boys and Home Girls

While idols are meant to have broad appeal, hopefully inciting hundreds or thousands to purchase the products that they endorse, idols do have a core fanbase that they are at once beholden to and considered responsible for (especially online.) Otaku, a word commonly understood in China, is the Japanese term for one obsessed—with idol culture, video games, fanfiction, Hello Kitty, Legos, figure skating, and so on. While many otaku individuals do have rich school or work lives outside their hobby, being *hikikomori* is associated with the most hardcore of otaku.[53] In China, the terms 宅男 *zhai nan* (home boy) and 宅女 *zhai nü* (home girl), or the more recent phrases "lying flat" and "free idler,"[54] are often used. Another (pejorative) moniker, NEET, an acronym which stands for the English phrase "No Education Employment or Training," is used throughout East Asia to denote youth with low employment potential. Previously, in the 1970s, the three no's (no drive, no interest, no sense of responsibility) were used to describe such youth,[55] though this term belies the quite strong interests that otaku have in their particular hobby or fandom. As Saito Tamaki, author of *Hikikomori: Adolescence Without End*, explains, "I would like to emphasize once again that what I have been calling 'withdrawal' does not necessarily mean the same thing as apathy. It is true that people who are in social withdrawal might look 'inactive' or 'idle,' but they are not 'apathetic.' I am sure of that."[56] Essentially, withdrawal does not equate to apathy.

The concept of *hikikomori* gained a bit of fame in the West through the animated series *Neo Yokio* (2017), set in a curious anime amalgam of New York and Tokyo, which appeared on Netflix. In the series, Helena Saint Tessero is a young socialite and fashion influencer (or KOL—Key Opinion Leader—as they are known in China). Her followers, the Helenists (the word no doubt a play on late classical Hellenism), hang on her every word and make great efforts to dress as their idol, down to her Chanel clothes and lilac hair. After a personal crisis, in which she suffers demonic possession (a Chanel suit has become a type of *yokai*—or spirit—known as a *tsukumogami*, an object that has cultivated independent spiritual power), has passed, she "goes *hikikomori*." Tamaki defines *hikikomori*, or youth social isolation, as "A state that has become a problem by the late twenties [or earlier], that involves cooping oneself up in one's own home and not participating in society for six months or longer, but that does not seem to have another psychological problem as its principal source."[57] Further, people who have gone or become *hikikomori* were twelve to thirty-four years old when their social withdrawal began, with an average age of 19.6, and overwhelmingly come from middle-class or upper-class backgrounds.[58] Once a shut-in, Helena eschews fashionable dress, wearing instead a simple white tunic and bandages around her head. Ironically, her online followers adopt this new form of dress, believing it to be a new trend, even while Helena attempts to use her platform as a KOL to decry what she now views as a decadent fashion industry, eventually returning to society to continue this work against the fashion industry.

I include this fanciful anecdote about *hikikomori* and Helena Saint Tessero because, circling back to the beginning of this introductory chapter on male idols, understanding the fans of these idols is paramount to understanding their effectiveness as brand ambassadors, and many hardcore otaku fans of idols are—as well as being mostly young, mostly middle class, and mostly women—*hikikomori*, or *zhai nü*, to some extent. Far from apathetic, otaku are passionate fans and are often prolific online shoppers. In his translation notes to Tamaki's *Hikikomori*, Jeffrey Angles, using Michel Foucault's *La volonté de savoir* and its discussion of categorization in the field of abnormal psychology, comments on groups who commit an aberrant behavior that comes to be defined by language, such as *hikikomori*: "For instance, the group that medical doctors had identified as 'homosexuals' adopted this label as an identity that went mainstream and became the basis for political identification and an equal rights movement that sought fairness in the workplace and under the law."[59] *Hikikomori* may well become another such group in the years to come, and though as shut-ins they are largely unseen, their power as fans and consumers must not be underestimated.

Idols and BL

Related to this idea of the sexualized aspect of idols' labor is the intersection of idol fan culture and BL, or boy's love, fan culture in Asia. Even viewed from the United States, one can see that there is a sizable amount of BL media coming out of China right now in the form of both *wuxia* and *xianxia* dramas and *donghua* (Chinese anime series): *Mo Dao Zu Shi/Chen Qing Ling/The Untamed*, *The Emperor's Stratagem*, *Scum Villains Self-Saving System*, *Heaven's Official Blessing*, *Silent Reading*, *Spirit Pact*, *Society of Four Leaves*, *Act Wildly*, *Immortality*, *Those Days I Inherited a Zoo*, *A Tale of the Wanderers*, *Your Name Engraved Herein*, and *Soul Snatcher* (a film about a scholar and a fox spirit yaoguai with some BL elements). In researching BL idol fandom in China, it is a good strategy to look at the real-life or real-person (RPF) idol BL fan culture as coming from the lineage of *fujoshi* and manga and anime in Japan. Added to this is the idea of "skinship" in K-Pop fan culture in Korea, in which fans of groups want to see their idols bestow platonic, but very public, affection on each other. (And the groups' managers make them.) This includes being made to hug or kiss fellow same-sex idols on television chat shows or at fan meetings.

Idols and Body Bleaching: Like a Monster

To use another example from popular culture, in the *Twilight Saga*, vampire Edward Cullen's inhumanly white alabaster skin sparkles like diamonds in the sunlight. The 2018 UNIQ single, "Monster," written by UNIQ member Zhou

Yixuan, was inspired by the *Twilight Saga* vampire novels, and describes a fatal attraction for the female listener in which the male narrator "*Chongpole yiqie*" (broke everything), is "*Bupei ni di mei*" (not worthy of your beauty), a love who is "*ruci ruci de wanmei*" (so, so perfect).[60] Not in fantasy but in reality, idols' brown bodies are unnaturally whitened to sell first their own fame, and then fashion, cosmetics, and skincare products. In a livestream, for example, a fan compliments UNIQ band member Kim Sungjoo that he is looking very fair these days, to which Kim replies that he had just been to the spa for a full body bleaching. Wang Yibo laughs, admonishing Kim that he is not supposed to tell that to the viewers at home.[61]

Skin bleaching as a cultural practice is prevalent throughout much of the world, including East and South Asia, Africa, and the Caribbean. The practice is, unfortunately, a major public health risk in these parts of the world, leading to mercury poisoning, among other health consequences. According to an article published by O. E. Dadzie and A. Petit in the *Journal of the European Academy of Dermatology and Venereology*, "Skin bleaching is the practice of applying hydroquinone and/or other depigmenting agents to specific or widespread areas of the body, the primary function being to lighten normally dark skin. This practice typically occurs in men and women with Fitzpatrick skin phototypes IV to VI. It is a dangerous practice associated with a diverse range of side-effects, including mercury poisoning."[62] One could argue that the practice is ultimately a form of violence against brown and black skin, both in its colonialism and in its negative health outcomes. In "The Body, Cosmetics and Aesthetics in South Korea: The Emergence of a Field of Research," Valérie Gelézeau reminds readers, however, that:

> Luxuries and the use of luxury products, body care (from the spice baths of the ladies at court to the application of various preparations to lighten the skin and/or blacken the teeth) were all part and parcel of the very sophisticated traditional culture of the members of the Korean aristocracy. Thus, the infatuation with aesthetics that I described in the first section is *also*, or rather *above all*, part of a particularly Korean history in terms of the body, aesthetics and luxury. We should note here that the interpretation of the quest for lighter skin as simply a desire to look more Western is challenged (as the researchers who have studied this matter have pointed out) by certain facts: a lighter skin was a sign of social superiority compared with the great mass of peasants and common people who worked outdoors in the fields. We should also note that in this respect Korea is again aligned with the general tendencies that have been analysed in a number of countries, in particular in 16th century France.
>
> Lanoë 2007[63]

The desire for whiter skin in Korea actually predates Western colonial involvement there, and to rail against it blindly is ultimately its own brand of colonialism.

Celebrity Styling

In her 2020 book, *Fashioning China*, Sara Liao writes, "Celebrity endorsement is a time-honored marketing practice for brands; companies around the world have for decades paid top dollar to popular names in entertainment, sports, fashion, and so on as a means to establish a connection with celebrities with the expectation that their fame and popularity will boost sales."[64] Perhaps nowhere is this more true than China. Liao defines celebrity styling as the process in which:

> "... a product, or less often, a service, is endorsed by a celebrity with or without an official announcement of a partnership with the corresponding brand ... Although the practice is by no means a recent innovation, it has spread with the proliferation of digital mobile media and social networking sites such as eBay, Amazon, Facebook, Pinterest, Twitter—a good example being the aforementioned Instagirls fad (Okwudo, 2016)—or, in China, where the Great Firewall dutifully blocks the majority of foreign social media sites, Weibo, WeChat, and Taobao ... For example, the Chinese woman actor Yang Mi has been described as "the queen who drives sales," for every item that she owns, wears, or shares becomes highly sought after by her fans and replicated by numerous Taobao sellers.[65]

Liao notes a litany of A-list celebrities—Fan Bingbing,[66] Zhang Ziyi, Zhou Xun, Gong Li—to name a few.[67] Chanel, Chopard, Dior, Gucci, Louis Vuitton, and Miu Miu are among some of the Western luxury brands that work with Chinese idols and celebrities as brand ambassadors in Eastern markets.[68]

Roses Only: The Rise and Fall (and Rise) of Xiao Zhan

Xiao Zan (no "h"), born in 501 CE, was a minor prince (and a bastard son, at that) who fled his home in the year 525 for the city of Luoyang, capital of the Northern Wei (Bei Wei). The young emperor there was Yuan Ziyou, born in 507, and despite his lowly status as a minor bastard prince, Xiao Zan must have quickly fallen in the emperor's good graces, because he was allowed to marry the emperor's own sister. It is a possibility, though there is no direct evidence to support it, that Xiao Zan and Yuan Ziyou were lovers, hence the latter warming to the former so

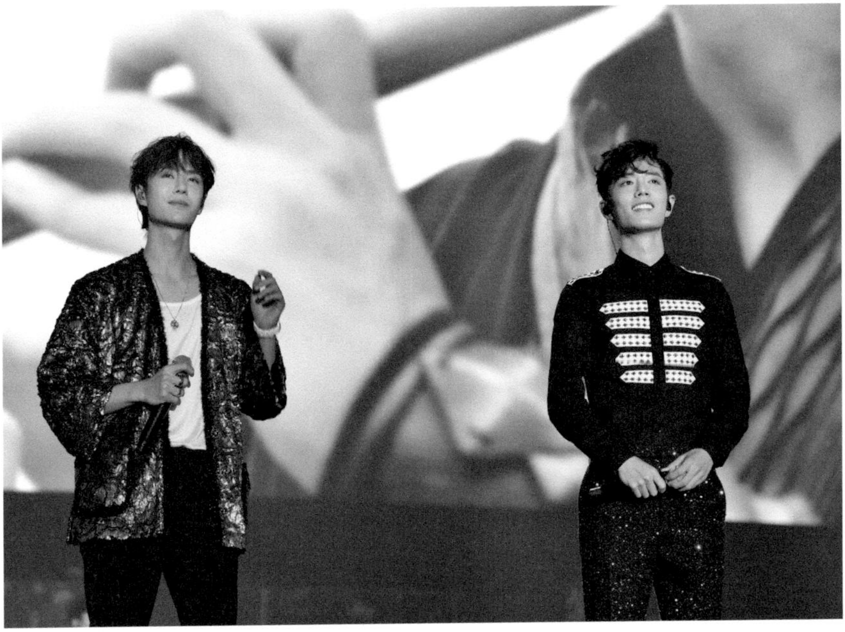

Figure 1.9 The Nanjing *Untamed* Fanmeet. Sean Xiao Zhan (R) and Wang Yibo (L) perform on stage during The Untamed National Style Concert on November 2, 2019 in Nanjing, Jiangsu Province of China. Photo by VCG/VCG via Getty Images.

quickly. The story of Xiao Zan and Yuan Ziyou—whatever it may have been—did not last long. There was a coup in the Northern Wei in 530 and both Xiao and Yuan died in 531. I present these characters from ancient Chinese history here because there is a popular fan theory[69] that Xiao Zan and Yuan Ziyou are the prototypes of contemporary idols Xiao Zhan (of the idol group X Nine, b. 1991—current and past endorsements include Gucci, Tiffany & Co., Cartier, Estée Lauder, and Olay) and Wang Yibo (of the idol group UNIQ, b. 1997—current endorsements number more than twenty and include Chanel, Swarovski, and Shu Uemura). Xiao and Wang co-starred together in the global hit BL[70] *xianxia*[71] TV series *The Untamed* (*Chen Qing Ling*) in 2019 (see Figure 1.9).

There are coincidences which "support" the reincarnation fan theory. Xiao Zan's name is one letter away from Xiao Zhan's, while both Yuan Ziyou and Wang Yibo were in the city of Luoyang. Xiao Zan and Xiao Zhan were both born in a year ending in -1 and under the astrological sign of the sheep, while both Yuan Ziyou and Wang Yibo were born in a year ending in -7 and under the sign of ox. Much as a romantic relationship has been suggested as a reason for Yuan patronage of Xiao Zan, Xiao Zhan and Wang Yibo are commonly "shipped" (purported to be in a romantic relationship) by fans. This reincarnation theory may seem a bit obsessive or farfetched, but it nevertheless illustrates the fervor and creativity of these idols' fans online.

The AO3 Incident

Sometimes, the fervor and creativity of fans manifests itself in the form of fanfiction, stories written by fans using existing characters or celebrities and posted online to databases such as Archive Of Our Own (AO3). Much of the RPF (real person fanfiction) pairing Xiao Zhan and Wang Yibo tends to be homoerotic in nature,[72] expanding upon the close friendship of their characters Wei Wuxian and Wang Yibo in *The Untamed*. Unfortunately, in early 2020, some Xiao Zhan fans were offended when they discovered this fanfic and reported AO3 to the Chinese authorities, because while homosexuality was legalized in mainland China in 1997, it is still somewhat censored in the media. In retaliation, Xiao Zhan anti-fans, or haters, boycotted Xiao and the brands he endorsed.[73] According to Marrian Zhou, contributor to *Nikkei Asia*: "'227' [another name for the AO3 incident in China] participants started flooding Olay's customer service line demanding receipts for products they had purchased weeks or months ago. This action is based on the Chinese tax law that customers have the right to ask for replacement receipts no matter how long after the purchase. If Olay did not give them the receipts, they would report the company to Chinese authorities. Olay had already been called to the appropriate government agency for questioning, according to Chinese media."[74] Extra staff time to answer complaints and produce past receipts was costly to Olay, not to mention the loss of prestige caused by the AO3 episode.

As a result of the incident, AO3 is no longer available in mainland China, while Xiao Zhan lost his endorsements with Estée Lauder (and later Olay), even though in the minutes after Xiao Zhan's 2019 Singles Day[75] commercials for his signature Estée Lauder Pure Colour Envy lipstick shades #333 (Persuasive Matte) and #314 (Desire Matte), the products sold out in China in less than an hour.[76] Having lost face—and major endorsements—Xiao Zhan's career looked to be in jeopardy. In my essay for *Bloomsbury Fashion Business Cases*, "Idols as Brand Ambassadors in China: The Rise and Fall and Rise of Xiao Zhan: Crisis Management at Estée Lauder and Olay," I noted that "while Wang is—much like a major American automaker—likely 'too big to fail,' Xiao's career and popularity, catapulted as it was by *The Untamed*, was still in March 2020 in its early stages and not immune to scandal. Additionally, many fans wish for the idols—straight or gay—to maintain at least the veneer of celibacy, so that they may pretend that the idol is their 'husband.' This idea of male idol as celibate has been suggested in the case of Wang Yibo by female idols Cheng Xiao (also managed by Yuehua) and Song Zuer, who have suggested that Wang is a bit like Tang Monk[77] (a character in the classical Chinese novel *Journey to the West* who is more concerned with his quest than with romance)."[78] Before proceeding further, it is useful to have a rudimentary understanding of the people who create fanfiction. As cultural theorist Henry Jenkins explains:

> Fans are consumers and producers. Those with the power to produce have access to the possibility of capital—in this case, cultural capital. Fans, whom Jenkins describes within a cultural economy as "peasants, not proprietors", both consume and produce (Jenkins 27). This very action has the power to destabilize this classed system, the boundaries of what is acceptable taste, of what is art, and how art itself can be consumed (16). Fans engage with texts in a fluid, constantly shifting, negotiated way. They take meaning and make meaning. This very action has the potential to break cultural codes; not just to break them, but to recreate, rebuild and manipulate them. Fan communities, even within their own sub cultures, experience and recreate this constant struggle over meaning.
>
> Hills xi[79]

In this way, fics can be useful for researchers studying the fan culture surrounding idols. Some well-received (based on the number of kudos and hits) RP (real person) fics that feature the Xiao Zhan and Wang Yibo CP are "Across a Lake of Glass," "Bring Your Secrets to Me and I'll Drink Them All Down," "The House on the Hill," "Hyacinth," "Once Upon a Time . . .," "A Tide in Two Seas," and "We'll Get Him Falling for a Stranger (or a Catfish)."[80] Additionally, there are, as of March 18, 2021, 20,716 stories on Archive of Our Own featuring the pairing of Xiao and Wang's characters from *The Untamed*, Wei Wuxian and Lan Zhan (and this is in spite of the fact that the platform was taken offline in Mainland China in 2020 due to the AO3 scandal). A well-written, G-rated story featuring the pairing is "Yiling Poltergeist" by Jaemyun.[81]

It should also be noted that Wang Yibo appeals to authors of homoerotic fanfiction as a subject even in the absence of Xiao Zhan. There is a Chinese idiom, "old cow chews young grass," meaning something akin to a "cradle robber" in English; that is, someone in a romantic relationship with someone younger enough than them to be seen as socially inappropriate. This is the basic theme of a fanfiction serial called *The Gege Collector*[82] in which Wang Yibo encounters a different male celebrity in each chapter—Lay, Jackson Wang, cast members from *Summer Surf Shop*, the Roman gladiator from the Italy episode of *Day Day Up*, and several others—and he ends up being penetrated by the said celebrity. *The*

Gege Collector in particular could be read in light of what Henry Jenkins has noted regarding good taste, propriety, and lowbrow culture:

> Fandoms—fan communities that is—are intrinsically disruptive, subversive spaces. Fans, (and by this I mean those actively engaged in the participatory culture of fandom) disrupt boundaries of dominant culture and what counts as "culture" in regards to the arts. What is constructed as true culture is a part of an inherently classed system. It is those in the privileged class that have the power to establish what culture and art are. The establishment of a thing, however, necessitates the establishment of another, of a set of exclusions and exclusionary practices, and/or of a boundary. Boundaries must be enforced, reinforced and policed. This is how "taste" is deployed, as a construct, to police the border between what is art and what is lowbrow; "proper taste must be separated from improper taste".
>
> Jenkins 16[83]

The only chapter without an explicit content rating is the one with UNIQ bandmate Zhou Yixuan, who tries to set Wang straight and get him back on the path to propriety. On variety shows, Wang Yibo has a reputation of only interacting well with older males, or *geges* (literally older brothers), rather than younger guys or women.

520: Roses Only

Following the AO3 Crisis, Xiao Zhan kept a low profile for much of 2020, while his new TV series *Duoluo Contient* had its premiere date pushed back. Xiao focused on poverty alleviation work for farmers in Yuxian, Hebei Province, in response to falling agricultural prices due to the Covid-19 pandemic.[84] Xiao Zhan did eventually step out of the shadow of the AO3 incident, and as I noted in "Idols as Brand Ambassadors in China: The Rise and Fall and Rise of Xiao Zhan: Crisis Management at Estée Lauder and Olay," his scandal could have been much worse:

> For brands, when idols are involved in controversy, it is a matter of crisis management. And as scandals go, certainly, it could have been much worse. Take for example the scandal that effectively ended the career of female idol Zheng Shuang when her ex-partner revealed that she abandoned two secret children that she had via a surrogate in Pueblo, Colorado.[85] Surrogacy is illegal in China and deemed immoral, never mind child abandonment. The resulting Internet backlash forced Zheng to leave her position with Beijing Satellite Television and

> has likely ended her career. Prada, the brand that she endorsed, dropped her contract like a hot potato. Xiao Zhan's controversy was quite minor in comparison to the Zheng Shuang surrogacy controversy.[86]

For Xiao, "getting back on the horse" of brand endorsements was a matter of finding the right fit. Known for his love ballads, a company with a romantic brand image was ideal. Many popular songs in China deal with themes of love, for example Xiao Zhan's song "Kepler," which includes the line "I Love a Lonely Star." In fact, saying the words "wo ai ni" (meaning "I love you" in Mandarin) is done sparingly in China. The sentiment behind the phrase generally feels too strong for everyday use in Chinese culture, and is saved for when one is overcome with emotion, much unlike the United States, where lighthearted phone calls with relatives and even friends are often ended with "I love you." A less emotionally intense means of saying "I love you" or similar sentiments suitable for everyday use is achieved through texting or messaging numbers to loved ones. The following numbers are frequently used as texting slang in China: 520: "I love you" ("*wo ai ni*"); 530: "I miss you"; 770: "Kiss you"; 880: "Hug you"; 1314: "Forever"; and 5201314: "I will love you forever." These numbers are so ubiquitous in common parlance that retailers will often incorporate them into their phone number or even the name of a shop, such as a florist called "520." 5/20, or May 20, is also known as "Chinese Valentine's Day" because of the number's association with love, and flowers and other gifts are typically bought for sweethearts for that day.

The Qixi Festival of the seventh day of the seventh lunar month (usually around August 25), however, is also known as Chinese Valentine's Day, and is a major day for giving flowers and other romantic gifts. According to a Chinese folktale, two lovers, the stars Vega and Altair (Zhi Nü and Niu Lang, respectively), were separated across the Milky Way from each other by Vega's disapproving mother, and can only meet once a year, on the night of the Qixi Festival. Xiao Zhan's "I love a lonely star" is perfect for this night. On August 17, 2020, in advance of this Chinese Valentine's Day and in spite of the continuing AO3 scandal, Xiao Zhan, as brand spokesperson, did a livestream for the Rose Only floral delivery service that received a staggering 8 million views and 300 million comments.[87]

Flesh and Blood and Virtual Idols

To conclude this introduction on male idols, which supposes a young man of flesh and blood humanity, it is worthwhile to explore a potential future—a future that seems increasingly likely with the growing popularity of the metaverse—that is, one of virtual idols as brand ambassadors. Virtual idols already exist, to be sure, and have even endorsed products. Virtual idols are also more bullet-proof, literally of course, but also figuratively in that, in having no personhood, they are effectively immune from personal scandal. In "Beauty Brands Face China's 'Cancel Culture,'" Sky Canaves recounts the beginnings of the AO3 (Archive of Our Own) controversy that rocked Xiao Zhan's career and ended his endorsements with Estée Lauder and Olay, and offers as an alternative to flesh and blood idols—virtual idols, who, by their nature as programmed images incapable of conscious thought, are immune to controversy:

> Given the trouble that real-life celebrities can cause for brands, it's no surprise that virtual idols have been gaining commercial success, and some brands have even created their own influencers to stay on message with consumers. Among the current crop of youthful, anime-inspired virtual stars Luo Tianyi is by far the best known, amassing millions of fans since her creation in 2012 as a singer. Luo Tianyi has appeared in collaborations with numerous brands, including KFC, Nestle, Procter & Gamble, and Pechoin cosmetics. Video-streaming platform iQiyi has also created a very different style of virtual celebrity with its hip-hop band, RiCH BOOM. The street-style characters of the group help to act as a bridge between brands and its popular reality competitions such as "Rap of China"[88] (中国新说唱) and "Idol Producer" (青春有你). The band both appears on shows and in music-video commercials for sponsors including Tsingtao beer and Pinduoduo.[89]

Virtual idol Luo Tianyi also appeared and performed at Alibaba's Singles Day launch party in October 2019. (The importance of the Singles Day shopping holiday for brands in China cannot be overstated, and a discussion of human idols Wang Yibo, Zhou Yixuan, and Li Wenhan's participation in Singles Day activities can be found in this book in the case study chapter on Wang Yibo.) But is Sky Canaves correct? Do virtual idols really offer brands a more lucrative, stable ambassador? And what of fans and consumers?

A Brief History of Virtual Idols in Japan

To understand the virtual idol concept, it is best to begin in Japan, where the virtual idol was "invented." As Daniel Black, a leading scholar on virtual idol culture, writes in "The Virtual Idol:"

> The virtual idol, a computer-generated media starlet largely confined to Japan, takes the logic of corporately managed celebrity and simplifies it to the point of

> caricature. However, despite the simplicity of the motivations behind virtual idol production, this figure also constitutes a point of intersection for discourses of femininity, technology and corporeal aesthetics. Part machine, part cartoon character, part media-disseminated pop star, part toy, part pin-up girl, part game, part doll, part puppet . . . in the design, function and aesthetic evaluation of the virtual idol can be seen an interplay of seemingly quite disparate themes, each of which has a much wider resonance in the culture of contemporary Japan, but also elsewhere in the post-industrial world . . . As suggested by its name, the virtual idol is a computer-generated equivalent of the Japanese aidoru, or idol, a pop star cum actor who can be taken as an extreme example of corporate attempts to prefabricate celebrity. According to Hiroshi Aoyagi, "becoming a female idol is to be wrapped up in a package of toylike femininity designed by idol manufacturing agencies to attract consumers and enlarge profits" (2005: 86). The fact that the management of girl idol group Tokyo Performance Doll sought to internationalise the market for the group's songs by selecting a group of young Chinese girls to form Shanghai Performance Doll—singing translations of Tokyo Performance Doll's songs—further illustrates idols' status as mass produced and interchangeable value-added commodities.
>
> Iwabuchi, 2002: 102; Aoyagi, 2005: 238[90]

If idols truly are "mass produced and interchangeable value-added commodities," does it not make sense for brands to protect their investments by contracting with low-risk virtual idols? As Black notes in "Digital Bodies and Disembodied Voices," "However, a central problem for the production of celebrities is that, '[u] nlike factory-built products, celebrities have minds of their own and the capacity for independent action' (Turner, 2004: 35)."[91] Besides lacking a personality, motivations, emotions, and self-interest, virtual idols, as it transpires, also make handy models and brand ambassadors during a global pandemic.

Due to the Covid-19 pandemic, many fashion week shows were either canceled or held virtually, with a combination of livestreams, videos, and photographs. Helsinki Fashion Week was unique in that it transpired largely within the metaverse, inviting fashion world elites to attend as avatars in a virtual world. The experience, reminiscent of Second Life (a virtual world that will be much discussed in this book), was chronicled by noted fashion journalist Kristen Bateman for *Teen Vogue*:

> On the morning of Helsinki Fashion Week's first day in late July, I entered what is called the "Digital Village," the first entirely 3D fashion week, as an avatar. My first stop was the Sanctuary, where a glowing, moving orb vibrated in a forest environment with lots of clouds, trees and a lake. The orb responded and moved

> according to background noise. According to HFW, everyone's Sanctuary was slightly personalized and the 3D fashion week was open to everyone. While the Sanctuaries are mainly natural environments this season, in the future it will look more like a traditional fashion week and users will see a front row with recognizable industry faces. For now, though, the concept is more abstract and each user is an "avatar" floating through the space, though you cannot actually see yourself. After exploring the environment, I decided to go to the fashion shows, which have their own schedule but can be accessed at any time. From alien-like space environments with the aurora borealis overhead, to crystal palaces and underwater oceans, the "runways" of each designer were definitely unlike anything else you've ever seen at fashion week. 3D models walked down the runway, wearing pieces from each designer's respective new collection. IRL scans of the models were done by New Aliens Agency, while the 3D planets and environments for each show were designed by HFW creative partner NDA Paris and Soldats films . . . When I first saw my digital avatar by Paolo Pinna, I was really surprised how life-like it was. One of the most interesting things about attending fashion week as an avatar is the fact that we're already interacting with AR on a daily basis through Instagram filters. The Avatar didn't look too far off from some of the more extreme filters I've tried.[92]

Technology can become a Faustian bargain. Certainly, it is sometimes very useful, and indeed a blessing, but can also lure us in with its ability to give us new power over ourselves, each other, and our environments—trapping us in situations with sometimes negative consequences. Two of the consequences of technology are the creation of new, unanticipated needs, and the creation of new problems. Technology creates new needs (and problems) while satisfying previous needs, and brands must consider that virtual idols as yet offer "unknowable unknowns," while flesh and blood idols, even in times of scandal, are a "knowable unknown." Flesh and blood idols, because of their fanbases, also have the potential to weather, and even grow beyond, scandal.

Xiao Zhan, Ascendant Again

Clearly, the selling power of Xiao Zhan's personal brand has withstood the 227 incident (see Figure 1.10). Toward the end of 2020, he was crowned the Most Handsome Man in Asia after a lengthy web vote with over 1,000 million social media impressions (Wang Yibo came in fourth). Since the AO3 episode, as a follow-up to his role as Wei Wuxian in *The Untamed*, Xiao is now also known in China for his starring role as Tang San, a spirit master with both plant and

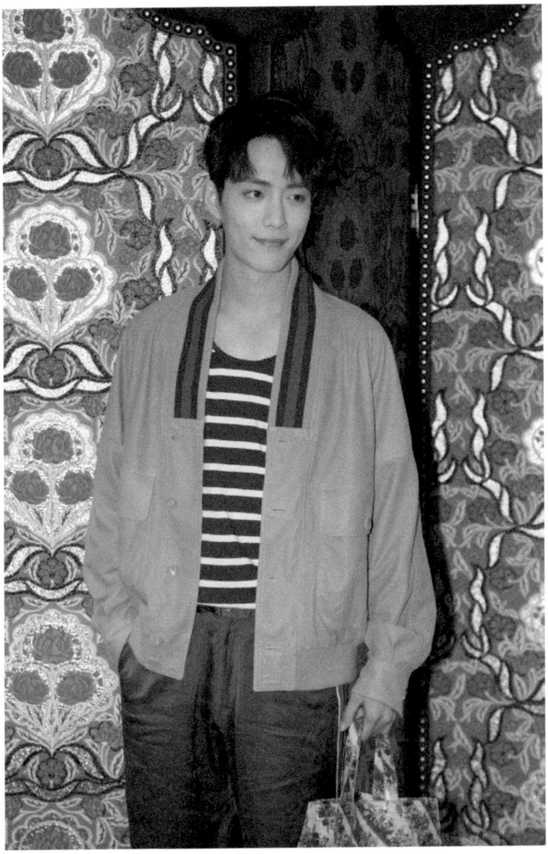

Figure 1.10 Xiao Zhan attends a Gucci event. Actor Xiao Zhan attends the opening ceremony of Gucci concept store on June 27, 2019 in Beijing, China. Photo by Visual China Group via Getty Images/Visual China Group via Getty Images.

warhammer powers who falls in love with a rabbit spirit at school, in *Duoluo Continent*, which broadcast on CCTV (China Central Television—China's main, state-controlled network) in early 2021. Xiao Zhan has also picked up endorsements with Li Ning (a Chinese sportswear company), luxury jeweler Tiffany & Co., Tod's, and Zenith watches. On Weibo Night (the awards show of Weibo, one of China's biggest social media platforms) in February 2021, Xiao wore a Gucci suit (another of his endorsements) emblazoned with a collection-level Tiffany's brooch worth several million US dollars. It would seem that netizens quickly forgot the AO3 controversy . . . or simply did not care in the end and love Xiao Zhan regardless. The next chapter will delves more deeply into Xiao Zhan's role as brand ambassador.

2

Exploring the Relationship Between Fashion Brands, Culture Idols, and Fans: The Power of Naming as Market Strategy

Peng Liu and Lan Lan

Introduction

As luxury fashion brand ambassadors, male idols are being successfully used in fashion marketing to improve the brand image, boost sales/profits, and attract potential customers. Fashion brands need to approach potential consumers and market certain products, and they require various levels of collaboration with male idols known as brand-idol endorsers who have local influence with their substantial fan bases. Utilizing celebrity endorsement to promote sales[1] is no exception in China. Instead of being simply called ambassadors, idols are categorized by fashion brands into a "hierarchical-like" naming system in the China market to match and differentiate various collaborative engagements.[2] The level of complexity and variation of names have not been seeing elsewhere—generally speaking, in descending order from the most prestigious role, they include: "spokesperson" (Dai Yan Ren/代言人), "brand ambassador" or "muse" (Da Shi/大使), "brand face" (Mian Mao/面貌), and "brand friend" (Zhi You/挚友).[3] However, these names and many more have not been used and applied consistently across all fashion brands competing in the China market. For instance, the name "brand face" might be regarded as the highest-level endorsement at one brand but considered secondary and less prestigious at other brands. This rather haphazard use of naming across fashion brands has caused ambiguities among the fans of the idols within the fan economy in this cultural context. Acknowledging that obtaining an endorsement with a top-end luxury fashion brand can be regarded as a great achievement for the idol who always pursues greater influence in the social and cultural context and more commercial value, fashion brands seem to be manipulative in creating and giving new names to the appointed celebrities. This can be regarded as a deliberate marketing strategy in terms of engaging with potential consumers and gaining higher visibility in social media, for example, in this mass market cultural context.

Giving people a name is the "bestowal of status honours"[4] in sociological terms that demonstrates the power of the authority to define discursive positions in its political culture in which the given names are precise and indisputable. However, the current endorsement relationship between fashion brands and idols is more than a classificatory strategy of fashion brands to place idols into the hierarchically arranged naming categories; it is a strategy to connect fans via name making. The debates and discussions on the wordings of the names can be examined as a means to understand the perceptions and interpretations of fans. This chapter also analyzes the parallel naming practice taking place as a cultural practice between idols and fans—nicknames that are given to idols by their fans. Acknowledging the note from Richard D. Alford that personal naming is a universal cultural practice,[5] our study examines the various nicknames given to idols by their fans to reflect the exercise of the power to name, as well as the naming of the body as social practice, as "[t]o name oneself, and to be named, is both to distinguish oneself from and to attach oneself to a world of symbolic exchange."[6]

By including the two practices of naming, the chapter argues that naming a male idol as an ambassador can be seen as a kind of "top-down" authoritarian appointment according to the fans' sentiments reflected in our survey, while giving a nickname to beloved idols can be seen as a "bottom-up" expression of their support. Both practices show the exercise of defining and controlling the idols, via the practice of naming in the fan economy, where the idol–fans relationship is indicative of the power relations between idols and fans in contemporary Chinese society. The given nicknames unveil hidden characteristics of the male idols in the eyes of the female fans that can guide fashion brands when appointing appropriate endorsers to reach potential female customers, which further reflects on cross-gender endorsements in marketing the products in China. Meanwhile, the idol–fan relation also reflects that Chinese female fans, evidenced through the vocabularies they choose to name their idols, position themselves in passive terms with regard to gender relations in Chinese society. Within China's fan economy, female fans see themselves as maternal, caring for their male idols like their own children;[7] this is called fan circle culture (飯圈文化). This chapter, therefore, focuses on the case study of male idols' endorsement of luxury fashion brands in marketing skincare and cosmetic products,[8] a market in which female consumers/fans of the idols make up most of the total product sales. The chapter explores the naming practices between fashion brands, male cultural idols, and female fans in the Chinese fashion market.

Investigation of the practices of naming in the China fashion market is actualized in analytical writing. To support our qualitative approach, a pilot study was conducted using an online survey, which was conducted in October 2021. The survey collected interpretations by respondents regarding the naming practices. The participants of the online survey were reached by the authors using WeChat, a popular multi-function social media app. The participants are current or former university students who are existing "friends" on the authors' WeChat. The app is used by the authors' affiliations for professional communication. There are 2,351 "friends" accessible on our app, of whom 465 were selected to participate in the survey. The group was selected based on their proactive attitude and sensitivity in relative terms toward popular culture. Firstly, most of the participants majored in the subject areas of Fashion Design, while a small portion of them majored in Interior Design, Visual Communication, and Fine Arts at undergraduate and/or postgraduate levels including research-based higher degree levels. Secondly, all selected participants are from middle to high socio-economic backgrounds, and they are self-identified fans of male idols. Thirdly, 345 respondents (or 74.2%) are aged between seventeen and twenty-eight. The online survey was designed to have three sections. The first section gathered demographical information about the participants in terms of gender, age, and yearly spending on skincare and cosmetic products. The question on yearly spending is to locate respondents who have adequate first-hand experience of using the products themselves and that are making decisions in selecting the brands and products while being exposed to the relevant marketing, such as celebrity endorsement. The majority of the 465 survey respondents were females (353, or 75.91%) and the rest comprised 108 males (or 23.23%) and four non-gender persons (0.86%).[9] Some 234 respondents (or 49.88%) spent between 500 and 3000 RMB a year on skincare and cosmetic products, with 81 people (or 17.42%) spending less and 152 people (or 32.69%) spending more. The second section sought opinions on the adaptation of names/titles in various celebrity endorsements in the China market. The third section collected nicknames of cultural idols given by respondents/fans both in the public domain and as a private cultural practice. The collection of nicknames spans from 2016 to 2021, as this particular period has seen a boom in male idols endorsing fashion brands in promoting skincare and cosmetic products in China. Correspondingly, the past five years have also seen the emergence and development period of fan circle culture in the fan economy. Investigation of the naming practices also involved online observations throughout 2021 of the major social media websites, such as Bai Du Tie Ba (百度貼吧), Weibo (微博), and Dou Ban (豆瓣).

Male Idols as Brand Ambassadors in Marketing Skincare and Cosmetic Products

Brand Personalities and Celebrity Endorsement as Marketing Strategy

The notion of brands possessing personalities was first brought up by Burleigh Bradford Gardner and Sidney Jay Levy;[10] this definition is rooted in anthropomorphism whereby human characteristics are transferred to non-humans. Max Blackston took the idea of personifying brands further by proposing the concept of a brand relationship—between brand and consumer—involving a "complex of cognitive, affective, and behavioral processes."[11] As noted by Martin Kornberger, "brands are things, they are tools, they are processes; they explain, they seduce, they corrupt."[12] Like individuals with a combination of all facets that a person is supposed to have, the personalities of brands appeal to the senses and emotions in social and cultural environments. Defining brand personality as "*The set of human characteristics associated with a brand*,"[13] Jennifer Lynn Aaker created the Brand Personality Scale (BPS), which is a widely cited work used to examine various cases regarding brands in relation to consumer behaviors in marketing and consumer psychology studies. Since then, studies dedicated to brand personality have flourished with many either mobilizing the BPS model for examining the relationship between brand personality and brand trusts/affect—Youngjun Sung and Jooyoung Kim's study, for example[14]—while some other investigations have adopted new models, such as the study of professional sports[15] and fashion stores.[16] The BPS definition has been debated and revised to accommodate the increasing number of product categories in the market. More accurate descriptions in terms of the scope of human personality traits that are only relevant and applicable to brands are needed, which has been revised by Audrey Azoulay and Jean Noël Kapferer as follows: "*Brand Personality is the set of human personality traits that are both applicable to and relevant for brands*."[17] The revised definition of brand personality is further refined by Jillian C. Sweeney and Carol Brandon who conceptualized brand personality in relation to human personality as follows: "*Brand personality is the set of human personality traits that correspond to the interpersonal domain of human personality and are relevant to describing the brand as a relationship partner*,"[18] emphasizing the interpersonal and relationship-based characteristics of human personality.

Of particular interest to this discussion, which also relates to brand image, is that brand personalities rendered in human terms can, for example, project a sense of elegance to customers through their rich cultural residuals, or connection to long and intense histories to convey a sense of arrogance and toughness.[19] Such perceived qualities tell customers what the brands specialize in and, in turn, customers can determine their attitude towards the brands and thereby be influenced by the brands they choose. In Kornberger's word, brands have "turned faceless commodities into personal and emotional goods . . . [and] goods [have] became social objects"[20] that are "props and scripts that help us to perform our identities."[21] Appropriating the symbolic meanings of brands can help consumers to build up their self-concept.[22] The higher the congruence between brand personality and consumers' self-concept, the more preferable the brand becomes to the consumers, thus increasing the purchase intention of these consumers.[23] Celebrity endorsement is being used to increase this congruence.

To reach out to potential consumers, celebrities/cultural idols are appointed as brand ambassadors according to the local market where they have large fan bases that can be influenced. As Charles Atkins and Martin Block note, celebrities are seen as being in possession of dynamic qualities such as attractiveness, likability, credibility, and so on.[24] Celebrity endorsement is defined as "any individual who enjoys public recognition and who used this recognition on behalf of a consumer good by appearing with it in an advertisement."[25] In other words, brand ambassadors function to materialize the brand's personality via real human beings, and their interactions with consumers/fans help the brands to achieve their economic goals. The use of celebrity endorsement and its effects and influences upon consumers in terms of marketing communication have been examined extensively by various scholars. Bayram Zafer Erdogan's literature review investigates the source factors of celebrity endorsement as marketing strategy, specifically how credibility and attractiveness models work in various endorsement cases,[26] which is further addressed by Ronald E. Goldsmith, Barbara A. Lafferty, and Stephen J. Newell in terms of credibility.[27] Nevertheless, there are unsuccessful cases where, despite the qualities of celebrities being transferred onto products via marcom activities, the endorsement did not lead to an increase in sales.[28] Celebrity endorsement can be rather "a two-edged sword."[29] Studying previously published academic articles in marketing and advertising journals, Lars Bergkvist and Kris Qiang Zhou have done a comprehensive review of celebrity endorsement research over a seventeen-year period since Erdogan's first review came out, which updates his definition while analyzing new directions.[30] Of particular relevance to our chapter are the source factors of celebrity endorsement, namely celebrity attractiveness[31] and celebrity likability.[32]

Meaning transfer between the endorsers and the brands/products endorsed requires a high-level fit,[33] as emotional attachments to celebrities through parasocial interaction[34] can translate to emotional connections with brands/products,[35] through which the purchase behavior for the brands/products is anticipated. Meaning transfer is explained in detail by Tony Proctor and Philip J. Kitchen, where "the symbolic properties of the celebrity first become associated with the brands that he/she endorses. Next, these meanings are transferred from celebrity to consumers as they rush to select brands loaded with meanings congruent with their self-concept. When the symbolic properties associated with brands via celebrities are used to construct the self or to communicate the self-concept to others, a self-brand connection is formed."[36] Acknowledging that there are studies that only partially support, if not entirely reject, the match-up hypothesis that high-level fit celebrity endorsement would lead to stronger effects, Jung-Gyo Lee and Esther Thorson argue that the condition of involvement between idols and brands can significantly impact on the effect of the fit, for example.[37] It is essential that there is a fit between the values of the endorsed brand and the values that the brand endorsers bring. However, while male idols endorsing beauty and fashion brands in skincare and cosmetic products are becoming popular with female consumers, the product gender image and endorsing celebrity gender are not considered an effective fit, or even perhaps mismatched according to the traditional matchup hypothesis. While the underlying mechanism of female consumers' response to the "mismatch" is worthy of investigation, this chapter focuses on a certain type of male idols in cross-gender endorsement that sheds light on the role of the male idol in marketing skincare and cosmetic products.

Cross-gender Endorsement: Male Idols in Marketing, and Female Customers in Consuming Skincare and Cosmetic Products in China

1. The View Held in Chinese Society of Males Consuming Cosmetic Products

The consumption of beauty products by male consumers has been increasing in Asian countries such as South Korea and China in recent years. Male consumption of skincare and cosmetic products, for example, is regarded as a positive move in terms of self-care awareness, and having good skin is seen as a sign of a healthy body.[38] According to Euromonitor International 2013, China and South Korea were already the key markets in the Asia–Pacific region for the consumption of male skincare products in 2012. Since then, sales of male cosmetic and personal care products in China have increased, and was valued at US$1.9 billion in 2020,[39] with facial masks, BB creams, and eyebrow pencils among the most popular products, according to the report released in 2018 by Vipshop.com and JD.com.[40] A survey conducted in 2020 indicated that 88% of male respondents thought daily care of skin is essential and 65% of respondents thought skincare can increase self-image by making them feel better and more comfortable.[41]

Related to this phenomenon, endorsement by Korean male celebrities and the K-Pop phenomenon are significant driving forces in the trend towards male cosmetics and skincare products in South Korea. There is a certain type of male idol that seems to be favored by fashion brands, called Xiao Xian Rou, which literally means "little fresh meat." This name reflects the idols' appealing physical appearance in catering to the female fan/consumer aesthetic. The "little fresh meat" is considered one of the main factors "commanding high engagement and pushing male beauty trends forwards" in the China market, and has been adopted as a marketing strategy by fashion brands.[42] The "little fresh meat" endorsement in fashion brands serves to attract female consumers in marketing skincare and cosmetic products. It is a marketing strategy that brands use to target the female fans of the idols/ambassadors. Therefore, the use of male idols as endorsers of relevant luxury beauty and fashion brands is becoming common in the Chinese fashion market.[43]

It is nonetheless acknowledged that the products of skincare and cosmetics are not gender exclusive. The gender-specific male idols' endorsement is, therefore, also an opportunity to reflect on gender relations in Chinese society by unveiling the underlying mechanism of the response of female customers to cross-gender endorsements. In other words, the traditional view of gender relations held in patriarchal society, where the male dominates the female, is challenged by the phenomenon of male idols using and promoting skincare and cosmetic products in China. However, there is a negative connotation in mainstream culture in terms of male idols using and promoting skincare and cosmetic products in China, where the "little fresh meat" are criticized as beauty obsessives and for projecting an unhealthy body image in the public domain through Chinese official channels.[44] The negative view of males being "girly" and "feminine," or displaying alternative/soft masculinity, is allied with traditional thinking about male–female relations in a patriarchal society.

2. *Male Idol Endorsement in the Chinese Luxury Market*

Apart from the standard names, such as "brand ambassadors," "muse," "brand face," and "brand friends," that are relatively clear in terms of the name hierarchy adopted in the China market, further complexity has been added by inserting wordings and vocabularies with information about the location, such as global ambassadors, Asia-Pacific ambassadors, greater China ambassadors, and China ambassadors. Moreover, information about product coverage has also been incorporated into the names, such as the particular product series, the entire product line series, and so on. Hence, names can have variations. The following are a few examples of male idol endorsements for brand products in 2019: Wang Yibo became Shu Uemura's "global brand ambassador" (全球品牌大使);[45] Kris Wu was Lancome's brand ambassador but only for the Asia–Pacific region (亞太區品牌大使);[46] Estee Lauder had two "little fresh meats" on board for specific areas, with Li Xian appointed to endorse its skincare and beauty line in the Asia–Pacific region and titled as "cosmetics and skincare spokesperson for the Asia–Pacific region" (亞太區化妝品及護膚品代言人), while Xiao Zhan was named the "brand face for fragrance and beauty line" (香水和美容系列品牌面貌).

Furthermore, various vocabularies have been added to differentiate and distinguish the names from others. Names are created to resonate with the brand's spirit, reinforcing the brand's specialties, or reaching out to certain groups of consumers, which makes the hierarchical naming systems even more confusing in the China market. For example, Deng Lun became one of Biotherm's brand ambassadors, with the given name of "Biotherm female brand ambassador" (碧歐泉女士品牌大使); this means that the brand clearly believes that the "little fresh meat" can help to boost the sales of products designed for female consumers in particular. Similarly, Zhu Yilong became the L'Occitane "China Bath & Body Brand Ambassador" (中國沐浴及身體品牌大使) and Xiao Zhan endorsed Olay as "Body care ambassador" (身體護理大使). Both appointments reflect the specialized categories of products that the two idols are supposed to promote. Wang Yibo endorsed Origins, and was named as "China Chief Exploration Officer" (中國區首席探索官), which is coherent with the brand's spirit of Never Stop Discovering[47] in terms of finding new recipes for skincare.

The Practice of the Power to Name

The Notion of Power

According to Michel Foucault, power is understood as the multiple relations that operate in the social sphere immanently and constitute their own organization.[48] The relations of multiple forces are contextualized within certain social and cultural environments where the process of power being transformed, strengthened, and/or reversed between people is always accompanied by struggles and confrontations. According to Foucault, the relations of power are the immediate effects of the divisions and inequalities which occur in social relations,[49] whereby power relations operate indirectly, consisting of actions that modify the actions of others. As Foucault notes, "what defines a relationship of power is that it is a mode of action which does not act directly and immediately on others. Instead it acts upon their actions."[50] The technologies for governing oneself and others are bound together by the notion that the truth of these experiences, such as madness, sickness, punishment, and sexuality, is firstly internal to the self, and secondly "can be discovered, hermeneutically extracted, and exploited through the intervention of others."[51] Furthermore, the ever-shifting power relations are regulated by authorities via controlling how people perceive and discuss realities. In other words, power influences behavior.[52]

Of relevance to this chapter, power, as a notion that has been studied extensively in social science, is seen as one of the dimensions that reflects social hierarchy. There has been substantial research on examining power-related themes, particularly its relation to other concepts, such as status, control, and influence. This chapter, therefore, borrows the ideas on how power operates to interpret the connection or "tie" between the male idols and their female fans as seen in the practices of naming that reflect their interactions in terms of gender relations in Chinese hierarchical society. For example, Nathanael J. Fast, Nir Halevy, and Adam Daniel Galinsky examine the interaction of power and status in terms of social psychology where power refers to an asymmetric outcome control over valued resources,[53] and status is the respect that one (such as male idols) has in the eyes of others (female fans as their counterparts) that represents a dimension of social hierarchy.[54] Status in relation to social hierarchy has been studied via the lens of psychology supported by empirical evidence.[55] Eric F. Dépret and Susan Tufts Fiske's investigation, which focuses on powerlessness with regard to "how power differentials constitute a social-structural form of control deprivation"[56] in psychology, can also help in understanding the interrelationship situated in the fan economy. Fiske further investigates the interpersonal dynamics of stratification in relation to hierarchy, status, power, subordination, and oppression, which can also apply to this interrelationship.[57]

Adam Daniel Galinsky, Deborah H. Gruenfeld, and Joe C Magee investigate the impact of power upon power beholders whose action orientation increases.[58] John C. Georgesen and Monica J. Harris examine situational power between perceiver and target where perceiver power leads to self-enhancement and derogation of the target through a task-oriented dyadic interaction.[59] Deborah H. Gruenfeld, M. Ena Inesi, Joe C. Magee, and A. D. Galinsky mobilize the concept of objectification as a process of subjugation in which people are treated as a means to an end, and is a response to social power.[60]

To Name is to Exercise Power

The idea that language is used as a device to manipulate human society is not new. Scholars have provided significant insights on this understanding, such as Peter Burke and Roy Porter's idea of the social history of language which claims language is a social institution that shapes socio-political reality.[61] Giving names creates categories and guidelines, and language control is a practical administrative method in social management[62]—or to borrow Foucault's words, in terms of the theory of knowledge and power, naming gives form to modes of knowledge.

Naming, creating, and giving a vocabulary to someone in the form of a name or nickname, therefore, can be understood as an interactive power relation between and among the parties involved. In other words, naming and calling out names are a performative power of negotiation. As Janet Brennan Croft notes, "[t]he namer, the one who bestows a new name or uses an already-given name, reveals, through the choice of name they use, their relationship to that which they name."[63] The interaction between the one who names and the one named reflects the power relationship and power shift. In a parallel discussion about the power of the state in relation to moral order, Anagnost notes that the "bestowal of status honours . . . [and] demonstrates the power of the state [the authority] to define discursive positions in political culture through its classificatory strategies—its power to name and to sort persons into the hierarchically arranged categories of a moral order."[64] The naming practice in celebrity endorsement shares the idea that fashion brands act as the authority that creates new names to sort the idols into hierarchically arranged categories of ambassadorship in order to match up with the increasingly segmented and sale-driven market in China. Moreover, the vocabulary given in the name, or the name read as a whole, always reflects, for example, the closeness/aversion of the two, one exerting power over the other, or one bowing down to the other, which not only demonstrates the relationship between the two parties, but also the impact on others who hear and see the name.

Furthermore, giving people a name as a political power exercise is no stranger in Chinese philosophical thought. Naming, as a part of the political ritual in social construction, is omnipresent in China's history. In a parallel discussion in *Confucian Analects*, Confucius pointed out that the first thing that needs to be done in terms of administering the government is "to rectify names,"[65] or naming. Confucius suggested that every political movement needs to be named first (well reasoned), so that the subsequent activities carried out under its name (reason) are justifiable and reasonable, and to ensure that the outcome of the movement will be politically legitimate, morally justifiable, and culturally acceptable. The political act of naming is comparable in its application to the case of the idols' endorsement of luxury fashion brands in the China market. The endorsement strongly displays the political nature of the business action—an action that starts from those at the top who do the naming, to those at the bottom who are named—and also demonstrates the extraordinary capacity of the bodies of the male idol in their adaptation of these "glorified" abstract names/concepts.

Apart from the philosophical approaches, there have been various material case studies that have investigated naming practices across the field of humanities. For instance, the exploration on the relation of body and name in recent research by Jenny Edkins reflects the practice of naming by authorities and investigates people missing after wars whose names were recorded without their bodies being recovered and taken back home for burial, as well as the bodies found without names, such as unidentified migrants who drowned in the sea.[66] Unlike Edkins' s approach to naming practice that situates and assumes the one-to-one correspondence between body and name, where each body shall have and can only be one name in terms of their cultural identity in society, giving nicknames to idols is a collective action conducted by fans creating multiple nicknames for their idols. An anthropological study on similar names shared between the two largest ethnic groups in Nigeria examines how the connotation of naming is deliberately used as a tool of power, whereby the authorities can sort people into different categories by giving them specific names.[67] The connotation of naming as a form of manipulation similarly reflects the sense of control involved in our case study involving nicknames. In addition, the naming practice of the characters in David Foster Wallace's literary writing is examined by Clare Hayes-Brady who notes that the name in Wallace's writing "operates as a signpost to one's physical or metaphysical reality … [which is] fundamental to the sense of one's identity."[68] Names, given to the characters, function to identify the characteristic of, and construct the relationship between, each role in the storytelling, where the connotation of each name is complex and enriches the readership experience. As Hayes-Brady claims, "[a]n allusive name ruptures the boundary of the text in which it exists by inviting the reader to recall the text alluded to, forcing an intertextual characterisation that both enriches and destabilises the narrative and characterisation, colouring events and actions by association."[69] Therefore, the vocabularies chosen by fans for their idols are examined in our case study, where the Chinese characters express the strong sense of the relationship between male idols and female fans in which one is eager to control the other.

In addition to the aforementioned, Susan Debra Blum investigates Chinese naming practices, and notes that "the Chinese person as thoroughly embedded in a world of speakers and hearers whose relationships to each other and the world are constituted through speaking certain terms, and where sound, object, and name are in some important senses combined."[70] In particular, our research has found that naming practices in the contemporary Chinese context mainly concern English name adoption in the Greater China region. For example, Justina Cheang studies the practice of naming in English that reflects one's identity management because it projects the desired image or personal characteristics to the public.[71] Peter Sercombe, Tony Young, Ming Dong, and Lin Lin elaborate on the reasons for Mainland Chinese students and professionals adopting English names, including the selection of names with appropriate criteria for the self, that might fulfill one's desire to become international, and accommodate the needs of foreigners.[72] Hao Wang and Mingfa Yao examine the use of English names in terms of nationalism and authenticity.[73] Acknowledging the above approaches, this chapter wishes to extend the investigation on naming practices to the interrelationship between fashion brands, male idols, and female fans with a focus on cross-gender endorsement in marketing cosmetic and skincare products.

Case Study: Naming Practices in the Fashion Brand–Idol–Fan Relationship

Naming Practice as Marketing Strategy

Luxury brands would consider the suitability of the selected male idols in terms of their fame, characteristics, and fan base to help achieve the two main purposes of the branding partnership: firstly, to improve the brand's image in the China market in order to attract potential customers; secondly, to increase sales and profitability. As noted by Wided Batat, "luxury consumption is a response to a search for emotions, pleasure, uniqueness, consideration, and greatest services."[74] Brands need to appoint several male idols and differentiate between them using various names in order to deliver certain objectives, while maintaining the sense of luxury being offered to customers as embodied in the endorsed products. Luxury brands cannot survive financially on their haute couture and ready-to-wear clothing lines only, so their more affordably priced accessories, cosmetics, and perfumes are the battlefields. The "little fresh meat" and their multimillion fan bases become the main driver for sales in the fan economy where luxury consumption comes at a reasonable price. Appropriately choosing and naming the endorsers are crucial in making the luxury brands appeal to the fans, as the fans are not buying lipsticks of any kind, for example, but buying the lipstick of that particular luxury brand endorsed by their idols. The purchase behavior of the fans for the products endorsed by their beloved idols is one of the main means for supporting their idols.

The naming practice of brand–celebrity endorsement as a marketing strategy has important implications when a naming term is created by fashion brands and given to idols. This name needs to be specific in referring to a certain level of engagement in the hierarchy that should not be confused with, and at the same time allow differentiation from, other names. For example, some idols are named as a brand friend at the beginning, which is an entry level of endorsement, then later they are promoted to be the brand face or brand ambassador/muse for deeper engagement, followed by further promotion to be the brand spokesperson as the top role in endorsement. However, the perceptions of our survey respondents on the commonly used and clearly distinguished names show some mix up and even confusion (see Table 2.1). For the survey, we listed four names in no particular order and 465 participants were asked to rank the most prestigious title (with 1 being the highest, to 4 the lowest), in their opinion, with reference only to the vocabularies/wording in the names. Brand Face (品牌面貌) is ranked with the highest score at 2.93, followed by Brand Ambassador (品牌大使) and Brand Spokesperson (品牌代言人) at 2.68 and 2.51 respectively. The lowest score of 1.76 is given to Brand Friend (品牌摯友).[75]

Based on the four commonly used names, fashion brands have created more names containing information of specified locations and product lines, for

Table 2.1 Four commonly used names/titles in brand–idol endorsement in the China fashion market

	Commonly used ranking	Respondents' ranking
1 Most prestigious name	Brand Spokesperson	Brand Face
2	Brand Ambassador	Brand Ambassador
3	Brand Face	Brand Spokesperson
4 Least prestigious name	Brand Friend	Brand Friend

example, to further diversify and complicate the "naming system" in brand–idol endorsement in the China fashion market. The case analysis to follow provides close examination of the means of making up new names as well as the fans' perception and interpretations of this.

2.1. Case Analysis

Based on our survey responses, the cases of Wang Yibo and Li Xian provide a straightforward comparison of the naming practice in the China market. They are prominent figures in the fashion industry who respectively have endorsements with two luxury fashion brands, namely Shu Uemura and Estee Lauder. Wang Yibo was named a global brand ambassador for Shu Uemura in 2019, and Li Xian became Estee Lauder's cosmetics and skincare spokesperson for the Asia–Pacific region. Both of these male idols were extremely popular in 2019 and had huge fan bases.[76]

Firstly, comparing and analyzing the two titles in terms of wording only, both titles indicate the geographical coverage of what they can and cannot represent. The wording "global" in Wang's title "global brand ambassador" means all global products of Shu Uemura are promoted by Wang Yibo. In contrast, the wording "Asia–Pacific region" in Li's title "cosmetics and skincare spokesperson for the Asia–Pacific region" indicates that he only represents certain products within a certain geographical market for Estee Lauder. Wang is in a better position than Li. Apart from the distinction based on geographical scope, Wang is a "brand ambassador," which is considered as less prestigious than Li's title as "spokesperson," which is the top-end endorsement. Yet, Li's title also specifies certain products to promote, namely cosmetics and skincare, which is again considered relatively less prestigious. Therefore, it is clear that "global brand ambassador" is more prestigious than "cosmetics and skincare spokesperson for the Asia–Pacific region." Our survey respondents backed up this idea with an overwhelming number of 356 respondents (or 76.56%) selecting this response. Only 66 respondents (or 14.19%) thought the reverse, while 43 respondents (or 9.25%) chose "not able to tell" which one is more prestigious than the other.

However, according to the survey, the gap in the perception between the two titles is significantly narrowed after unveiling the name of the brands. Some 253 respondents (or 54.41%) believe that the "global brand ambassador—Shu Uemura" is more prestigious than "cosmetics and skincare spokesperson for the Asia–Pacific region—Estee Lauder", while 161 respondents (or 34.62%) thought the other way around. The number of respondents that chose "not able to tell" remained at a similar level at 10.97%, or 51 respondents. There was less than a

20% gap between the two titles when the brands' names were shown, but there was a 62.37% gap without the brand names shown. Although both Shu Uemura and Estee Lauder enjoy similar fame as luxury brands in the global market, one is perhaps better positioned in terms of publicity than the other in the China market.

The next question in our survey continued to compare the two titles, where the two idols' names are respectively added, namely "global brand ambassador—Shu Uemura—Wang Yibo" and "cosmetics and skincare spokesperson for the Asia–Pacific region—Estee Lauder—Li Xian." A total of 234 respondents (or 50.32%) ranked Wang's title as more prestigious than the other; however, 145 respondents (or 31.18%) thought Li's title was better. While both sides suffered a bit of a decrease, the number of respondents that chose "not able to tell" almost doubled, sitting at 86 respondents (or 18.49%). There is more confusion when there are idols' names attached to the abstract titles.

Therefore, the initial titles without brands and idols can be recognized and distinguished in a hierarchical order straightforwardly according to geographical coverage and other information. The recognition becomes more difficult after the attachment of a specific brand, as brands have personalities that appeal to individuals' senses and emotions in social and cultural environments. Moreover, the differentiation between titles becomes more challenging for respondents after they know the titles associated with and allocated to certain idols, who bring their own qualities to the products, thus impacting on the respondents' opinions. Furthermore, the doubled number of respondents who chose "not able to tell" at the end of the set of questions reflects the complexity and confusion in the comparison in the current naming practice. Nevertheless, this leaves a space for fans to argue and talk up the achievement of their idols in terms of celebrity endorsement.

2. *What and How to Talk up from the Perspective of Fans?*

The fans in our survey selected four main aspects in considering the success of an idol in endorsement from the perspective of fans.[77] The four main aspects are determined by the four most popular ones selected by more than 50% of the respondents in the multiple-choice questions. After further analysis, the four main aspects were found to contain keywords that appear to be associated with the history, publicity, and product price of the luxury brand in the collaboration, which are the areas in which to talk up their idols' achievement in terms of becoming more influential and gaining commercial value. Starting with an open question asking,

"What aspects do you think can reflect the success of your idol in endorsement?", respondents can either type in their thoughts or select from a list of answers provided. The set of multiple-choice questions in the survey let the respondents select the aspects that can be considered signs of having successful achievement in celebrity endorsements. The most selected aspect, chosen by 309 respondents (or 66.45%), is the rich cultural heritage of a luxury brand. It is closely followed by association with the publicity of a luxury brand in terms of it being popular rather than niche, as chosen by 305 respondents (or 65.59%). The third most selected sign by the respondents is the prestige of a luxury brand and the price of its products, as chosen by 301 respondents (or 64.73%). The fourth aspect selected by more than 50% of the respondents is the commitment of a luxury brand towards sustainability, as chosen by 234 respondents (or 50.32%). In contrast, other aspects are relatively less important for the respondents/fans regarding brand endorsement as the idol's individual achievement, such as the total number of endorsements that an idol has had, which only 151 respondents (or 32.47%) selected.

By comparing and further analyzing the titles of the two idols in this way, the names given by the endorsements can be interpreted. For example, our pilot study suggests that Wang's title given by Shu Uemura is better than Li's at Estee Lauder (234 respondents or 50.32% versus 145 respondents or 31.18%). However, Li's fans would think the opposite, as getting an endorsement role at Estee Lauder is highly competitive due to its relatively longer and richer history, thereby having greater influence.[78] In other words, the long history of the luxury brand, which is shown as "rich" history embodied with (in)tangible cultural heritage advertised in the brand's advertisement through storytelling, compounded also by the highly priced products in the retail market, are considered as evidence by Li's fans in talking up their idol's endorsement of having a greater influence.

Furthermore, in a separate case, Wang Yibo has been named "China Chief Exploration Officer" for Origins, which was established in 1990 as a sub-brand of Estee Lauder that specializes in cosmetic and body/skincare products. Apart from the vocabulary which defines the geographical scope, the name sounds unfamiliar and has no reference to other existing names in the China market. Instead of providing information on certain product lines that the brand specializes in or using familiar representative roles such as brand ambassador or brand spokesperson, Wang's name is enhanced by using information reflecting the brand's spirit of Never Stop Discovering in terms of finding new recipes for skincare. Creating a brand-new name with less relevance to other names used by other brands in the China market leaves more space for fans to interpret and express their opinions in terms of the naming hierarchy.

Naming Practice as a Cultural Phenomenon in the Fan Economy

Typically, purchasing items associated with and products endorsed by the male idols can be interpreted as the collective actions of fans in the fan economy. The collective actions are purposefully conducted and guided by self-organized idol support communities that have millions of members. It is worth noting that the male idol is no longer a role model adored by fans in the traditional idol–fan relationship. The interaction between male idols and female fans in the fan economy is manifested as a mother–son relationship, derived from the so-called fan circle culture. Interestingly, the equivalent writing of the term in Chinese is 飯圈文化, which literally means "food circle culture." The literal word-by-word translation back into the English language does not make sense. Because the pronunciation of "fan" is the same as "food" in Chinese, "fan culture" can be substituted by "food culture," which in turn reflects the implied relationship between idols and fans in the fan economy, whereby it is expected the fans would need to feed their idols. The fan (food) culture is driven by the idea that fans actively cultivate their idols instead of being passive followers, like the type of simulation games where players train virtual characters to reach higher levels as the main goal. Sharing this similar concept with simulation games, the pathway in "guiding" an idol to success is seen as the journey of self-realization of fans in which idols are the fans' subjectivity, satisfying the self-imagination of viewers/fans. At the same time, idols are also the objects of fans' desires, filling the absence of ideal partners, for example. Fans are endowed with new characteristics as the "guardian" of the idol, and they become (partially) responsible for the development of the idol.

Therefore, being together with the idol is interpreted and actualized as helping the idol to become more influential and valuable in the cultural and commercial sense. In concrete terms, there is a strong willingness on the part of the members of the self-organized idols' support communities which are mostly female fans that spend money to support the male idols. Many of these fans would see it as their duty to help the careers of their favourite idols by ensuring that their endorsements are successful. Therefore, borrowing the idea from the simulation games that players may have to purchase additional items or equipment with virtual currency in the game to level up the character, fans purchase an album, a movie ticket, gifts, and so on, as their way to support and cultivate their idols in reality. There are always new sales records made by fans' purchasing behaviors, given the colossal number of the fan base, whereby the bigger sale made, the higher the value of the idol in fulfilling their career goals to be more influential.

On the other hand, the fan culture and fan economy in China have created some sociological concerns in recent years. Typically, in relation to financial activities, raising money online or crowdfunding can reach a huge number of fans which becomes the main way to increase idol-related sales, but some illegal financial acts, such as monetary fraud, have caused some legal and sociological concerns. Government reports have been released and subsequent updated regulations have been issued in the past two years to address the growing concerns about the fan culture in China, which shows that the authorities are determined to regulate fan culture, including the report on the fan-related black industry in 2020,[79] the announcement on special rectification of the network environment in 2020,[80] six government departments making a joint effort against cyberspace abuse and violence in 2020,[81] and further strengthening of controls on five types of fan culture-related chaos in 2021.[82]

Despite the above, the engagement between female fans and their male idols can be observed in name giving as a cultural practice. The naming, titling, or categorizing of people is a social political practice that can break through the boundaries of gender, ethnicity, and geographical specificity by including terms and vocabularies borrowed from other traditions and languages throughout human history. At the same time, these given names, titles, and categories can consolidate the cultural specificity of the groups and communities using these names so that the self-affirmation of members within are enhanced, despite the varied social, cultural, and economic backgrounds. In other words, far from being intermediaries of information striving for objectivity and neutrality, in selecting terms and categories to name, organize, and celebrate their relation to the "little fresh meat," female fans give nicknames that not only express their commitment as members of a support community, but also project their personal emotions regarding the private and indeed one-way relationship with the male idols. The content and the way of making the nicknames reflect the characteristics of the idols in the minds of the female fans as well as the desired private relationships with their idols that perhaps will never be realized.

Our survey respondents were asked to provide the five idol nicknames known in public and/or among any private groups for the current super-popular male idols widely regarded as "little fresh meat" in China in 2021, namely, Xiao Zhan, Wang Yibo, Yi Yang Qian Xi, Yang Yang, and Li Xian. The survey indicates that 302 respondents (or 64.94%) are aware of the multiple nicknames of the given idols, and nearly one-third (141, or 30.32%) of the respondents admit that they have been involved in creating nicknames for their idols in private. There are more than 200 nicknames collected by the survey, with 86 identified for analysis after we had eliminated repetitions, typos by respondents, nicknames with negative connotations, and those composed using numbers and/or English letters. The nicknames were arranged into three categories with further subdivision into sections where applicable, and analyzed in terms of the content of the vocabularies that reflect the following: intimacy/family relationship, characteristics of the "little fresh meat," and appearance of the "little fresh meat," such as being cute, young, and adorable.[83]

Taking note of Bruce Mannheim and Dennis Tedlock's point that a relationship can emerge and start by simply calling out the name,[84] it can be asserted that certain relationships between male idols and female fans emerge from and are reflected in the selection of appropriate vocabularies in the nickname making. The first category in our analysis consists of twenty-five nicknames, each with a key word displaying a sense of family/intimacy relationship between fans and the idols. The contents of names are analyzed and subdivided into four sections according to the level of intimacy shown in the content. Rather than stating that the fan–idol relationship in the fan economy is deemed as a mother–son relation regardless, the subdivisions reflect the subtle changes in between the nicknames which in turn suggest the closeness between fans and the idols (see Table 2.2).

Table 2.2 The nicknames listed in category one suggest a sense of family/intimacy in the relationship between the fans and idols

Category one	Nicknames[85]	Level of intimacy
Section A	王一宝 (big baby Wang), 现世宝 (baby of life), 火羊宝 (fire lamb), 羊宝宝 (baby lamb), 玺宝 (baby Xi), 啵仔 (baby Bo), 赞比 (baby Zan), 啵比 (baby kiss)	Mother–son relationship
Section B	国民老公 (national husband), 现男友 (boyfriend)	Couple/partner relationship
Section C	土豆哥哥 (big brother potato), 博子哥 (Big brother Bo), 玺子哥 (big brother Xi), 波子哥 (big brother Bo), 现哥 (big brother Xian), 训哥 (big brother Xun), 战哥(big brother Zhan), 哥哥 (big brother), 一宝肖哥 (big brother baby Xiao), 有钱哥 (rich big brother), 四字弟弟 (little brother Sizi), 千玺弟弟 (little brother Qianxi), 一博弟弟 (little brother Yibo)	Brotherhood relationship
Section D	赞姨 (Aunt Zan), 坚果叔 (Uncle nut)	Other family relationship

The nicknames in section A convey the most intimate type of relationship. The linguistic use of Bao,[85] which means most treasured possession, creates a sense of a mother–son relationship that implies an immediate family relation. The nicknames in section B refer to a couple/partner relationship with terms such as Laogong (husband) and Nanyou (boyfriend, de facto couple), which are still related to the immediate family, but without the ties of kin. The nicknames in section C contain terms like Gege (older brother) and Didi (younger brother), where the relationship is further weakened in the choice of wording. Gege and Didi can be used to refer to a family member; however, at the same time, they can also apply to any males who are respectively older and younger in age. Section D includes other family titles such as Yi (aunt) and Shu (uncle), with even fewer close ties suggested in the fan–idol relationship. Our analysis of the category 1 names has examined the contents of the nicknames in terms of family relations and shown the descending level of intimacy of the fan–idol relationship as exemplified in the nicknames. According to the traditional patriarchal society in China, the ties of kin in family and ancestral relations determine the closeness or alienation between people and towards others. The closer the tie, the stronger the trust derived, where (in)tangible effects, including a sense of control over each other, emerge. As reflected in the nickname making, the closer and more intimate the idol is called, the stronger the emotional attachment the fans would have, accompanied with a stronger sense of control. Most importantly, the degression of intimate relationship also suggests the proportionate downgrading of the control of fans over the idols.

There are thirty-six nicknames in the second category collated to explore the contents of nicknames that reflect how female fans consume and control their idols through the act of nickname making. In a parallel discussion, Ben Caplan suggests that "the content of a name is not the object it refers to . . . but rather a mode of presentation of that object, where a mode of presentation is something that picks out that object."[86] Hence, the content and the ways of making nicknames show what stands out in the idols for their fans. The image and characteristics of the "little fresh meat" held in the minds of female fans are manifested in the content of the names, such as cuteness, youth, and naivety that contribute to an overall sense of control. The nicknames can be subdivided into three sections according to the means of making (see Table 2.3).

It is common to see a child with double Chinese characters as her/his childhood name in accordance with Chinese tradition. The nicknames in section A are made by doubling Chinese characters, which convey a strong sense of being cute and young in the Chinese language. Moreover, it is a cultural practice to precede one's name with the term Xiao, which means little, such as little Wu (小吴) and little

Table 2.3 Category two shows nicknames made with the female fans realizing the characteristics of the idols. A sense of control is achieved over the idols, which female fans express through the nickname making

Category two	Means of making	Nicknames
Section A	A sense of being cute: doubling the Chinese characters is a common way of making cute names in Chinese culture.	咩咩羊 (lamb bleat), 美洋洋 (beautiful lamb), 咩咩杨 (bleat Yang), 羊咩咩 (sheep bleat), 羊毛羊 (fluffy lamb), 洋洋 (lamb lamb), 兔兔 (bunny bunny), 咩咩 (bleating), 羊羊 (lamb), 博博 (bobo), 饱饱 (plump), 战战 (Zhanzhan), 站站(Standing), 烊烊 (lamb), 现现 (Xianxian), 千千 (little thousand), 啵啵 (kiss kiss), 赞赞 (Zhanzhan), 拢龙 (little dragon), 肖肖 (Xiaoxiao), 王甜甜 (sweet Wang)
Section B	A sense of being young: starting the nickname with the word Xiao (little) can make the object young and naive when called out.	小羊羊 (little lamb), 小王子 (little prince), 小赞 (little Zan), 小吴 (little Wu), 小波 (little Bo), 小战 (little Zhan), 洪荒少女小飞侠 (Prehistoric girl & peter pan), 小飞象 (Dumbo), 小狮子 (little lion), 小兔子 (little bunny)
Section C	A sense of being controlled: referring to docile animals in the content of the nicknames.	绵羊 (sheep), 羊毛 (wool), 千纸鹤 (a thousand origami cranes), 千纸鹤呆桃 (cute goose of thousand paper cranes), 兔子 (bunny)

Zhan (小战), collected and shown in section B, to indicate the person with that name is at a young age. The nicknames in section C are made up of information containing animal names, which can refer to the naive and compliant character of the persons being addressed, such as sheep (绵羊), crane (鹤), and rabbit (兔子). The imagery of vocabularies in nicknames can be enriched by referring to actual animals, for example, as the given vocabularies can activate vivid metaphors in people hearing or reading these names who already have the stereotyped characteristics of these animals in mind. According to the discussion on metaphor by George Lakoff and Mark Johnson, "[*t*]*he essence of metaphor is understanding and experiencing one kind of thing in terms of another*";[87] thus, the naming with reference to docile animals would convey the idols as soft and controllable characters. All three ways of nickname making can be used in combination to

Table 2.4 The third category contains nicknames with overall appreciation expressed for the idols' achievements

Category three	Features	Nicknames
	Presenting a traditional relationship between fans and the male idols.	一博王炸 (Yibo bomb), 一博君 (Yibo Kun), 惊喜啵 (surprise kiss), 战神 (god of war), 战子 (son of war), 火盆内娱天花板 (entertaining ceiling for mainland showbiz), 全才 (allrounder), 枪神 (sharpshooter), 吴博 (Dr. Wu), 酷盖 (cool guy), 阿博椰(耶)啵 (Abo kiss)

create a character that is cute, young, and adorable, such as little sheep sheep (小羊羊), which is an essential characteristic of the "little fresh meat." In this way, a sense of control is formulated by means of the name calling.

Apart from the first two categories, there are nine nicknames in the survey that construct a rather traditional relation between fans and the idols via name making. Unlike the nicknames in the previous categories with clear patterns to investigate, the third category contains ones with an expression of appreciation for the idols' achievements reflected in chosen vocabularies that have little expression of the idols as "little fresh meat" (see Table 2.4). The contents of the nicknames suggest the affection of fans for the idols' achievement that is equivalent to idolatry, displaying a clear sense of the traditional fan–idol relationship between the one adoring and the one adored. For example, 战神 (god of war), 天花板 (ceiling), and 全才 (all-rounder) are expressions to appreciate and describe one's extraordinary capability in popular culture, which are used as keywords in the nicknames.

Conclusion

This chapter has explored the interrelationship between luxury fashion brands, male idols, and female fans in terms of sociological naming practices reflected in celebrity endorsement activities in marketing skincare and cosmetic products in China and in nickname making as a cultural practice. The relationship is situated within the fan economy in which the endorsement partnerships between luxury fashion brands and cultural idols are designed for and driven by the collective purchasing power of millions of fans. In other words, when it comes to marketing skincare and cosmetic products for mainly female consumers, the fashion brands have determined that the endorsers cannot be any celebrities but increasingly the male idols deemed as beautiful young men with millions of fans whose physical appearance and characteristics cater to the taste of female customers, as reflected in the name of this category of idols, namely "little fresh meat."

Despite criticism in China's state media of the male idols for using and promoting skincare and cosmetic products as going against the cultural value embedded in the traditional image of masculinity, cross-gender endorsement as a marketing strategy works well for these products, with soaring mega-sales being recorded in the China market. The rather "loose" but creative way of naming endorsers for various collaborations across different fashion brands has led to vibrant interpretations and discussions among fans in social media platforms. Acknowledging that there is not yet a practical and widely recognized standard to refer to in terms of the naming practice, most of the survey respondents do not think this is necessary. The survey showed that only 138 (or 29.68%) respondents think it is necessary to establish a universal standard to name endorsers in an instructive and precise way. In contrast, nearly half of the total of survey participants, 218 (or 46.88%), selected "it won't affect me," while 109 (or 23.44%) respondents agree that a universal standard is not needed. Therefore, the various names created by the fashion brands is a business practice that impacts on the fans of endorsers and beyond, which in turn benefits the fashion brands in the market.

To further investigate the aforementioned interrelationship, another type of name making by the fans of male idols was analyzed. According to our survey, 311 (or 66.88%) respondents who are not necessarily fans of any one of the given five "little fresh meat," can name at least one or more nicknames for the five. Therefore, nicknames are a common cultural phenomenon and widely accepted practice in China. Giving nicknames to the male idols is a means of grouping together with and/or differentiating from those sharing similar ideas and values in the popular cultural domain. The analysis and the categorization of the collected nicknames in the survey emphasizes the means of making in relation to the known characteristics of the "little fresh meat," as reflected in the use of Chinese characters in the nicknames. Alternatively, these collected nicknames can be grouped in different ways, such as under each of five individual idols to see what and how many nicknames each idol has, whereby associated analysis can reflect the characteristics of each idol in the eyes of fans, or, relatedly, how the popularity of an idol can be reflected in the quantity of nicknames he has from his fans. The analysis on nicknames provides an overall assessment of the idol–fan relationship which is an important reference in the fan economy when it comes to selecting the appropriate endorsers.

3

Idol Case Study—Wang Yibo, Aloof White Peony of Luoyang: Subverting Celebrity Styling

Amanda Sikarskie

Wang Yibo (王一博, b. 1997), the so-called "Dance King of Asia," is a gifted and versatile performer and a super idol who serves as ambassador for dozens of brands in China. Wang left home at the age of thirteen for four years of intensive training at an idol school in Korea under Yuehua Entertainment, returning to China at seventeen as the *maknae* (Korean term for the youngest member of a group of friends, commonly used as a role in K-Pop groups), rapper, and main dancer for the K-Pop/C-Pop group UNIQ (*Falling in Love*, *EOEO*, *Monster*). At eighteen, he became a co-host[1] of the popular Chinese variety/talk show *Day Day Up* (*Tian Tian Xiang Shang*).[2] Wang Yibo skyrocketed in popularity after he co-starred in the global hit costume drama *The Untamed* (*Chen Qing Ling*, 2019). He was also a dance mentor on the reality girl group talent bootcamp competition show *Produce 101* and on the urban/hip-hop dance competition show *Street Dance of China 3* and *4*, appeared in the skateboarding reality show *One More Try*, the surfing reality show *Summer Surf Shop*, *Bravo Youngsters* (alongside Huang Zitao, China's brand ambassador for Loewe), and has several other dramas—the role of Xie Yun in *The Legend of Fei*, *The Wind From Luoyang*, *Being a Hero*, *Gank Your Heart*, *Formed Police Unit*, *Faith Makes Great*—and variety show appearances to his credit. Youku produced a documentary about Wang—*Wang Yibo: A Better Self*—in 2021.

As a solo artist, Wang Yibo gained renown with "Dance on the Floor," which he performed on *Day Day Up* in 2018. His popularity exploded with his song "Wu Gan"[3] in 2019, which sold 10 million digital copies in under eleven hours, and "The Rules of My World," in 2020, which sold 7.5 million digital copies in under fifteen minutes.[4] His 2021 single "Starlight of Mountains and Rivers" was released in autumn 2021. He has also gained renown in the sporting world, racing motorcycles for Yamaha. Weibo is the most used social media platform in

China, and at the 2020 Weibo Awards, Wang won the Weibo Hot Figure of the Year award and the Weibo God award.

Given his popularity (and looks), Wang is in high demand as a brand endorser, working with fashion brands from Chanel to Japanese denimwear label Evisu/Evisukuro to Abercrombie to sportswear companies like Nike,[5] Anta Sports/Anta Kids and FILA,[6] Banana in, and Peacebird clothing. The Goldman Sachs June 2021 “Greater China Consumer Corporate Day Takeaways” investor briefing even rated Anta at “buy” as Anta “rebounded again following the debut of celebrity Wang Yibo [as brand ambassador].”[7] Wang also endorses jewelry brands Swarovski and Tiffany & Co., Casio watches, cosmetics and skincare brands Shu Uemura (as global ambassador), Origins, Miniso (see Figure 3.1), Abby’s Choice (and formerly L’Oréal and Korean beauty brand Laneige), and a variety of other brands including the Audi Q2L, DiDi (a popular taxi service in China), China Unicom, China’s Bank of Communications (Wang actually appears on three credit card designs), the Redmi 10X and K40 mobile phones (see Figure 3.2), Bang & Olufsen stereo equipment, Beddybear insulated thermoses, Bissell vacuum cleaners, Colgate

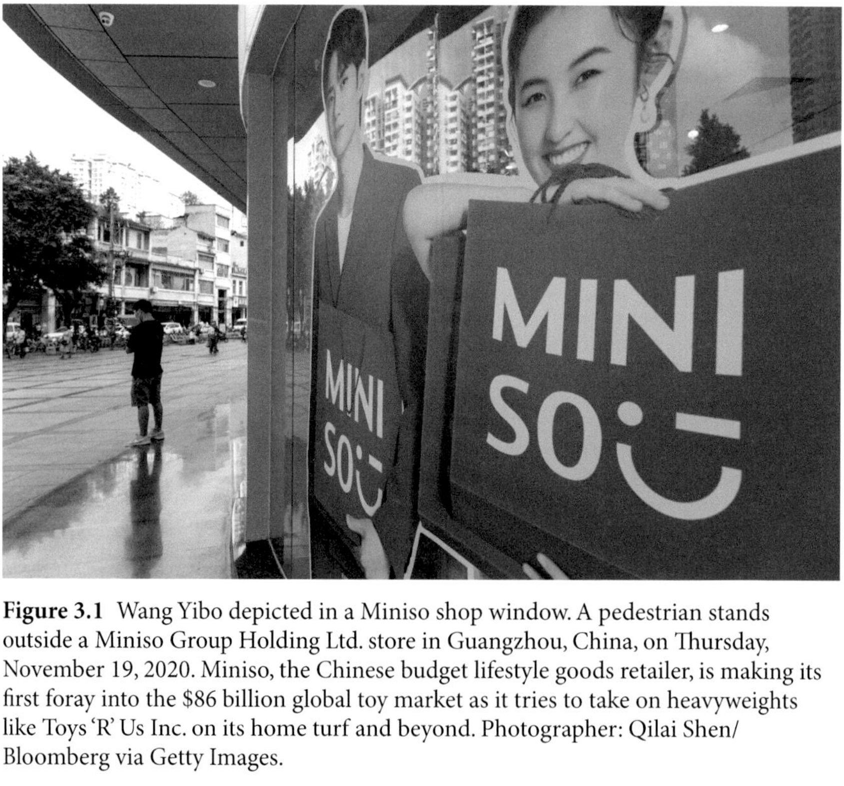

Figure 3.1 Wang Yibo depicted in a Miniso shop window. A pedestrian stands outside a Miniso Group Holding Ltd. store in Guangzhou, China, on Thursday, November 19, 2020. Miniso, the Chinese budget lifestyle goods retailer, is making its first foray into the $86 billion global toy market as it tries to take on heavyweights like Toys ‘R’ Us Inc. on its home turf and beyond. Photographer: Qilai Shen/Bloomberg via Getty Images.

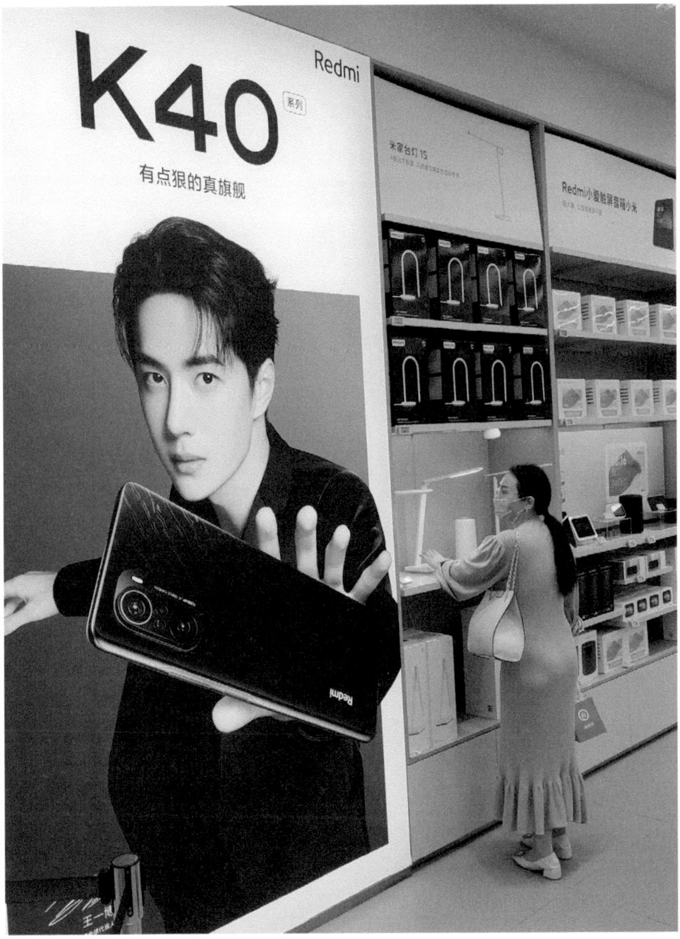

Figure 3.2 Wang Yibo—Redmi K40 advertisement. A photo taken on May 11, 2021 shows the newly launched Mi's first Mix foldable smartphone and Redmi K40 at the store in Shanghai, China. On May 26, 2021, Xiaomi Group announced that its total revenue in the first quarter of 2021 was 76.9 billion yuan, up 54.7% year on year. Photo Costfoto/Barcroft Media via Getty Images.

toothpaste, Eleme (a takeout food delivery mobile app), Helen Keller (eyewear), Himalayas (an audio app), KellyOne Popper (a carbonated beverage), Lenovo computers, Lowen white beer, Lyfen snacks, Minute Maid, Monster Energy (see Figure 3.3), PingAn insurance, Richora (New Zealand honey), Skittles, Stride gum, Wild Aid (a wildlife charity), Yangjin beer, and even KFC (and even this extensive list is not conclusive), as well as being the cultural promotion envoy of the 2022 Beijing Winter Olympic and Paralympic Games.

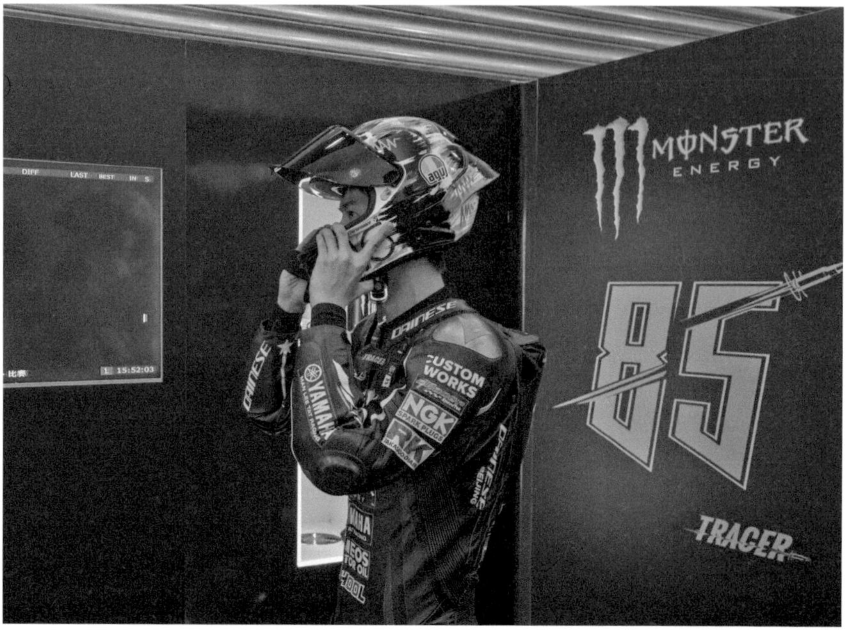

Figure 3.3 Tracer 85 (Wang Yibo), sponsored by Monster Energy, competes in motorcycle races at Zhuhai. Idol Wang Yibo takes part in a motorcycle racing held by Zhuhai Motorsports Association (ZMA) at the Zhuhai International Circuit on October 7, 2020 in Zhuhai, Guangdong Province of China. Photo by VCG/VCG via Getty Images.

Wang Yibo

In researching material for this chapter, I spent months reading posts by various Asian fashion magazines on Instagram and Weibo, and watched hundreds of hours of Chinese television, mostly Hunan Satellite TV uploaded to YouTube by the Mango app. It was through *Day Day Up*, a Hunan TV program, that I became familiar with Wang Yibo, and it was immediately clear that here was a person who must be an important figure in fashion marketing in China. My research questions eventually coalesced around the following themes:

- From his teenage years, Wang Yibo was styled as "cool and chic" and "Aloof White Peony of Luoyang" by Yuehua Management. "Cool and chic" is certainly what many young women hope to be and cool sells a lot of clothes. What else from his idol school training has helped to groom him to become a brand ambassador?

- Wang wears Celine menswear for many of his public appearances, yet he is not their brand ambassador (at least, not as of June 2020). Why Celine?
- As brand ambassador, Wang of course wears Chanel frequently. But it is usually Chanel womenswear. Is this because as brand ambassador he is mostly supposed to be marketing clothes to women? Or is it that they just fit his frame very well? Or is there another reason? (See Figure 3.4, below.)
- Wang wore a light blue tweed Chanel jacket at the 2020 Weibo Awards. This seemed like a shrewd move, because it suggested Lan Zhan's (the character he played) light blue wardrobe (and name) perfectly. Was this jacket his choice, or the stylist's? And was the blue a conscious reference to Lan Zhan?
- What do male idols and fans of all genders think of the term *xiao xian rou* (little fresh meats) as a descriptor of male idols in the media? Just how harmful is the term, and what could replace it? Could another term actually be better for brands as well?
- In the West, most commonly it is female stars who market cosmetics, but in Asia, male idols such as Wang often serve as brand faces for cosmetics. Why is it that male idols are so good at selling makeup in Asia?
- Wang has been an ambassador for Japanese cosmetics brand Shu Uemura in a number of campaigns. How involved was Wang in choosing the colors for the Wang Yibo x Shu Uemura eyeshadow palettes? And in the collaboration with the Japanese anime *One Piece*?
- It was said that Wang Yibo looks like the goddess Venus on the set of a *Harper's Bazaar* China photoshoot. How important is it for male brand ambassadors in China to channel a female sense of beauty?
- In his performance of "Trophy Child" with a would-be girl group on *Produce 101*, Wang and company did a song that encourages students who might not be as perfect as their peers, refraining "Kid, you're the best." Having gone through competitive idol school training, how might most idols relate to this idea? Is it important for a brand ambassador to have this mentality towards the brand's customers?
- Finally, and perhaps most importantly for brands and star management companies, can Wang Yibo's success be replicated?

Ubiquitous, to say the least, as of September 1, 2020, Wang Yibo has landed twenty-seven endorsements in twenty-eight months. While female actors still

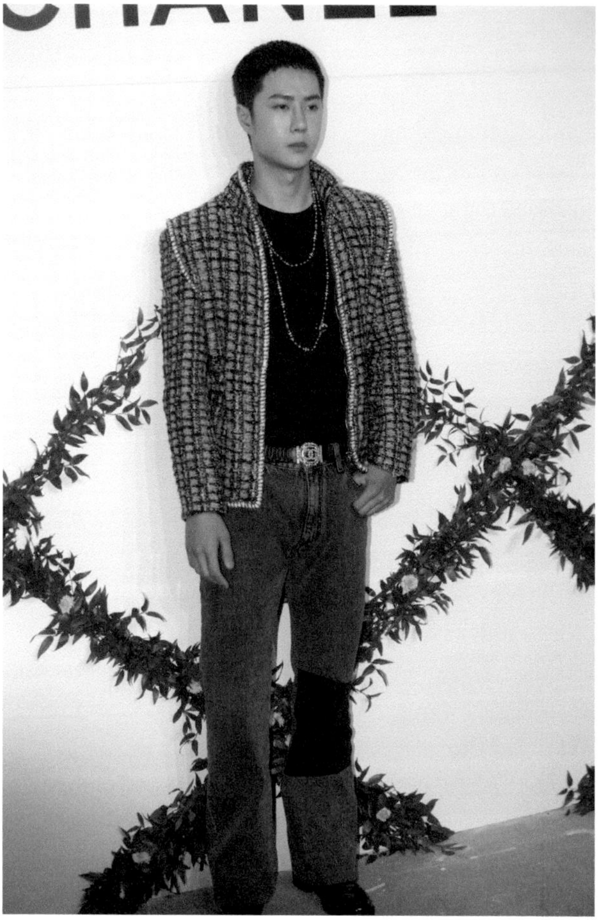

Figure 3.4 Actor/singer Wang Yibo attends a Chanel event in Shanghai, China, on June 1, 2021. Photo by VCG/VCG via Getty Images.

remain on top in terms of the number of endorsements in China—Liu Tao has fifty-seven and Dilireba (real name Dilraba Dilmurat—she is of Uyghur ethnicity) is currently second with forty-one brand endorsements—Wang Yibo is in fourth position and gaining fast. Can Wang Yibo's success be replicated? This chapter begins with a brief biography and then details how a middle-class boy became a pop idol, then an actor and brand ambassador with dozens of endorsements in his portfolio, focusing on personal qualities and characteristics that endear Wang to fans and consumers. No doubt many management companies would like to copy Wang Yibo's success, but, as of 2021, he remains a bit of a one-of-a-kind phenomenon in China.

Aloof White Peony

Friedrich Nietzsche once said that "To experience a thing as beautiful means: to experience it necessarily wrongly."[8] This is perhaps especially true in the case of idol and fashion and beauty ambassador Wang Yibo, who has a reputation—based no doubt in part on his performances in interviews and on variety shows over the years—of having a rather icy demeanor. Even his nickname from his UNIQ days, "Aloof White Peony," suggests a certain degree of coldness, a character trait which some fans dispute and others embrace. Fans of UNIQ—whose members included Zhou Yixuan, Kim Sung-joo, Li Wenhan, Cho Seung-youn, and Wang Yibo—are known as "Unicorns," beautiful and pure creatures from European folklore, aloof and known for their extreme rarity (see Figure 3.5). UNIQ was artificially short-lived; in response to a dispute with South Korea over an American missile defense system, the Chinese government enacted the notorious *hallyu* ban[9] in 2016, prohibiting the consumption of Korean Wave entertainment media and crippling UNIQ, which had only debuted in the autumn of 2014. The *hallyu* ban meant solo side projects for the five young men in UNIQ, in which only the maknae Wang Yibo found increasing fame (see Figure 3.6).

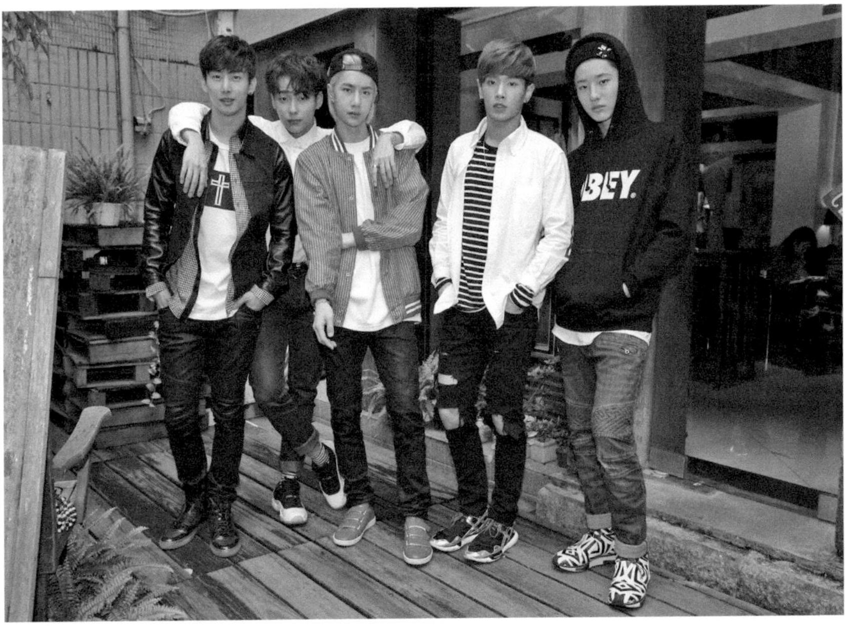

Figure 3.5 UNIQ takes photos together during an exclusive interview on December 2, 2014 in Taipei, Taiwan of China. Photo by Visual China Group via Getty Images/ Visual China Group via Getty Images.

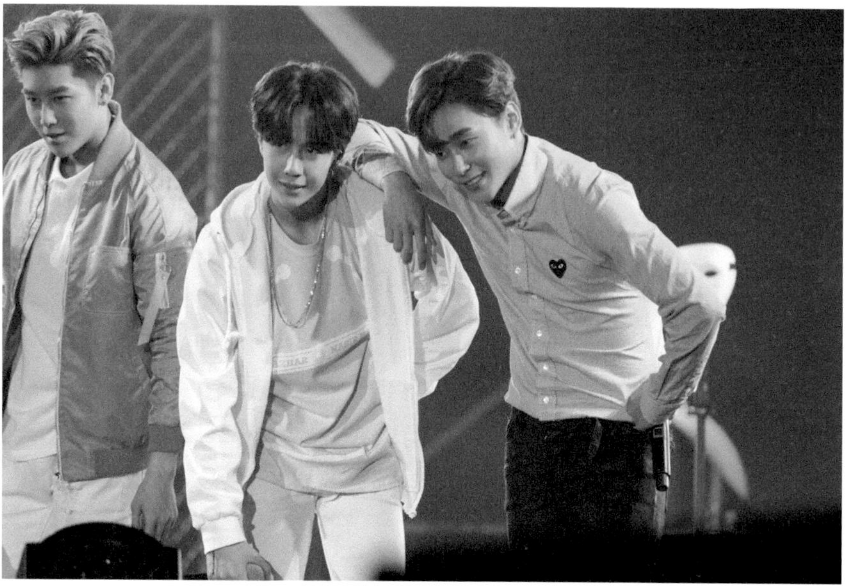

Figure 3.6 Chinese-South Korean boy group UNIQ (left to right: Zhou Yixuan, Wang Yibo, and Kim Sungjoo) perform onstage during the 2015 MTV EMA Chinese stars concert at the University of Science and Technology, Beijing, on October 11, 2015. Photo by Visual China Group via Getty Images/Visual China Group via Getty Images.

"Aloof" refers to Wang Yibo's temperament, "white" to his bleached blonde hair (until late 2015) or to his quite fair complexion (see the section on idols and body bleaching in the Introduction), but what of "peony"? China is a nation of flowers. Each season in China (and throughout much of East Asia) is represented by a flower: the orchid of spring, summer lotus, chrysanthemums of autumn, and plum blossoms of winter. Flowers also have strong regional associations in China. The two idol brand ambassadors featured as extended case studies in this book, Wang Yibo and Xiao Zhan, have both had the language of flowers figure heavily in their careers. Wang has been known as "Aloof White Peony of Luoyang" since his teenage days in the boy band UNIQ. The "Peony" portion of the epithet refers to Wang Yibo's hometown of Luoyang in Henan Province, which in addition to being the birthplace of Confucius, the site of the first Buddhist temple in China, and one of China's ancient capitals, is also the city of peonies and boasts a nationally popular peony festival each spring.[1011] Meanwhile, the Chinese rose is native to Sichuan and Chongqing provinces, Xiao Zhan's home region. Xiao, whose career was in a precarious position following an anti-fan incident online in March 2020, very much proved that he could still pull fans to a brand with his August 2020 livestream for Rose Only florists, which was watched by over eight million people.[12]

Schopenhauer wrote, "That the outer man is a picture of the inner, and the face an expression and revelation of the whole character, is a presumption likely enough in itself, and therefore a safe one to go on; borne out as it is by the fact that people are always anxious to see anyone who has made himself famous."[13] And Wang Yibo often described himself as "chic and cool" in interviews with his UNIQ bandmates (see Figure 3.7). Known for becoming quite cantankerous in interviews, Wang Yibo is not above telling an interviewer that questions that he

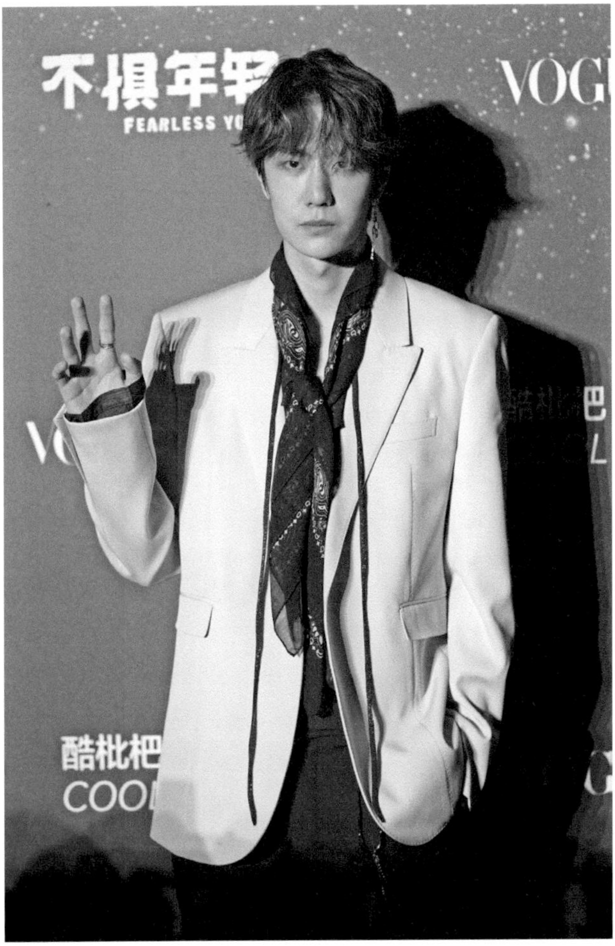

Figure 3.7 Singer Wang Yibo attends the Vogue Me 'Cool People' party on April 19, 2019 in Shanghai, China. Photo by Visual China Group via Getty Images/Visual China Group via Getty Images.

feels are too personal, too prying are "boring" (see the *Cosmopolitan* interview).[14] To be sure, Wang is naturally quite introverted and shy—often mistaken as cold and aloof—and while highly engaging while modeling, dancing, or rapping, when doing interviews and live streams, Wang has a track record of struggling. Wang Yibo's behind-the-scenes persona projects that of the quintessential INTJ—a person with introverted, intuitive, thinking, and judging personality traits—on the Myers-Briggs Type Indicator (MBTI). But I would argue that this characterization, as the quotation by Nietzsche suggests, is inaccurate, and certainly, if true, Wang would not be quite so good at hawking clothes and cosmetics. His cultivated aloofness, in fact, results in a coolness that effectively markets product precisely, but paradoxically because it subverts the conventions of celebrity styling.

Celebrity Styling

Celebrity styling, defined in the Introduction to this book as "a product, or less often, a service . . . endorsed by a celebrity with or without an official announcement of a partnership with the corresponding brand,"[15] is a key vehicle in making younger stars visible and available to fans and getting the fashion brands that they endorse seen by consumers. And, as Sara Liao observes:

> In addition, the practice of celebrity styling also benefits from platform algorithms created and dominated by media corporations to maximize the visibility and profitability of certain content over others. Celebrity styling establishes a direct link between consumers and beloved fashion brand ambassadors, encouraging an interactive consumption experience through the continuous feeding of consumers' appetites for glimpses of their idols. Celebrities may, for example, post selfies of themselves at home in silky pajamas, captured in a chic look by the paparazzi, or in a television drama wearing a trendy outfit.[16]

The styling in the *Cosmopolitan* interview, with a neck ornament somewhere between an ascot and a choker mixed with a black leather jacket, suggests masculine and feminine simultaneously. The ensemble is Celine, a label that super idol Wang Yibo frequently wears for public appearances—he donned Celine suits at the 2019 TenCent Awards, GQ China's 2019 Man of the Year Awards, and the *Untamed* concert in Nanjing, and often wears Celine for *Day Day Up* tapings (see Figure 3.8).[17] Appropriately, for his performance at the 2021 Douyin Awards, Wang Yibo wore a Celine black leather motorcycle jacket from their "The Dancing Kid" line.

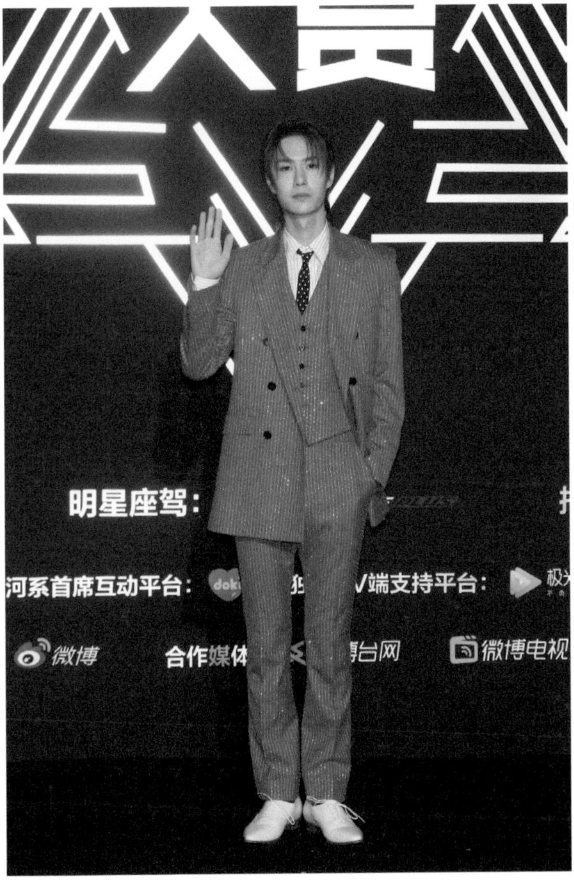

Figure 3.8 Actor/singer Wang Yibo arrives at the red carpet for the 2019 TenCent Star Awards on December 28, 2019 in Beijing, China. Photo by VCG/VCG via Getty Images.

Subverting Celebrity Styling

Interestingly, Wang Yibo frequently challenges or subverts traditional audience expectations of celebrity styling. Though he is regularly obliged to do livestreams—I say "obliged" because the introverted Wang clearly does not enjoy doing them (and who could blame him after the infamous twenty-first birthday livestream on August 5, 2018 in which he was gratuitously verbally abused by trolls in the comments)[18]—Wang has learned to circumvent our expectation of 30 or 45 minutes of endless prattle by eating during his livestreams. This is a quite clever way to fill the time—he doesn't need to say much—but also plays with the concept of consumption: he consumes a meal while the fans consume him.

Wang Yibo and his UNIQ bandmates also defy expectations of airport style (see Figure 3.9). Rather than using the airport as a platform for chic, on-trend styling, Wang—who is snapped by paparazzi at airports multiple times per week commuting between the taping of *Day Day Up* and other projects—dresses instead as an appeal for privacy (a luxury seldom accorded to top idols in China), usually wearing not only a face mask but also a hooded sweatshirt and then a floppy hat over the hoodie. In most paparazzi pics of Wang Yibo at the airport, the viewer cannot even see his face; he is really only recognizable by the skateboard he carries. Part of being an idol means looking fashionable online in livestreams and paparazzi and fan photos posted to Weibo and other social media. But Wang—who wishes to closely guard his private life in so far as he can—simultaneously performs this online celebrity styling while also subverting it. There are trolls and anti-fans out there, of course, but judging by his massive and so-far enduring popularity on Weibo, his fans do not mind, and many probably even find it endearing. Where fans do get to see Wang Yibo (and the products he represents) in his fashionable glory are in fashion magazine shoots, advertisements, awards shows and red carpets, webcast interviews, and organized fan meetups.

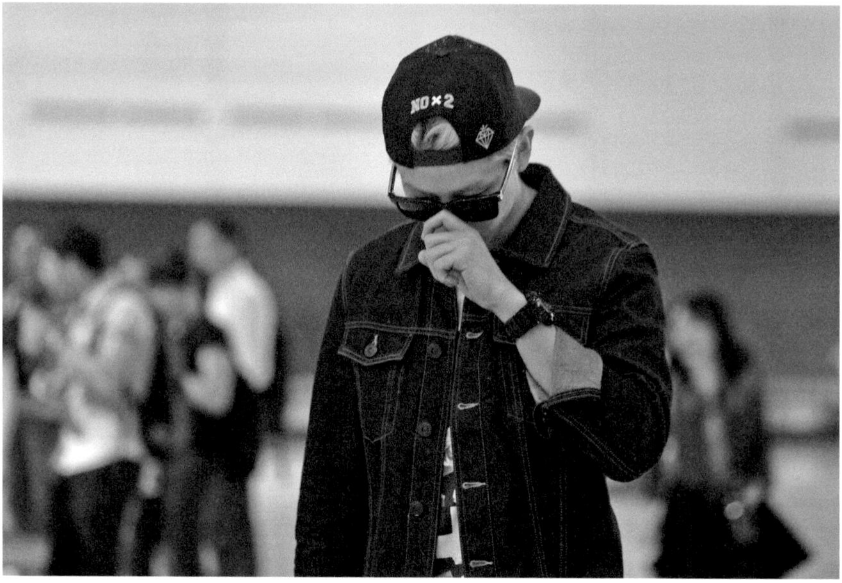

Figure 3.9 Zhou Yixuan's airport style. Chinese singer Zhou Yixuan of Chinese-South Korean boy group UNIQ arrives in Nanjing, Jiangsu Province, on September 13, 2015. Photo by Visual China Group via Getty Images/Visual China Group via Getty Images.

Day Day Up

Wang Yibo whooshes down an indoor snowboarding hill in January 2021 on *Day Day Up* (*Tian Tian Xiang Shang*), the variety show which he co-hosts on Hunan Satellite TV. In skiing into modernity, Andrew Denning notes that in the early twentieth century, choreographers became interested in alpine skiing for its beautiful, fluid movements: "The cultural historian Hillel Schwartz shows, for example, how commentators interpreted torsional movements beginning in the upper body and 'spinning out from a soulful center' as physical expressions of internal fluidity, rhythm, spontaneity, and harmony."[19] Who better than an idol, then, who is by necessity a professional dancer, to serve as ambassador for downhill events at the Winter Olympics? Wang, a super idol with numerous brand endorsements, is also, as an official ambassador of the 2022 Beijing Winter Games, selling not only the promise of winter fun but also national pride and hope for the future of China's youth. Over one hundred years ago, alpine snowsports were described by cultural theorists as formative and transformative of social character: "In the modern period, according to Sigmund Freud, Georg Simmel, and others, individuals had become alienated from themselves and from one another as the real or imagined former foundations of society—harmony with nature, social unity, and balance between mind and body—had evaporated."[20] Twenty-first-century China is working through a similar crisis of alienation, and the grace and emotional uplift of the snowboarding pop idol seems to satisfy these foundational social longings. While an idol has an important social, even nation-building, function in contemporary China, the idol's chief function is the commercial one, which is at the heart of this book and this chapter—the ability to gain visibility and increased profitability for brands. In the conclusion to this chapter, "Kid, you're the best," the idol as economic engine and as an instrument of social uplift and youth aspirationalism come back together.

In the January 4, 2021 episode of *Day Day Up*, the hosts of the show learned about traditional Chinese opera, particularly Peking opera, and even trained to stage scenes from popular operas in full stage makeup and costumes. Wang Yibo played Zhao Yun, the God of War. Statues of Zhao Yun are often seen at the entrances of Daoist temples in Wang's home province of Henan. Zhao Yun is based on an historical personage (died 229 CE), a general who lived during the Three Kingdoms period of the Eastern Han dynasty. Siu Wang-Ngai describes Zhao Yun's character, as portrayed in opera, as follows: "In a Peking opera, the old general Zhao Yun holds his armour in a typical military pose, demonstrating spirit, discipline and severity. He listens soberly to the judgement on the commander who lost a strategic location by disregarding careful advice and through reckless pride. The commander must now pay with his life."[21] In addition to being a popular character of the Peking opera, a form which appeals chiefly to older audiences, Zhao Yun is also a known character in youth popular culture through his appearance in the *Sanguo Yanyi* (*Romance of the Three Kingdoms*) video games franchise. According to game scholar Celeste Rain Johnson, Zhao Yun "was made the series' poster boy for the 8th iteration"[22] of *Sanguo Yanyi* (SGYY). "Further, each poll shows a decent amount of fluctuation between favorites, and a clear bias towards the more beautified and youthfully designed characters, except for one case."[23] While Wang has been styled as China's god of war, he has at the same time been likened to the Roman goddess of love and beauty.

On the set of the *Harpers Bazaar x The Untamed* photoshoot, Xiao Zhan was overheard on camera telling Wang Yibo that he looked like Venus.[24] Wang had been styled head to toe in a creamy marble color, with a loose, flowing skirt as a bottom. In Greco-Roman mythology, Venus (or Aphrodite) was the goddess of love and beauty and lover of Mars (Aries), the god of war. Her son, Cupid, is the cherub associated with Valentine's Day who shoots potential couples with his golden arrows to make them fall in love. When one types "fall in love at first sight" on an iPhone, the heart with an arrow through it emoji (Cupid's heart) appears. Wang Yibo frequently wears the Chanel double "C" with a Cupid's heart logo. In his seminal essay, "The Work of Art in the Age of Mechanical Reproduction," Walter Benjamin wrote, "The uniqueness of a work of art is inseparable from its being imbedded in the fabric of tradition. This tradition itself is thoroughly alive and extremely changeable. An ancient statue of Venus, for example, stood in a different traditional context with the Greeks, who made it an object of veneration, than with the clerics of the Middle Ages, who viewed it as an ominous idol. Both of them, however, were equally confronted with its uniqueness, that is, its aura."[25] In both antique statuary and Italian Renaissance painting, there is a tradition of the "modest Venus," in which a nude Venus just exiting the bath (or newly born, as in *The Birth of Venus*) makes a half-hearted attempt to cover herself, coming across instead as rather immodest. Venus is also sometimes depicted as pregnant, as in Sandro Botticelli's quattrocento painting *Primavera* (Springtime). In many of her guises, Venus is as Lan Zhan (Wang's character in *Chen Qing Ling/The Untamed*) would put it: shameless.

Perhaps a better classical comparison to Wang Yibo than Venus is the figure of Helen of Troy. Helen was legendarily the most beautiful woman in the Western world. According to Homer's epic, the *Iliad*, Helen lived during the Mycenaean period, prior to the classical Greek civilization. She was married to the King of the Greek city state of Sparta, but fled him to take Paris, Prince of Troy, as a lover. This was, in literature at least, the flashpoint of the Trojan War. Helen was fabled to be the "face that launched a thousand ships," as her beauty was so striking that it sent the Greeks sailing across the Bosphorus to war. Similarly, Wang Yibo is, hyperbolically, the face that promotes a thousand brands (not technically a thousand, but after the first dozen, it does seem like rather a lot). Helen, incidentally, was of semi-divine origin: in mythology, she hatched from an egg laid by her mother, Leda, who had taken Zeus, King of the Olympian Gods, as a lover. . . while he was in the form of a swan. While Wang obviously does not have any swans, cranes, or other similarly handsome fowl in his family tree, he does have, as (relatively long-time) brand ambassador, the mystique of Chanel.

Blue for Chanel

Wang Yibo has nearly 34 million followers on Weibo; Chanel, by contrast, has about 3.5 million Weibo followers.[26] With roughly ten times the followers on mainland China's most popular social media platform, Wang's significant online presence makes him a logical choice for Chanel. As brand ambassador, Wang Yibo regularly wears Chanel when making official public appearances. While Wang seems to favor Celine menswear, when he wears Chanel, he generally wears pieces from womenswear collections, perhaps because, as brand ambassador, he is marketing to a largely female fanbase, or perhaps because they are just cut well for him. He sported Chanel from women's collections at the *Produce 101* final concert; the *Untamed* fanmeetings in Tianjin, China and Thailand; for his performances of "*Wu Gan*" on Hunan Television's New Year's Eve 2019 special and at the 12th annual Yuehua Family Concert in Suzhou in 2021; for *The Rules of My World* on Hunan TV's 2020 New Year's Eve Special; and in 2020 on *Happy Camp* and *Street Dance of China 3*.[27] At the 2020 Weibo Night awards, Wang Yibo wore a women's blue tweed Chanel suit jacket from the 2019-20 Cruise collection, and again in 2021, Wang wore a women's blue Chanel jacket—albeit a more cerulean shade, paired with a jaunty beret and a handbag charm (of a handbag) looped to his belt—to Weibo Night.

Understanding and using symbolic dressing, especially color symbolism, is useful for any public figure, but particularly for brand ambassadors. In the case of the 2019-20 Cruise blue Chanel jacket, the color was likely a conscious choice on the part of Wang—or his stylist—the light blue perfectly echoing the ethereal sky blue of the robes worn by his character, Lan Zhan, on *The Untamed*. (The name Lan, incidentally, can mean either "orchid" or "blue" in Mandarin.) (See Figure 3.10.) In *Blue: The History of a Color*, art historian Michel Pastoureau calls blue the West's favorite color,[28] while noting that in many African and Asiatic cultures, "There are certain situations in which little importance is placed on the line separating red tones from brown or yellow, or even green from blue."[29] The color blue conjures deep layers of meaning in Western art, visual culture, and advertising, however. According to Pastoureau, "As people began to associate blue with the Virgin Mary, the color became a powerful element in church decoration and symbolism. Blue gained new favor as a royal color in the twelfth century and became a formidable political and military force during the French

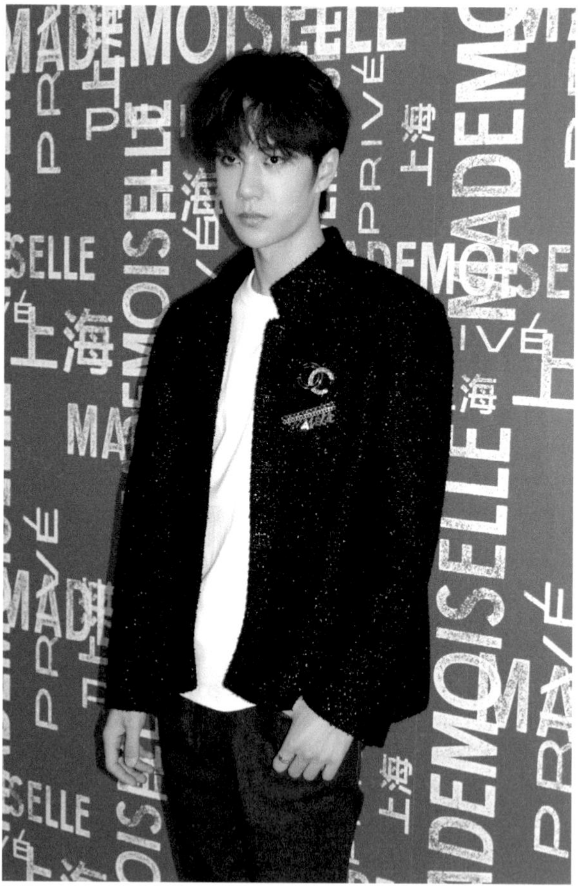

Figure 3.10 Actor/singer Wang Yibo attends the Chanel Mademoiselle Privée exhibition at West Bund Art Center on May 5, 2019 in Shanghai, China. Photo by Visual China Group via Getty Images/Visual China Group via Getty Images.

Revolution. As blue triumphed in the modern era, new shades were created and blue became the color of romance and the blues ... into contemporary times, when military clothing gave way to the everyday uniform of blue jeans and blue became the universal and unifying color of the Earth as seen from space."[30] The theme of blue was echoed in the modeling work Wang Yibo did to promote the Bleu de Chanel fragrance, a masculine scent created in 2010 and "embodied by Gaspard Ulliel in a film directed by Martin Scorsese."[31]

Interestingly, China, while a dominant player in global luxury consumption generally, has heretofore only been lukewarm as a consumer of fine fragrance. Casey Hall wrote for *Business of Fashion* that,

> China dominates almost every aspect of the consumer market: it is the world's biggest apparel market; the biggest luxury market; the biggest source of growth for fashion and beauty brands the world over. But fragrance has remained an anomaly. As of 2017, only one percent of worldwide perfume sales happened in China, and less than one percent of Chinese consumers used perfume daily, according to market research firm Mintel. But that's changing fast, thanks to a new generation of consumers, who are adopting perfume as a way to express their personal style. Now it's obvious that the ones who aren't using fragrance, just aren't using it yet. "The youngsters are all so much about wanting to tell who they are and why they are unique. Fragrance is the ideal way to convey who you want to be in a really subtle way," said Dao Nguyen, founder of Essenzia, a boutique creative strategy agency specialised in fragrance and beauty. "Now it's obvious that the ones who aren't using fragrance, just aren't using it yet." China's fragrance market was valued at 10.9 billion yuan ($1.7 billion) in 2020, according to data from Euromonitor International, around 5 percent of the global market. It's expected to surge past 30 billion yuan ($4.7 billion) by 2025. Nguyen noticed a change in the way young Chinese women were talking about fragrance as early as 2014. Where earlier in the decade many viewed perfume as a pragmatic tool to mask body odour (largely viewed as a Western problem in China), suddenly the conversation shifted to fragrance as a means to express identity, Nguyen said. She knew a major disruption was on the horizon.[32]

Ambassadors like Wang Yibo, himself a high-profile member of Gen Z, are crucial to the Chinese market strategy of Chanel and other luxury houses as they strive to remain relevant to young consumers in China. Hall continues, "To be sure, established luxury giants like Chanel and Dior top the fragrance market in China too, but the most impressive growth is being driven by younger consumers, who are seeking out new brands. 'Generation-Z doesn't like to follow trends, or to be told what they should purchase,' said Chen Ye, a research analyst at market intelligence firm, ChemLinked. 'They are more inclined to take the initiative to try and form their own judgements, they are the main driver pursuing niche perfumes.'"[33] For its 100th anniversary, Wang Yibo also promoted the iconic Chanel No. 5 fragrance. Numbers and numerology still carry strong significance in China, and in a Weibo post, Wang used numbers to tell his Chanel story: 5 (for Chanel No. 5 and for Wang's birth date) + 8 (Wang's birth month of August) + 17 (the age at which Wang debuted) + 24 (Wang's age in 2021) + 46 (the number of his favorite motorcycle racer, Valentino Rossi) = 100.[34]

Chanel entered the imaginations of a new generation of Chinese consumers in part through a major exhibition, *Culture Chanel*, which was exhibited at the Shanghai Museum of Contemporary Art (MoCA) and the National Art Museum of China in Beijing in 2011. The exhibition was reprised two years later in 2013 at the Guangzhou Opera House.[35] *Culture Chanel* took place while Wang was training in Korea, but despite his youth and middle-class background, Wang Yibo has a relatively long history with Chanel. An early identified public appearance by him in Chanel was at the 2017 Sina Best Taste Awards, where he won New Artist of the Year. At the 2017 Sinas, Wang wore a jacket from the 2017-18 Cruise collection, which was endorsed by celebrities such as Bai Bai He, Keira Knightley, Liu Wen, Katy Perry, Kristen Stewart, Tilda Swinton, Pharrell Williams, Zhou Xun, and a favorite musician of Wang Yibo—K-POP star and fashion icon G-Dragon.[36] (Wang Yibo and UNIQ bandmate Cho Seung-youn covered G-Dragon and Taeyang's song "Good Boy" in a music video in 2015.) Karl Lagerfeld had described 2017-18 Cruise range as "a chic and offbeat collection,"[37] words that suit Wang Yibo's personality and reflect his own self-description from his UNIQ-period interviews, circa 2014–15. Wang's highly decorated and accessorized style of dressing for public events—for example, often wearing multiple strings of pearls, as at the Chanel "*Le Chateau des Dames*" pre-Fall 2021 party in Shanghai on June 1, 2021—also fits in with Chanel's penchant for costume jewelry. As Laetitia Cénac put it, "With Chanel, there is a rich heritage of costume jewelry that is revisited with a recurring vocabulary: pearls, jeweled belts, medallions, plate glass, and braided, quilted, or linked chains."[38] Both in his style and his aspirations and demeanor, Chanel was a perfect fit for Wang Yibo.

"I am that Dragon"

While blue is the color associated with the Chanel fragrance Bleu de Chanel and with Lan Zhan, Wang's character on *Chen Qing Ling/The Untamed*, green is the colour most associated with Wang Yibo's personal brand. Wang frequently uses a green microphone and earpiece when performing, green "王一博" ("Wang Yibo") LED signs are held up by his fans in the audience at concerts, awards ceremonies, and the like, and green is his team color on *Street Dance of China 3* and *4*. In China, the color green is associated with spring and youth (a key element of Wang's personal brand), cleanliness, the East, and with the dragon. Dragons are powerful beings in Chinese mythology and folklore, with the people of China's central plains said to be descended from dragons.

Wang Yibo performed Jay Chou and Vincent Fang's rap song "Dragon Fist" for the August 18, 2020 Hunan TV gala. The lyrics of "Dragon Fist" are nationalistic and forward-looking, indicating that now is the time for China to rouse itself after 5,000 years of slumber.[39] The song ends with the refrain of "*wo jiu shi na tiaolong*," or in English, "I am that dragon." In a commercial for the Casio G-Shock watch, a large men's watch with a green-toned case, brand spokesperson Wang Yibo models the item and is then joined by a CGI dragon that coils behind Wang and the watch approvingly, perhaps protectively. The commercial was read by netizens as a nod to Wang's "Dragon Fist" and has been remixed as such, combining scenes of the actual commercial with scenes from the performance on Hunan TV.[40]

Singles Day: A Major Shopping Holiday for Jewelers

Singles Day is a major shopping holiday in China, observed on November 11. It has become a day, simply, to treat oneself, and people may buy themselves goods like clothing or jewelry for the holiday. Testimony to the importance of the day to retailers, at L'Oréal in 2019, "Fourth-quarter growth was driven in particular by the exceptional performance of Singles' Day (11/11) in China, where sales have been growing throughout the year, and the Group is making significant market share gains."[41] While this case study chapter deals with Wang Yibo, it is worth noting that second-tier idols also serve as brand friends for major shopping days such as Singles Day. Fellow UNIQ members Zhou Yixuan[42] and Li Wenhan[43] did not achieve anything like Wang Yibo's commercial success after UNIQ, but reunited in November 2017 to do a Singles Day infomercial, the Taobao Fans Party, featuring brands from the Proctor & Gamble family (see Figures 3.11 and 3.12).[44] The duo performed a mock theatre piece to showcase the Xiaomi cell phone and played various product-related games. Unlike when Wang makes a public appearance for a brand, arriving with a team bearing Wang Yibo-signed photographs, Zhou and Li were not expecting Unicorns to be in the audience and were completely unprepared when an audience member cried

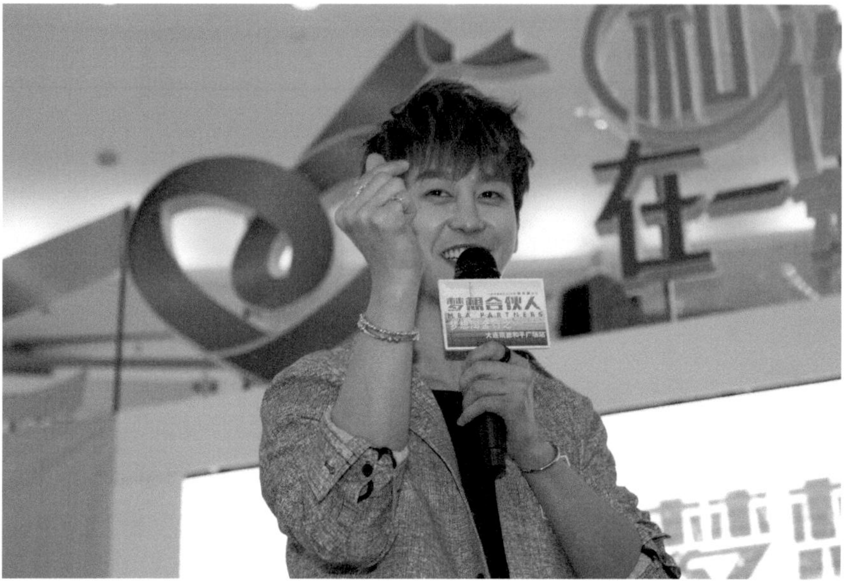

Figure 3.11 Zhou Yixuan does a fingerheart at the press conference of South Korean director Jang Tae-yoo's film *MBA Partners* on April 26, 2016 in Dalian, Liaoning Province of China. Photo by Visual China Group via Getty Images/Visual China Group via Getty Images.

because UNIQ was no longer performing together. Zhou Yixuan comforted the woman while Li scrambled to sign something for her. This incident is an example of the fact that idols often continue to work with brands (not as ambassadors, but on an event-to-event basis) even after they, or their management, believes their celebrity has largely expired.

On *Street Dance of China 4*, Wang appeared alongside Han Geng, Lay, and Henry Lau as one of four idol mentors of professional dancers. Each season, a few contestants on *Street Dance of China*—who are already internationally respected battle dancers or choreographers before coming on the show—become a bit like idols themselves after making a long run on the program, especially over multiple seasons. Choreographer Huang Xiao and b-boy Qiao Zhi, a popular pair from seasons 3 and 4 of the program, for example, had 2.3 million and 2.1 million followers on Weibo respectively as of November 1, 2021.[45] Many contestants on the show appear in TV commercials for brands that sponsor the show, but a few, like Huang and Qiao, branch out into doing advertisements for other brands, especially in the run-up to Singles Day, right after the program has concluded at the end of October, such as Huang Xiao[46] for Jo Malone London

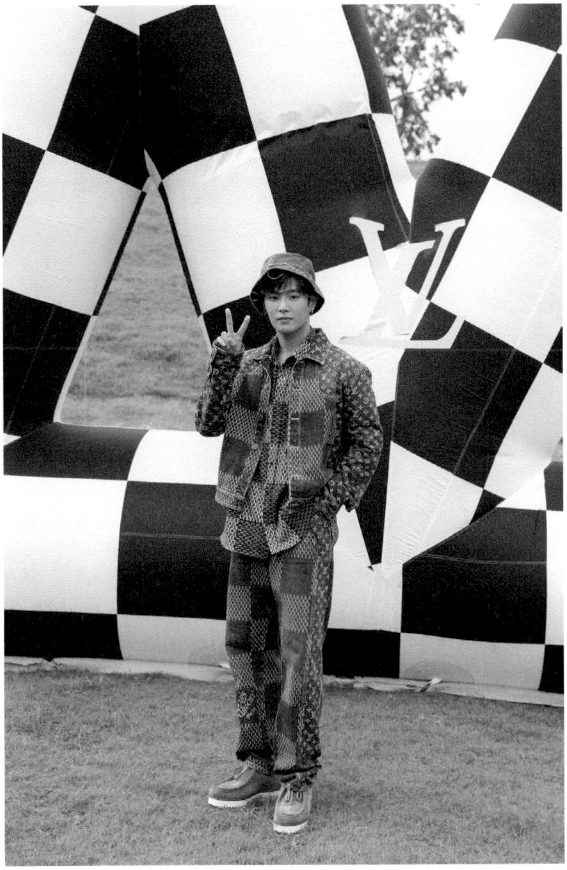

Figure 3.12 Singer Li Wenhan attends the Louis Vuitton S/S21 Men's Collection event at Shanghai Tank Art Park on August 6, 2020 in Shanghai, China. Photo by Lintao Zhang/Getty Images.

fragrance and Qiao Zhi[47] for Casio watches. Many dancers from the program participated in Singles Day activities for T-mall (*Tian mao*; see Figure 3.13), and some contestants from the show also appeared in features in fashion magazines that coincided with the airing of the program, such as Huang Xiao (*Harper's Bazaar* China, *Vogue* China), Qiao Zhi (*Vogue* China), Bouboo—a French expatriate street dancer (*Harper's Bazaar* China, *Elle* China), and choreographer Ma Xialong (*Neuf Mode* magazine). Ma Xiaolong also walked for Angel Chen at Shanghai Fashion Week during the airing of *SDC4*.[48]

Wang Yibo, of course, also participates in Singles Day activities, and in Swarovski's 2020 Singles Day campaign,[49] Wang wears green peridot (his favorite

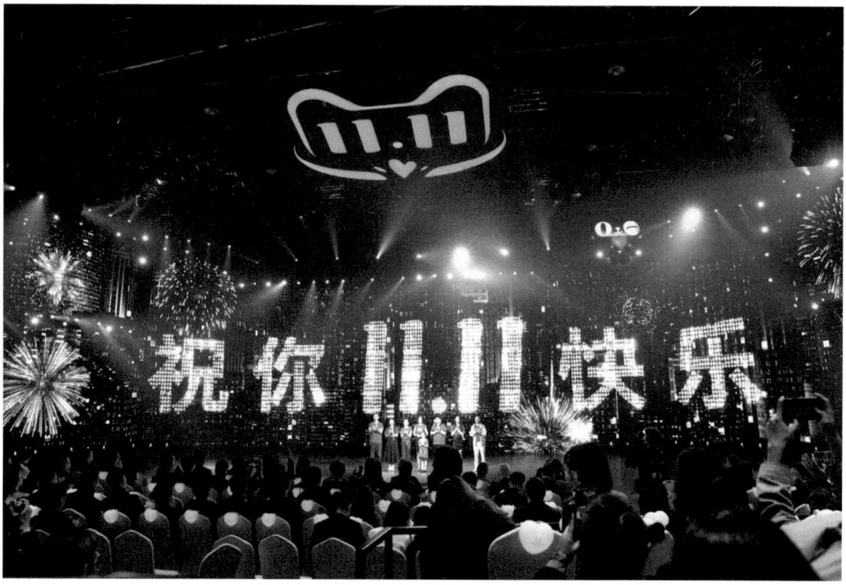

Figure 3.13 The Alibaba Group launches the 2021 Tmall 11.11 Global Shopping Festival on October 20, 2021 in Shanghai, China. Photo by VCG/VCG via Getty Images.

color and birthstone) earrings and attempts to crack a safe. The code, the viewer of the promotional video surmises from the loud heartbeat on the audio track, is the beat of Wang's own heart. Having figured that out, Wang Yibo cracks the safe and looks delighted to reveal a matching peridot and diamond necklace. Presumably, viewers should be moved to treat themselves to their own birthstone necklace from Swarovski, just like their idol Wang Yibo (or to the "Double 11" Singles Day limited edition necklace, earrings, bracelets, brooch, or watch, which retailed from $210 to $625).[50]

Interestingly, Swarovski's juxtaposition of the gemstone and the human heartbeat are quite at odds with seminal cultural theoretician Roland Barthes' understanding of the nature of gemstones and jewelry. Barthes wrote, "Extracted from hell, the gemstone came to symbolize hell, and took on its fundamental characteristic: the inhuman."[51] So for Barthes, the cold fire of the gemstone was profoundly inhuman, as if from another realm. The profoundly inhuman, of course, is not likely to sell a lot of jewelry on Singles Day (nor indeed any day). Haute jewelers like Swarovski rely on idols—and our affective connection to them—to humanize the cold, the hard, and the unyielding inherent nature of the gemstone.

Jewelry was of course, once primarily the preserve of high-borne aristocracy and religious sects. For Barthes, "having originated in the ancestral world of the damned, the piece of jewellery has in one word become *secularized*."[52] Now it has become *individualized*. Of course, many people still purchase jewelry for romantic partners and family members, but as with the Singles Day example, a growing consumer sentiment in the jewelry sector is to purchase for oneself. Certainly, jewelry also increasingly represents one's individuality. This could be as simple as wearing one's own birthstone (growing up, I remember a time in the 1980s in the United States when mothers would often wear jewelry with all of their children's birthstones on them, rather than wearing their own), or wearing jewelry that represents oneself in some way, such as Wang Yibo's Gucci ox head pendant.

For Barthes, the diamond in particular among the gemstones represented duality—pure yet seductive, both fire and ice:

> As for the quintessential stone, the diamond, it is beyond time: never wearing, incorruptible, its limpidness forms the moral image of the most deadly virtues—purity: in terms of substance, the diamond is pure, clean, almost aseptic . . . And yet, it seduces; hard and limpid, the diamond has a third quality: it glistens. Here it is incorporated into a new magical and poetic domain, that of the paradoxical substance, both lit up and stone cold: it is nothing but fire and yet nothing but ice.[53]

Echoing this duality is the common practice of styling male idols in women's jewelry for television and red-carpet appearances. In a July 23, 2020 post, Instagrammer @bjyxyizhan posted a photograph of Wang Yibo on the set of *Street Dance of China 3*, wearing a long women's necklace over a masculine black jumpsuit, writing:

> My baby lion is wearing a woman [sic] necklace, I always love how he doesn't care about gender stereotypes in fashion . . . but that is how you become a fashion trendsetter . . . you bend all the gender stereotypes . . . Like GD [G-Dragon] (although for me GD is a legend) he is invited in many well known fashion shows . . . lots of fashion designers want him to wear their brand and GD has always been bending all gender stereotypes, he wore lots of women attire and still nailed it! That is how my Yibo is [green heart emojis] he look beautiful in everything that he wear [more green heart emojis].[54]

Clearly, this blogger is enamored of Wang Yibo's masculine feminine duality. This, too, one can surmise, sells jewelry. And in fact, "More than half of Gen Z customers shop from both menswear and womenswear offerings, according to a recent survey by the New York-based brand consultancy Wunderman Thompson."[55] Gender-based categories of womenswear and menswear make sense to many Gen Xers such as myself, but for Gen Z, or the Post-95 Generation, dividing clothing based on gender seems increasingly restrictive and unnecessary. It is likely that in the future, such categories will cease to exist altogether. And it is all the less surprising, then, that Wang Yibo often wears Chanel womenswear or sparkly Louboutin shoes (such as Louis, Fun Louis Junior, and Sonny Low No Limit)[56,57] for public appearances.

"Versace on the Floor"

While Wang Yibo is not a global brand ambassador for Versace (as of 2020), for the 2020 Hunan TV Singles Day Global Shopping Festival Gala, an all-white clad Wang performed an extremely sensual dance to the Bruno Mars song "Versace on the Floor." The song refers to the Versace luxury brand, urging the listener—who, lyrically, could be male or female, but definitely wears Versace--into a sexual encounter with the singer, and the last verse of which implores, "Let's just kiss 'til we're naked, baby / Versace on the floor / Oooh take it off for me, for me, for me, for me now, girl / Versace on the floor."[58] It is a slow, 1990s-style ballad; *GQ* magazine wrote of the song, "This is pure Boyz II Men realness and I don't mind it! . . . I'm glad someone is owning the space of nostalgia and lightheartedness. An R&B song about sex? In 2016 that's downright sweet, in its own way."[59] Both the song and performance were entirely appropriate for the Singles Day shopping holiday, combining carnal longing and a taste for luxury goods.

China is foundational to Versace's global sales strategy, with a whopping sixty-one brick-and-mortar Versace boutiques in China as of November 2020 (or an even more impressive seventy-six, adding in nine stores in Hong Kong and five in Macau).[60] This compares to Versace's twenty-one in the United States, three in Canada, five in the United Kingdom, five in France, six in Germany, ten in Japan, five in South Korea, two in Singapore, three in Thailand, and three in Vietnam.[61] Versace boutiques by city in mainland China include:

Beijing	5
Changchun	2
Changsha	1
Changzhou	1
Chengdu	2
Chongqing	4

Dalian	1
Fuzhou	3
Guangzhou	2
Guiyang	1
Hangzhou	5
Harbin	1
Hefei	1
Kunming	1
Nanjing	2
Nanning	1
Qingdao	1
Shanghai	5
Shenyang	2
Shenzhen	1
Shijazhuang	1
Suzhou	1
Taiyuan	1
Tianjin	2
Urumqi	1
Wuhan	1
Wuxi	2
Xi'An	3
Xiamen	3
Xian'	1
Xuzhou	1
Zhengzhou	2

Ironically, though, Wang Yibo wore Fendi SS20, not Versace, for the performance. While China is essential to Versace, Fendi, after its Great Wall of China show in 2007, became something approaching synonymous with China. Miles Socha wrote in *WWD* that,

> The audacious spectacle, which luxury titan Bernard Arnault trumpeted as "the first fashion show visible from the moon," ignited the trend to event marketing and itinerant fashion shows, and was one of the earliest signals of China's importance for luxury consumption. It positioned Fendi as a global brand, and made a powerful statement about cultural appreciation and exchange. The sunset parade on a picturesque section of the Juyongguan Pass northwest of Beijing is also a potent reminder of the emotional charge of physical fashion events. To this

> day, Fendi clients in China still talk about that chilly October night, according to Venturini Fendi . . . Mounting big fashion shows in China seems commonplace now, but not in 2007, when most European heritage brands were still operating small boutiques in luxury hotels, and China had yet to demonstrate its potential for luxury. According to consultancy Bain & Co., Chinese consumers accounted for only 2 percent of global consumption of personal luxury goods in 2006, just ahead of the Fendi event. (Bain now projects that Chinese consumers will account for 50 percent of all luxury purchases by 2025.)[62]

The growth from 2% to 50% of global market share in the span of just nineteen years is truly remarkable. It is no wonder that songs like "Versace on the Floor" are so popular in China and no wonder that European and American luxury houses are pivoting their long-term market strategies to increasingly China-focused plans.

Balmain's Asia Strategy

The sequined Balmain menswear jacket that Wang wore for the final episode of *Street Dance of China 3* also suggested this duality of male and female. Classic French fashion house Balmain was once worn by such celebrities as Marlene Dietrich, Ava Gardner, and Queen Sirikit of Thailand (now the Queen Mother of Thailand). Today, with Olivier Rousteing, a French millennial (born 1985) of Ethiopian, Somali, and Djiboutian descent, the brand has modernized considerably. Rousteing, in particular, has focused on the brand's Asia strategy, adding Asian design elements to Balmain collections.[63] Is Wang Yibo being courted as a brand ambassador by Balmain?

The Importance of Male Idols in the Marketing of Cosmetics: Xiao Xian Rou 小鲜肉 (Little Fresh Meat)

The men's cosmetics market is growing, particularly in Asia. In a 2019 article for Reuters.com, Haejin Choi, Sarah White, and Sam Nussey noted that, "Asia's male grooming market is still a relative minnow, accounting for under a fifth of the $49.5 billion industry globally in 2017, according to data from market research firm Euromonitor . . . Beyond showbusiness circles or the limited realm of beauty bloggers, the brands have other clients—such as image-conscious executives—in their sights, as they emphasize the undetectable aspects of some products . . . But an increasingly receptive audience in markets such as South Korea—where wildly popular 'K-pop' boy bands and their cute, flawless looks have helped redefine ideas of the comely male—points to growing potential for this niche."[64] These makeup-loving men, known as *jingzhunan*, or "luxury pig men," in China do indeed represent a growing market for high-end cosmetics in East Asia.[65] For now, however, consumers identifying as female continue to make up the lion's share of the cosmetics and skincare market, and unlike in the West, where cosmetics intended for females have female brand ambassadors, in Asia cosmetics intended for female consumers often appear on males in advertisements. As Dzireena Mahadzir has noted,

> Getting a trending star to front a brand can see great returns. For example, Estee Lauder's official Weibo post on its collaboration with Li Xian was shared more that 430,000 times with more than 30,000 comments. The article also said that a report by Yingxiao Huabao showed that 23 beauty brands (mostly international) have signed 25 male celebrities this year, with the majority born after the mid-1990s. From January 2018 to the present, in rankings of top celebrities by fan activity, male stars commanded 36 of the top 50 spots. Only one female celebrity ranked in the top 10 list as of late September. It stands to reason that given all that, these male celebrities will continue to be the main picks in beauty endorsements.[66]

In East Asia, at least, this male-to-female marketing strategy for cosmetics and skincare is highly effective. According to Xiaomeng Li in "How powerful is the female gaze?":

> If one turns on the television or goes to a shopping mall in China these days, one may be surprised to find that most of the cosmetic brands for women are using male celebrities as their brand ambassadors or spokespeople. According to recent market research, this trend of using males for the promotion of female products has been rising steeply. In the first 7 months of 2018, 18 cosmetic brands have signed male celebrities to promote female-targeted products in the Chinese market ("18 Brands Have Signed 'Little Fresh Meat,' Cosmetics Market Entering the Nan Se era," 2018). Most of these brands belong to large transnational corporations, including Lancôme, Maybelline, Elizabeth Arden, Sisley, L'Oréal, and so on.[67]

Significantly, as of May 1, 2021, the requirement for animal testing on imported cosmetics in China will be lifted, allowing Western cruelty-free brands to enter the Chinese market. Casey Hall has reported:

> The Chinese agency that regulates drugs and medical devices says imported ordinary cosmetics will no longer be tested on animals, as of May 1, according to

> a notice posted on the National Medical Products Administration website. Authorities have been reviewing the animal testing rules since last year, and these revisions will level the playing field with domestic Chinese manufactured goods, which have been exempt from animal testing since 2014, and French cosmetic companies, which were the first to be exempt from mandatory animal testing in January of this year. This opens the door for a slew of cruelty-free brands from Fenty Beauty to Drunk Elephant to enter the massive Chinese market, which is the second largest market for beauty consumption in the world, behind only the US.[68]

It remains unclear whether these new Western players in the Chinese market will tap male or female celebrities as brand faces.

Much of this success of male ambassadors for cosmetics and skincare stems from the soft masculinity associated with K-Pop (and Mandopop/C-Pop) groups, such as Wang Yibo's UNIQ. Young men in these groups have flawless skin, and wear not only eyeliner but also eyeshadow and lipstick. (The same could be said of many male performers of the classic rock era in the West, such as Mick Jagger, in the 1970s.) According to Li, "Some discourses may criticize the 'little fresh meat' or male celebrities with 'soft masculinity' for lacking professional skills and experience and only using their outstanding appearance to attract female fans; however, given today's promising fan economy in China, their popularity is largely substantiated by women's growing economic power and agency … Indeed, by branding these young and attractive men into stars and placing them in ads, the corporations behind them can quickly draw massive female fans' interests, media traffic, and, consequently, financial gains from the powerful female consumers."[69] That the young men representing these cosmetics brands are collectively known as *Xiao xian rou* ("little fresh meats") in Mandarin (or sometimes as *xiao gege*—literally "little older brothers") speaks to the pervasiveness of the female gaze in contemporary consumer culture in Asia. Male idols often wish to distance themselves from the "little fresh meats" image. In an infamous photograph taken with UNIQ bandmate Cho Seungyoun at the Yuehua Family Concert red carpet in 2018, Wang Yibo wears a pair of Dsquared2 jeans which carried the words "my cock is gluten free" on the front of them; however, the viewer senses the opposite effect, that Wang Yibo (or his stylist) is inviting the female (and male) gaze down to his trousers. Similarly, in 2021, in the promotional photos for season 4 of *Street Dance of China*, Wang wears a pair of crystal-studded Givenchy love locks on the belt loops of his jeans. The padlocks are a nod to the romantic Love Lock Bridge in Paris, France, but again, have the effect of compelling the viewer to look at Wang's crotch area. These were not the first such sartorial choices for Wang—just after UNIQ's debut in 2014, Wang Yibo was on film wearing a sweatshirt that read "Escort Boys" in English.

Gong Cai

Wang Yibo and Xiao Zhan have repeatedly worn the same clothes, particularly Nike shoes (prior to the 2021 brand boycott in China). As brand ambassador for Nike, Wang Yibo had access to limited edition styles, and likely gifted them to *Untamed/CQL* co-star Xiao Zhan as well. There is also a popular fan theory that Xiao Zhan, as brand ambassador for Gucci, gifted Wang Yibo his Gucci ox head pendant necklace (Wang's Chinese zodiac sign is the ox). Wang Yibo is also said by fans to give candies (hints) that he and Xiao Zhan are indeed a couple in his social media posts. Fans argue that his posts are often time-stamped with numbers significant to Xiao Zhan (Chinese people often confess romantic love using numbers). And for October 5, 2020, Wang changed the number on his Yamaha racing team motorcycle helmet to 29, the age that Xiao Zhan turned that day. (The number on Wang's helmet is usually the same as that of his racing idol, Valentino Rossi: 46.)

On the set of *Street Dance of China 3*, Wang Yibo happened to stand next to the character for *zhan* that appeared in an (unrelated) sentence written in neon lights. Many people would argue that these instances are coincidences. The so-called "gong cai incident," however, does seem to give some credence to the theory that Yizhan[70] is real. The gong cai incident occurred when Wang Yibo ordered hotpot with gong cai and mountain yam on camera on the set of *Street Dance of China 3*. Gong cai (pronounced gong "tsai") are lettuce stems uniquely eaten in Sichuanese/Chongqing style hotpot. Gong cai look a bit like shriveled green noodles and are associated with the older generation—not exactly a trendy food with younger people. Luoyang, as the center of Chinese Buddhism, is known for its mildly flavored foods, so it seems unlikely that a young man from Luoyang would know about gong cai, let alone order the dish for his castmates on the set of *Street Dance of China*. (The other three mentors did not know what gong cai were.) Chinese fans took this incident to mean that Wang Yibo and Xiao Zhan have been eating hotpot together . . . a lot. (Humorously, the phrase "eat ramen and go" is the Pan-Asian equivalent of "Netflix and chill.") In light of this incident, I would like to suggest the term gong cai as an alternative to the overtly sexual and sexist *xiao xian rou*. Gong cai, or lettuce stems, are long and slender, much like these young male idols, while their vegetarian nature suggests a more restrained, less wolfish manner of consumption.

Wang Yibo x Shu Uemura

Shu Uemura[71] is the eponymous brand founded by Japanese makeup artist Shu Uemura (1928–2007). Uemura gained notoriety working in Hollywood with stars such as Lucille Ball, Shirley Maclaine, and Frank Sinatra during the 1950s and 1960s. In 1960, he began marketing his own skincare products and began creating cosmetics a few years later, opening his first Japan Makeup boutique in Tokyo in 1967. He changed the name of the company to Shu Uemura in 1983, and by the time of his death, had stores in Hong Kong, New York, London, and Paris, as well as Japan. Today, Shu Uemura is retailed globally—including in China—and is available in Sephora stores in the United States.[72] As a testament to the brand's global popularity, Shu Uemura eyelash curlers are mentioned in the film *The Devil Wears Prada*. A post featuring an eyeshadow palette on the Shu Uemura Instagram feed on June 18, 2020 describes the makeup as "colors inspired by Asian eyes."[73] Lucia Pica famously said, "I defend the freedom of using makeup to express one's personality,"[74] and to this, one must also add the freedom to celebrate one's heritage.

Wang Yibo represents Shu Uemura globally,[75] and collaborated with the brand to create two custom Wang Yibo x Shu Uemura collections—an eyeshadow palette and special edition lipsticks.[76] In his step-by-step tutorial on "How to Get K-Pop Makeup," cosmetics expert and author of *Pretty Boys*, David Yi, notes that "It's about using eyeshadow to elongate the eye outward. Warmer tones are popular for K-Pop stars—think copper, red, burnt oranges, and browns. Try going with the lightest color first and then blend in darker shades."[77] The colors of both the lipsticks and the eyeshadows in the Wang Yibo x Shu Uemura collection are warm hues, mostly with orange or peach undertones, reflecting Wang's usual look for public appearances—peach-colored lips and a tangerine shadow around the corners of the eyes. Exclusive colors in the Yibo x Shu Uemura collections include Desert Rose, Sunset Rose, Roast Tea, and Tangerine Tea. Wang Yibo also modeled the Chromatics Digital Orange palette in October 2020.[78] These *Xiao xian rou* are not merely eye candy for the cosmetics counter and fashion magazines. Like the women purchasing the cosmetics they hawk, these men must be knowledgeable about color palettes which flatter their own skin tones, as well as skilled in the art of eyeshadow effects. Idol trainee Candace Park, heroine of Stephan Lee's novel *K-Pop Confidential*, writes lyrics to a song called "Monolid Girl" in the story:

> My eyes are wide open, they see just fine
> Maybe your double eyelids make you see two
> You can't tell what's real and what's just illusions[79]

The Shu Uemura Instagram feed regularly offers tips on eyeshadowing for monolid eyes. In June 2020, the account posted, "Feel how easily you can blend and create a beautiful gradation on your eyes with the new color atelier eye shadow in M261. #shuuemura #shuartistry #pressedeyeshadow"[80]

Numerous English-language beauty blogs and magazine articles also offer tips for making up Asian faces. Cosmetics writer Faith Xue advocates that Asian women (and men) frame the eye rather than attempt to follow rules from makeup tutorials for Western eyes: "If you've ever tried to follow an eye makeup tutorial only to get to the part where it says 'blend into your crease' and stared at your creaseless eye in the mirror confusedly, we feel you. When it comes to applying makeup for Asian eyes, all traditional makeup rules fly out the window—and with it, our interest in attempting anything beyond a simple swipe of black liner if that. But before you throw down your eye shadow palettes at the injustice of it all, know this—there *is* a way," adding, "You want to frame your eyes—you don't want them to look worlds apart."[81] Buzzfeed contributor Peggy Wang suggests, "If you've been following ye olde western makeup tutorials all your life, you might be familiar with the traditional 'dark shadow in the outer corners' trick, which was always hard to get right without a lot of lid surface area. Instead, try using eyeshadow to make a gradient, with the darkest color closest to the lash line."[82] In her article for *Marie Claire*, "9 Best Foundations for Asian Skin Tones," Hana Hong notes that "most Asian women [and men] have strong yellow or golden undertones" and that "[a]lthough a handful of brands have recently diversified their shade ranges, Asian skin still tends to be something that many brands don't quite nail when it comes to foundation. Some brands still operate under the assumption that all Asians have the same skin tone (very much not true) . . . In any case, remember that not all Asian skin is created equal."[83] One of the most prolific cultural historians of cosmetics over the past twenty years has been Sara Berry, and in her essay "Be Our Brand: Fashion and Personalisation on the Web" (2000) she anticipated the growth in direct-to-consumer marketing of racially-conscious cosmetics precipitated by the rise of e-commerce, as well as traced its history:

> For Georg Simmel in 1904, fashion typified modern individualism in its tension between conformity and the desire to express individual subjectivity (Simmel 1971). Postmodernity, on the other hand, is in some way typified by mass customisation because it reveals the gap between the diverse ways people use and enjoy consumer goods and the market's attempts to exploit that diversity . . . Ethnic diversity is an aspect of social difference that Western fashion has explored throughout its history through the appropriation of "exotic" cultural motifs (as in Orientalism and Africanism). Cosmetics, in particular, have been

> marketed in terms of exotic ethnicity, if only because there was a limited range of products that could be sold in association with a demure "English complexion" ... For example, in 1928 Max Factor changed the name of his cosmetics line from "Society Make-Up" to "Color Harmony Make-Up" on the advice of his marketing agency, Sales Builders, Inc. Their research showed that if the need to buy personalised and "harmonised" products was stressed, women would buy more items in the same brand. The result was the Max Factor "Color Harmony Make-Up Chart," which indicated the complimentary shades of powder, rouge, and lipstick to be used according to complexion, hair, and eye colour (Basten 1995: 80). This personal colour-matching system was widely copied, and is still used today by brands like Clinique and reflect.com ... It avoided issues of race by describing differences in skin tones as "complexion types," although cosmetics advertising of the 1930s increasingly used exotic stereotypes like "Tropical," "Chinese," and "Gypsy" product lines. Other brands simply referred to women of colour with European euphemisms: a 1937 advertisement for Richard Hudnut "eye-matched" make-up features the Mexican-born star Dolores Del Rio, and describes her as having a "Parisian complexion type."[84]

This legacy of "Chinese" cosmetics as exoticized products for a then-predominantly white marketplace was no doubt one with which Shu Uemura contended when he began working as a makeup artist for films in the 1950s, in Japan, and shortly thereafter in Hollywood.

Shu Uemura x *One Piece*

Each holiday season for the past several years, Shu Uemura has unveiled a collaboration with a popular culture brand or phenomenon. In 2017, it was Super Mario Bros., and in 2019 it was Pokémon. Wang Yibo participated in promotional marketing for the 2019 Shu Uemura holiday collection, appearing with Pikachu, and idols are certainly no strangers to collaborations with the Pokémon franchise. According to L'Orèal's 2019 Annual Report for Asia Pacific, "Tokyo-based professional makeup brand Shu Uemura has reinvented itself to reach Gen Z and Millennials. Its products, such as Rouge Unlimited lipstick and Unlimited Foundation, are rapidly winning over younger generations, as are its collaborations with unique and inspiring celebrities. For example, Shu Uemura invited comedian Naomi Watanabe, the icon of her generation, to promote its new cosmetics range, Now Me, and has developed limited editions featuring young people's childhood heroes, like Pikachu."[85] Korean artist Kim Sungjoo of UNIQ, for example, did a promotional video when the Pokémon Go mobile game was released. The collaboration in 2020 was with the beloved pirate-themed Japanese anime and manga *One Piece*.

In his Shu Uemura x *One Piece* promotional video, Wang Yibo uses a spyglass to peer at the audience. He then proceeds to unveil his treasure, the Treasure Box Grand Line eyeshadow palette, and along with his wanted poster—he is a pirate, after all, despite the glitter on his face—also shows off a lipstick and eyebrow pencil from the *One Piece* collection. In the *Cosmopolitan* interview referenced earlier in this chapter, which took place nearly two years before the Shu Uemura x *One Piece* collaboration, Wang Yibo actually stated that the anime character that he most resembles is Roronoa Zoro from *One Piece*. Zoro is a pirate hunter turned pirate who vowed on the grave of his childhood sweetheart to become the greatest swordsman in the world and a practitioner of the absurdly difficult three-sword technique—he holds one of the swords in his teeth. Zoro is known for his strong heart and determination, unwilling to accept defeat even in the face of certain death, like Wang who was determined to study dance as a child, even though he suffered from complications of myocarditis.

Image-signs and Simulacra at Miniso Events

In a June 29, 2020 Instagram livestream hosted by the cosmetics brand Miniso, "Kevin" and "Jim" opened boxes of products for an online crowd of at one point over 300 guests. Products featured included nail polishes, eyeshadow palettes, eyebrow pencils, face masks, and handbags. The lure of the event was that one attendee would receive a signed photo of Wang Yibo, global brand ambassador for Miniso. Unsurprisingly, well over half of the comments were expressions of adoration for Wang Yibo rather than the merchandise, or, directives that the merchandise should be more Yibo-focused, such as a range of green nail polishes for Wang Yibo (who has stated that green is his favorite color; see Figure 3.14). Such promotions, since they only reach a few hundred people, many of whom are not even interested in the products (or, as at least, as one attendee commented, are too poor to be able to afford to purchase the products), are not the best way to leverage a celebrity brand ambassador's appeal. Livestreams are inexpensive (requiring only a staffer's time) and low stakes, though, and do not require the icon's actual presence at the event, just a (possibly autopenned) signed photo. Such promotions, however, are exploitative of the consumer, keeping them running a hamster wheel of comments on products for the better part of an hour in the vain hopes that they will receive a picture of their idol. Often, a more effective way for companies to utilize a celebrity brand ambassador is to dress

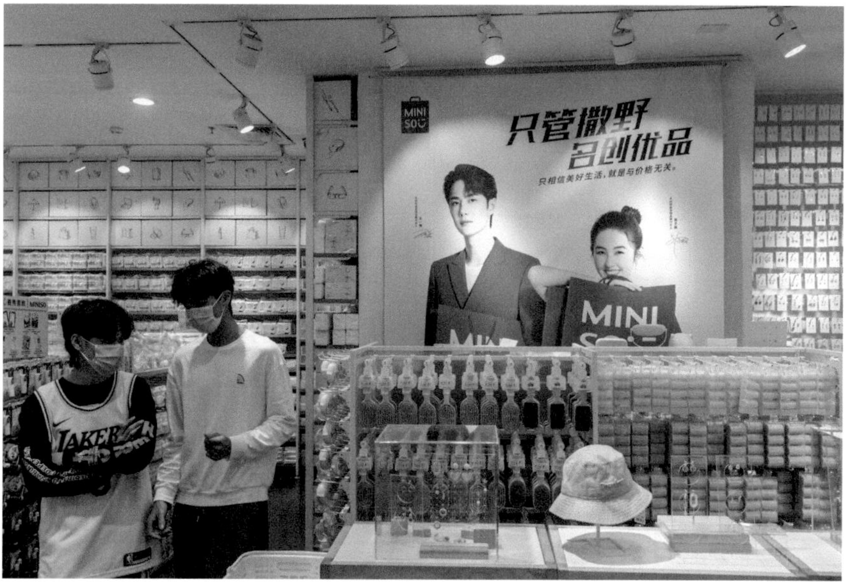

Figure 3.14 Customers walk through a Miniso Group Holding Ltd. store in Guangzhou, China, on Thursday, November 19, 2020. Miniso, the Chinese budget lifestyle goods retailer, is making its first foray into the $86 billion global toy market as it tries to take on heavyweights like Toys 'R' Us Inc. on its home turf and beyond. Photographer: Qilai Shen/Bloomberg via Getty Images.

the celebrity at high-profile events, guaranteeing an audience of thousands or millions, rather than hundreds, and likely an audience more interested in both fashion and fandom. (Although, the 8 million viewers and 300 million comments that Xiao Zhan attracted for his August 17, 2020 livestream for Rose Only florists suggests that if the idol is actually present for the stream, livestreams can be highly effective.)

At Miniso in-store events such as the one depicted here, signs and symbols of the idol abound: as drawings on the plastic bags, in small tabletop-size cutouts, as a large life-size cardboard cutout with which shoppers and fans can interact for air kisses and selfies, and finally, seated at the promotional table, a man who is not Wang Yibo but bears a faint resemblance to him in passing (see Figure 3.15).

In Jean Baudrillard's notion of the simulacrum, representational image-signs—such as those of Wang Yibo at the Miniso—go through four successive phases. In *Introducing Postmodernism*, Richard Appignanesi and Chris Garratt explain the four phases of the image-sign as follows:

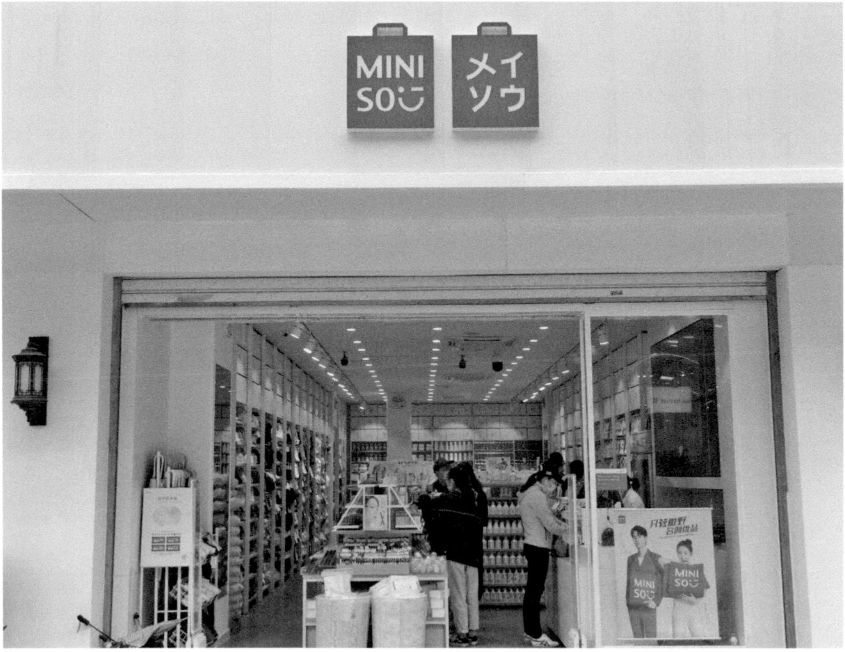

Figure 3.15 Signs and simulations: Wang Yibo for Miniso cardboard cutout, Miniso store in Wuhan, China, October 5, 2020. Note the Wang Yibo visual merchandising in the window. Photo by VCG/VCG via Getty Images.

1. It is the reflection of a basic reality.
2. It masks and perverts a basic reality.
3. It marks the absence of a basic reality.
4. It bears no relation to any reality whatever—it is its own pure simulacrum.[86]

Image-signs of Wang in so many different media in one small shop, complete with the not-Wang Yibo seated at the table, do mask and pervert the basic reality of the customer, placing brand ambassador events such as these in a state of nascent simulacrum.

To further unpack the Miniso representations of Wang Yibo as image-signs, let us take Jacques Lacan's algorithm of S/s, that is, signifier over signified.[87] Lacan demonstrated the algorithm with the example of the word TREE / 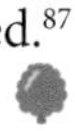 (the image of a tree, or that which is signified by the signifier—that is, the word TREE).[88] The situation becomes problematized when Lacan then proposed the equations LADIES / 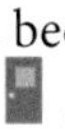 and GENTLEMEN / 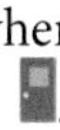. Here, different signifiers represent the same signified image-sign, even though the meanings of the signifiers are, some would argue, quite different.[89]

Jacques Derrida, in "Of Grammatology," bemusedly derides such faulty signifiers: "Writing, sensible matter and artificial exteriority: a 'clothing.' It has sometimes been contested that speech clothed thought. Husserl, Saussure, Lavelle have all questioned it. But has it ever been doubted that writing is the clothing of speech? For Saussure it is even a garment of perversion and debauchery, a dress of corruption and disguise, a festival mask that must be exorcised . . ."[90] (And as I write this in the notes app on my phone on Super Bowl Sunday, autocorrect unhelpfully tries to replace the word "dress" with the emoji, or image-sign for dress.) Do fans that flock to celebrity brand events such as these, even though the idol is not actually physically present, want to consume the image-signs, the signifier—the phrase "Wang Yibo" and all that linguistic clothing connotes, or the signified of the absent Wang himself? Answering this question satisfactorily would allow brands to make better use of idol image-sign merchandise and fan-consumers' time.

Kid, you're the Best

As the dance mentor on *Produce 101*, Wang Yibo assisted a group of contestants (Yamy Guo Ying, Kimberley Chen, Li Zixuan, Lu Xiaocao, Lucia Wu, and Angela Xu) with the choreography for their final song, "Trophy Child," and thrilled the audience by performing part of the song with the group as a surprise (see Figure 3.16). The number is a catchy tune targeted at the average East Asian high school student who feels extreme familial and social pressure to achieve greatness in school. The chorus urges the listener to "re- re- repeat after me, kid you're the best" and decries those "godly, peerless" students who are class reps in Chinese, English, math, and history. Mary Bergstrom notes the intense pressure that Chinese students feel to be successful for their parents: "From a Western perspective, it is hard to overstate the impact of family in China. Children are important to their families, and families are similarly vital for youth. This codependent dynamic often complicates how youth recognize success and support."[91] This pressure is compounded for idols, who leave the family dynamic at a young age to pursue the possibility of success as an idol (all the while lurking is the possibility of failure, indebtedness to the management company, and a lost youth and chance at formal education).

On his twenty-ninth birthday, October 7, 2020, Lay Zhang announced a plan, which he had been formulating since 2012, of opening an idol training school available even to third-gender children and to children from remote, rural

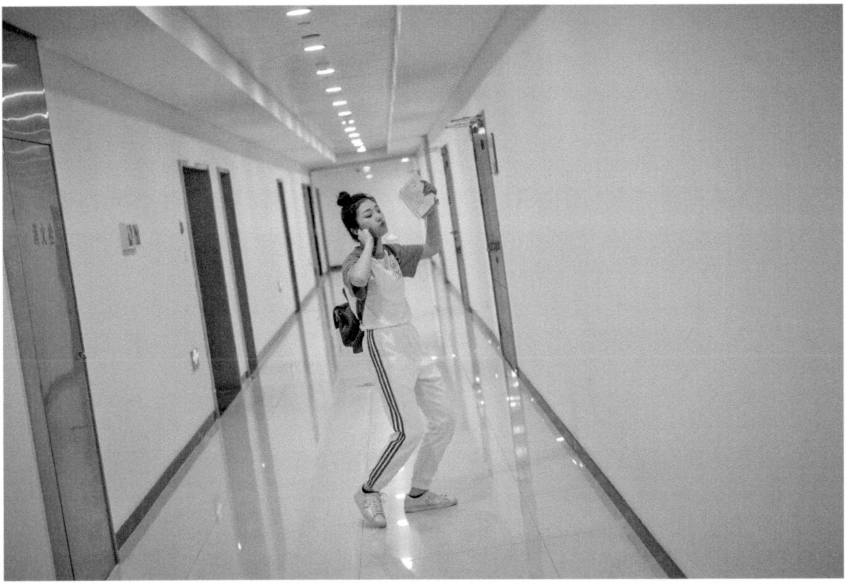

Figure 3.16 Contestant Yamy Guo Ying practices her rap song "Trophy Child" behind the scenes on *Produce 101* on May 11, 2018. *Produce 101 China*, held by TenCent, was a reality show filming from March 21 in Hangzhou, Zhejiang Province of China. During the three-month program, 101 girls took singing and dancing training sessions and performed in competition for the top eleven places, which were decided by the audience. At the final show, Meng Meiqi, Wu Xuanyi, Yang Chaoyue, Duan Aojuan, Yamy Guo Ying, Sunny Lai Meiyun, Winnie Zhang Zining, Sunnee Yang YunChing, Mimi Li Ziting, Jinna Fu Jing and Rainbow Xu Mengjie won and formed a girl group called Rocket Girls 101. Photo by Chen Zhongqiu/Visual China Group via Getty Images.

areas.[92] Talking about the ruthless competition in the idol industry, and how the deck is stacked against rural youth who want to break into the field, Zhang used the analogy of mineral water, noting that in China, if mineral water sells well, there will suddenly be 100 companies selling mineral water, and the competition will be vicious. Zhang hopes to use his own fame and extensive entertainment connections (Xiao Zhan, Wang Yibo, Jackson Wang, and Wallace Chung all expressed support) to give youth who would otherwise not even have access to idol school auditions the opportunity to form an idol group. Interestingly, Zhang believes that this intense competition is not as strong outside China. Using again the mineral water analogy, Zhang argued that in other countries, if mineral water sold well, other companies would look to invest in the whole supply chain—bottling, distribution, and so on—rather than focusing almost exclusively on direct competition. Zhang therefore proposes to invest in the entire idol supply chain, as it were. This is a most welcome change, as Dong-Yeun Lee points out:

> The number of teenagers who aspire to audition for the position of idol stars reaches several hundred thousand annually. JYP Entertainment, one of the representative entertainment agencies, tests approximately 50,000 idol aspirants each year. Unsurprisingly, competition is extremely high, and approximately one in 5,000 ends up becoming a member of an idol group. Even for those who pass the initial test, complete four-to-five years of idol training, and make a debut after fierce competition, there is less than a 10 percent chance that they will successfully build a solid profile through broadcasting media.[93]

A sample daily schedule for a fifteen-year-old trainee born outside Korea is as follows:

> 4:00am–5:00am: Workout/Shower
> 5:00am–5:30am: Healthy Breakfast (boiled eggs, sweet potato)
> 5:30am–11:30am: Korean Language Class
> 11:30am–12:30pm: Healthy Lunch (salad with no dressing, Greek yogurt)/Fresh Air Time
> 12:30pm–7:30pm: Group Practice
> 7:30pm–8:30pm: Healthy Dinner (fish cakes, radish soup, and purple rice)/Fresh Air Time
> 8:30pm–12:00am: Group Practice/ Self Practice[94]

This leaves just four hours for sleep, if the trainee falls asleep only when their head hits the pillow and wakes up only with their alarm.

From age thirteen to seventeen, Wang Yibo participated in such a residential idol school in Korea, far from his parents back in Luoyang, China, subjected to rigorous training in the Korean method: ten–twenty hours per day, waist measurement, and dreaded monthly tests in which peers and friends who could not handle the physical, aesthetic, etiquette, and intellectual (including fluency in Korean, and some English, in addition to his native Mandarin) requirements were unceremoniously expelled from idol school. Once a kid from a normal, middle-class family, he suddenly had to navigate one of the most high-pressure schools in the world. It is for this reason that Wang Yibo seems to sympathize with not only aspiring dancers on *Produce 101* but also with the lyrics of "Trophy Child." Fighting tooth and nail both alongside and against so many fellow "peerless, godly" students, Wang seems to have come to the realization that actually, we're all the best; that everyone who works hard for their dream is valuable and deserves a break.

So much of the luxury market is aspirational, young people who generally cannot afford to buy Chanel, but save for and buy a special piece here and there, in the hopes that someday they will be in a position to be a regular luxury customer. Take for example Audrey Yeung, a thirteen-year-old who attends the Christian Alliance International School of Hong Kong. In 2021, *South China Morning Post* published letters written by schoolchildren and submitted to the newspaper on the topic, "If you could swap lives with someone for a day, who would you choose and what would you do?" Some children wrote that they would like to swap with animals, older relatives, or even space aliens, but Yeung wrote, "I'd swap with a close friend of Wang Yibo, the Chinese actor, for a day. He is my favourite idol. If I were his friend, I could take a closer look at his face—he was one of the nominees for the 100 Most Handsome Faces of 2020. People say he has a great personality so I would be able to check it out, face to face. Of course, I'd also love to watch him dance in person. It would be even better if I could have lunch with him and other actors, for example, Xiao Zhan and Xuan Lu, from the famous TV drama *Chen Qing Ling*."[95] Even more than the mindless and sexually-charged idolatry of *xiao xian rou*, Wang Yibo's ability to empathize with those still struggling for their dreams—which is just about everyone—*that* sells a lot of clothes and cosmetics.

4

Capitalizing Yaoi/Danmei Fans: Fashion Brands and Male Popular Culture Idols as Brand Ambassadors in the Chinese Fashion Market

Peng Liu and Lan Lan

Introduction

This chapter examines the relationship between luxury fashion brands, male idols as brand ambassadors, and yaoi fans, known as danmei (耽美), in China's fashion market. Danmei is an abbreviation of dan yu mei se （耽于美色）, which literally means "immersing into romance," and it has become synonymous with Boys' Love (BL) in China. The investigation of the relationship is carried out with reference to multiple disciplines, such as BL studies, fanfiction studies, popular culture studies, and queer studies. The chapter investigates the consumption of male idols in terms of BL studies and the impact upon the idols as brand ambassadors in terms of fashion studies. Called "little fresh meat" (小鲜肉), these idols are made to cater to female desires; they gain hundreds of millions of fans and are appointed as ambassadors to reach female customers in the Chinese market. The chapter focuses on a particular event as a case study that involves Xiao Zhan, a Chinese actor and singer who starred in the drama *The Untamed* (2019) and is an ambassador for luxury fashion brands in China. This rather controversial event took place in March 2020 on the fanfiction social platform Archive of Our Own (AO3), centering on conflicts between Xiao Zhan's mimei (迷妹) fans and danmei fans in their consumption of the idol in the fanfiction community. Mimei is a Chinese term to describe fans in the fan economy who see themselves playing a maternal role in guiding and being responsible for caring and overseeing the growth of male idols in reality, while danmei fans normally see themselves as yaoi who are the readers and writers creating/consuming works in the fanfiction world featuring certain male idols.

These identities are, however, not mutually exclusive; one can be both mimei and danmei.

Fanfiction refers to stories produced by fans to create a new narration and/or direction extracted from existing story worlds, which is most commonly achieved by recasting characters from one or multiple texts and works. Scholarly inquiry concerning fanfiction varies, including debates in terms of cultural studies, literary and narrative theory, ethnography, and feminist and queer theory. For example, anthropological and psychoanalytical approaches are focused on the behavior and motivation of fans, while the identities and practices of fans are examined by scholars in cultural studies by contextualizing the written fanfic text as a socially situated activity (Thomas 2011). Electronic fanfiction platforms are digital sites powered by the internet where fans can access their communities to share and discuss works, such as The Harry Potter Lexicon. AO3 is a fan-run, non-profit, and internet-based fanfiction platform dedicated to and known for its archive of more than 7 million fan works including fanfiction. While the case study event reflects the interaction between the male idol and his danmei fans in both the fictive world and in social reality, our investigation of the event further unveils the involvement of international fashion brands and their intention to capitalize on danmei fans via the purposely selected ambassadors, namely the male idols. Despite the eagerness of fashion brands to capitalize on the collective purchasing power of the danmei fans, there is little presence of the fashion brands in online danmei communities. We can assume that this may be because the fashion brands want to avoid direct affiliation with the sub-cultural communities due to the sensitivities regarding these groups in China. Given that the number of danmei fans has grown into the millions in China and the potential they have for becoming consumers of fashion brands, this chapter will argue that fashion brands are approaching these potential consumers "indirectly" through their idols as a marketing strategy. In other words, certain types of male idols are increasingly being used as luxury fashion brand ambassadors, whose characteristics tend to be associated with the danmei community and whose aesthetics are used to appeal to this community. The use of the terms "characteristics" and "aesthetics" throughout the chapter draws a connection between male idols in reality and danmei characters in fictive worlds. This study shows that male idols, popularized as danmei characters in such fictive worlds, have a persuasive effect on the attitude of danmei fans towards the fashion brands and products endorsed by their idols, which can in turn lead to purchase activity.

This chapter draws upon ethnographic fieldwork combining participant observation, online surveys, and semi-structured interviews, which took place in

2020 and 2021. Participant observation was conducted throughout the two-year period by joining and observing online discussions in the major danmei websites, such as Bai Du Tie Ba (百度貼吧), Weibo (微博), and Dou Ban (豆瓣). Designed to provide demographical and essential information on the danmei community, the online survey was conducted with 249 participants who self-identified as danmei fans in July 2020. The survey was created and posted on the authors' WeChat app where all of their added "friends" can see and further share the survey with their "friends" on the app. The semi-structured interviews were used to gather danmei fans' perspectives and personal concerns regarding the AO3 event, and extended to interviewing them about danmei practices in the Chinese socio-cultural environment. We interviewed twenty-three senior danmei writers/readers aged between eighteen and twenty-eight, and the interviewees were anonymized for the purposes on the study and numbered as A1 to A23. The first two recruited interviewees were known personally to the authors and they helped to recruit the rest of the group through their private connections. Only the danmei community members who are considered senior, in the sense of being actively involved in danmei community practice and having a minimum of five years danmei experience, were selected by the authors to be interviewed for comments and opinions. The participants were either studying at university at that time (fifteen out of twenty-three) or in their early career (eight out of twenty-three). The interviews lasted between one and one and a half hours and drew on a flexible framework of questions subdivided into three sections regarding the AO3 event, the idol–brand–fans connection, and the subcultural community in China.

Originating in Japan, yaoi fans are mostly female, self-identified fujoshi (腐女)—which literally means "rotten girls"—who fantasize about BL characters in various genres, such as manga, animation, games, and so on. Acknowledging the extensive discussions of BL studies in contemporary literature, this chapter is particularly interested in the cultural phenomenon in which the subjective female gaze and the aesthetic of BL masculinity, initially applied to flat and two-dimensional bodies of fantasized male BL manga characters, is also being applied to real Chinese male idols as fictive characters in fanfiction. Chinese male idols are increasingly becoming associated with BL fandom through recasting and recharacterizing in texts and genres, as male-to-male romantic pairings, where the subjective female gaze is being re-directed and applied to the idols in the fictive world. Keeping the fandom and reality separate is considered one of the fundamental rules in the danmei subcultural field according to our senior danmei interviewees. The consumption of male idols as BL characters is prohibited within the traditional danmei community, as acknowledged by the majority of our twenty-three interviewees. Nevertheless, the alternative aesthetic of masculinity must also be noted, in which the male body, shown as feminine and androgynous in the form of beautiful-looking young men, is first applied on flat and two-dimensional fictive characters, then extended to idols-making in the cultural industry, and then finally to the real idols in the fictive world in China—with significant social impacts. Bringing real idols (back) into the fictive world, so that fiction and reality are mixed, resulted in the AO3 event, which stands as an example that has many implications for Chinese society. The research analyzes Xiao Zhan as a case study that reflects the engagement of fashion brands in capitalizing on danmei fans in marketing cosmetics and skincare.

BL/Yaoi/Danmei Theories

The Originating Japan Context: "Alternative" Masculinity and Bishōnen

BL refers to male homoerotic texts in genres like manga, animation, games, movies, and so on, which is conventionally understood as being written and drawn by heterosexual women for heterosexual women readers who claim themselves to be fujoshi.[1] BL studies have been approached from various perspectives in the past decades and have broad implications for gender, feminist, and queer studies. BL narratives were first analyzed from a psychoanalytic point of view.[2] This was followed by the examination of fan reception in cultural studies and queer theory, such as the analysis of responses to BL manga by gay males[3] and heterosexual males, as well as lesbian readings of BL.[4] When BL studies became transnational, other research themes appeared, including the emphasis on fan communities,[5] non-Japanese BL fandoms,[6] censorship of pornographic content,[7] perspectives from Western consumers,[8] fans in the English-speaking world,[9] as well as recent approaches in terms of the affective economy.[10] This chapter, therefore, reflects the trend of transnational fandoms by investigating BL fans in Greater China, particularly Mainland China. The local BL communities are in "negotiation" with Chinese mainstream popular culture in terms of the way of consuming male idols.

The creation and consumption of BL was originally developed in Japan in the early 1970s. At the beginning, as a subgenre of girl's manga, artists such as Keiko

Takemiya in the Year 24 Group created the work entitled *In The Sunroom* (1970), depicting male homosexuality, later known as shōnen-ai, which literally means "boy love."[11] The works featured tragic romances between androgynous beautiful boys in order to attract adolescent girls and young women as well as adult gays and lesbians who were among the readership.[12] During the same period, the first commercial gay manga magazine entitled *Barazoku* was published in 1971, which promoted shōnen-ai content. Dōjinshi, or self-published/amateur works, also emerged during the same period; these amateur artists gathered at Comic Market, a biannual fair in Tokyo as a platform to exchange ideas, where the term "yaoi" first appeared among some writers referring to their own works of self-published, male-to-male romance. The magazine titled *June*, which launched in 1978 and specialized in shōnen-ai content, was seen as a success in publishing yaoi works. Japanese women subsequently recasted the male characters in animations and manga into homosexual pairings during the 1980s, which is when the term yaoi appeared in reference to amateur anime-parody culture. It is understood this was a female-oriented community where amateur writings were produced, circulated, and consumed by writers and readers who were the same people, and eventually the self-published yaoi works took over mainstream commercial publications in the late 1980s.[13]

The term "boys' love" appeared during the 1990s along with publication of BL magazines in Japan, such as the launch of *Magazine Be-Boy* in 1993, which was the most influential among the thirty magazines devoted to yaoi between 1990 and 1995. BL manga has gained popularity since then, and expanded outside of Japan, and the stereotyped narrative has developed into a wide range of storytelling genres including romance, fantasy, historical, and contemporary stories with various character roles. BL and yaoi are the most popular terms[14] and they are generally treated interchangeably. These issues have been discussed in detail among scholars in recent years.[15] Some, like Kazuko Suzuki, distinguish between the terms in that BL is taken to refer to commercially produced manga with certain rules to follow from the publishers in terms of storyline, narrative structure, and so on, while yaoi is an umbrella term to cover most products including those by amateurs.[16] Nevertheless, the theoretical approach in this chapter is to treat BL and yaoi interchangeably with a focus on their application in the Chinese danmei community.

The aesthetic of masculinity in the BL love stories, called alternative masculinity,[17] is shown in the stereotyped characters of the *seme* (penetrator) and the *uke* (receiver) as feminine, androgynous, and beautiful-looking young men; this is the typical representation in BL fiction. The formation of such an aesthetic was made in response to the demand of BL consumers in Japan, as the result of "an effect of historically and locally specific socio-cultural conditions,"[18] namely, during the bursting of the economic bubble in 1990s. BL culture can be seen as a subculture in relation to traditional Japanese society, which is dominated by men who financially support the family and where the image of the salaryman is a form of hegemonic masculinity. The salaryman, or corporate warrior, *sarariiman*, or *kigyo senshi* in Japanese, refers to the postwar Japanese white-collar male worker who was employed on a full-time basis following the traditional Japanese work ethic from the 1960s to late 1980s. The figure of the salaryman "conjures up a mental picture of a neatly groomed, middle-aged, grey-suited, briefcase-carrying, white-collar male office worker who leaves his home in the suburbs early each morning, commutes in an overcrowded train to some faceless downtown office block, and ends the day by lurching drunkenly back to the suburbs on the last train after a drinking session with colleagues or clients."[19] Hegemonic masculinity is a sociological concept that is used to study gender order in society, which was first conceptualized by Raewyn Connell[20] and subsequently used to understand variations in local and regional masculinities.[21] Of particular relevance to this chapter, hegemonic masculinity enforces a patriarchal gender order in which men dominate and women and other gender identities are subordinate, so that men gain dividend from "cultural and sexual privileging."[22] As Lucy Glasspool notes, "since the collapse of the bubble economy in the 1990s … alternative constructions of masculinity [are] attempt[s] to redraw the fixed gender boundaries and heterosexual norms of the dominant salaryman discourse."[23] Therefore, male characters in BL fiction, that are made to cater to female aesthetic taste for female pleasure and reflected the female gaze on the male body as a sexual object, must be "beautiful boys."[24] In traditional East Asian societies, such as Japan and China, heterosexual sex is the activity which takes place "between an active [always seen as male] and a passive person [always seen as female], characterized by an imbalance of power;"[25] however, BL repositions the traditional power relation between male and female and explores gender identity in contemporary society.

Japanese society has a history of representing BL aesthetic masculinity, namely, *bishōnen*, involving a certain type of attractiveness found in adolescent males. *Bishōnen* is a term for beautiful boys and androgynous young men referring to their characteristics and mannerisms, and the aesthetic of *bishōnen* is influenced by ancient Japanese culture and literature, such as traditional Japanese kabuki theater in which effeminate male actors play female characters. However, the aesthetic of *bishōnen* differs from stereotypical feminine male characters and offers a non-traditional outlet for gender identity, as Gregory M. Pflugfelder notes when discussing male-male sexuality in the Meiji era, in which the beautiful boy of *bishōnen* is neither the "antithesis nor antecedent of adult masculinity."[26] The significant changes in the facial and bodily features of *bishōnen* characters in manga drawing styles from the 1970s to late 2000s can be regarded as an example of *bishōnen* masculinity and its relation to hegemonic masculinity in Japanese society from which BL/yaoi has emerged. Starting from the 1970s, the *bishōnen* character is drawn with a doll-like appearance with large and round eyes, and is interpreted, in a note from Celia Langford, as an object with a sense of emptiness that is awaiting readers.[27] However, the style changed from the late 1990s, when the character was drawn with an emphasis on the nose, eyebrow, and the almost identical triangular cheek; additionally, the "[n]oses are larger, and [there are] clear eyebrows ... [t]his is a sharp face, set in its angles and less receptive to the viewer's interpretations,"[28] which applies to both *seme* and *uke*, who are no longer distinguishable in the drawing style. Despite weakening the sense of the androgynous, the style created personhood in the composited image. The illustration of the characters changed again in the late 2000s, where the couples were clearly depicted and defined, differentiated in details such as hair color and with both characters "*drawn* in *two distinct styles*."[29]

Recent depictions of *bishōnen* are neither like the style of the 1970s, in which *bishōnen* was always drawn in a passive gesture as an invitation to readers, nor like the subsequent style in the late 1990s which begins to show active personality. Instead, the recent depictions have shown a sense of the "hesitation to grow up" in their appearance, manifested in a sense of ambiguity as a defining characteristic, whereby the androgynous needs to be discovered by and open to readers' interpretation, rather than as a given. With many other changes also taking place, such as young male characters aged above twenty becoming increasingly present, *bishōnen* is transforming in terms of its complexity, with more layers of meanings added and visual representations created, which creates its own type of alternative gender differentiation. Many scholars have responded to and examined *bishōnen*, and they tend to see it as something in between, or "interstitial,"[30] and as neither man nor woman, but a third sex/gender,[31] which is an alternative that operates outside of the "heteropatriarchal world."[32] Therefore, the appearance of the cute male impacts on the existing hierarchical power control in Japanese society, for example, in the way that that it "opens up the possibility of a woman, or even another man, assuming sexual control of a male body."[33] While beautiful (*utsukushii*) is used to describe a wide range of things, the word "cute," or *kawaii* in Japanese, is "beyond its denotative sense," in that the term *kawaii* is "often providing a democratic expression of resistance to gendered processes of aging, ideas of class and taste, and attractiveness in Japan's postmodern society."[34] In Glasspool's words, BL manga put the figure of the *bishōnen* "under the control of female authors and audiences" who "experiment with nonhegemonic gender and sexual practices."[35] This type of masculinity offers female audiences the opportunity "to consider alternative modes of desire and the possibility of shifting sexual power relations."[36] While the discourse regarding BL and its aesthetic is being internationalized, BL practices are correspondingly diversifying and changing when adopted into local BL communities—for example, the BL aesthetic applied to male idols in the danmei community in China, which causes conflicts among various fans.

The Internationalization of BL: Shifting Focus and Subjective Gaze

It is worth noting that slash fiction is commonly used to describe male-male homoerotic stories and developed in the Anglophone West during the early 1970s. BL and slash fiction are not equivalent terms and concepts, despite both having homosexual or homoerotic content. For example, fanfiction featuring sexual attraction between the Star Trek characters[37] can be misunderstood as a BL. As a combination of word and image, the manga form was easy to disseminate to the rest of world, with BL publications first appearing in the United States in 2004,[38] becoming a popular genre. There is already scholarly interest in investigating BL in an international context; as Turner notes, yaoi is transnational "as well as transcultural."[39] BL can reflect the social values from where it originates, and adjusts itself and provides alternatives in identifications and cultural meanings in different geographical locations. Therefore, recent studies have centered on the reception of female fans, and how fans interpret BL in different cultural/national settings, such as Björn-Ole Kamm conducting interviews in Japan and Germany.[40] Studies on the transnationalization of BL combine both qualitative and quantitative methods, such as the research surveying the demography of Western BL readers in the English and Italian language by Dru Pagliassotti,[41] and the more quantitative-driven, questionnaire-based studies on the motivations for yaoi consumption.[42] Moreover, the online survey conducted by AO3 on its own users in 2013 had 10,005 participants, where 9,974 (99.7%) respondents read and write in English language on the site, and 8,380 (83.8%) of the respondents are white. Some 90.3% (9,039) of the respondents self-identify as female.[43] The ongoing survey conducted by Anna Madill and Yao Zhao with a focus on Mainland China, Macau, Hong Kong, and Taiwan reinforces the finding that BL readers are predominantly females (88%) who are around twenty years of age.[44] Nonetheless, Turner notes that there is "a diverse range of alternative identities that exist in the fan community," which complicates any attempt to "categorise a large group of individuals into a singular heteronormative identity category [namely, heterosexual female fans]."[45] Research is being widened to pay attention to further ramifications among female fans, such as women with heterogeneous sexual identifications as well as gay male fans, to appreciate how BL is interpreted in multiple ways by different groups of fans.

Studies of the reception and interpretation of subcultural fans are being carried out in terms of gender and queer theories, for example to reflect the social functions of BL, such as the focus on LGBTQ discourse by Wim Lunsing,[46] Akiko Mizoguchi,[47] and Thomas Baudinette.[48] One of the findings is that, despite the diversity of BL subgenres, BL writers and readers are not only after sex in male-to-male relations, but rather romantic couplings, where the fans always identify themselves with the *uke* (receiver) and desire for the *seme* (penetrator), which is the usual pattern in the fandom.[49] Love plays an essential role as "an irresistible force in human life,"[50] which is demonstrated in diverse forms of BL storytelling, whereby the fans' "embracing [of the] sexual descriptions is by no means accepting pornography nor overly sexualizing same-sex relationships."[51] BL is differentiated from porn manga that only focuses on sex, and would rarely be considered pornography given its stylistic features[52] which are strongly associated with the visual elements and narrative literacies of *shōjo* manga, or young girls' comic.[53] For example, research in Taiwan shows that the subgenre called pure-love BL emphasizes "appreciation of young men's physical beauty without necessary recourse to explicitly sexual imagery."[54] Through interviews with local BL readers and writers, Fran Martin identifies distinctions between pure-love BL materials and others, such as gay narratives in which the flow of the central romance narrative is interrupted by detailed sex scenes.[55]

Discourse on female fans in terms of gender and sexuality has flourished, in which theorists investigate the social functions of the BL community, such as the perspective of feminist empowerment,[56] where female writers and readers can work with and against the "heteronormative paradigm in the exploration of alternatives."[57] In other words, BL is seen as "a form of female empowerment that endows women with subjective gaze,"[58] and is "a voyeuristic practice."[59] Specifically, the male's body becomes subjected to the female's objectification through BL fandom in which female fans challenge heteronormativity and hierarchical gender order by manipulating male characters in the idealized love and sexual fantasy worlds. As Dru Pagliassotti, Kazumi Nagaike, and Mark

McHarry summarize, BL "open[s] up sexually ambivalent spaces, de-eroticize[s] female subjectivity, contribute[s] to women's psychosexual self-therapy, and permit[s] expression of cultural, racial and sexual hybridity."[60] Being female voyeurs is a means of exploring sexuality and pleasure,[61] where female fans "enjoy the subversive thrill"[62] sexually and emotionally while watching/reading male characters being submissive in the story. Scholars such as Clay Calvert[63] and Jonathan Michel Metzl[64] analyze voyeurism as a psychiatric condition to understand producers and consumers in BL fandom, and to consider how the voyeuristic gaze of the female is not only related to sexuality but "imbued with power, gender."[65] In other words, writing and reading BL fiction is a political practice in which the female becomes the subject consuming the male as object; as noted by Chunyu Zhang, female readers are "empowered to objectify male figures to cater to female desires for men … [and] to control the way they interpret and make meaning of the story."[66] As the BL practice of recasting and recharacterizing male idols is a means of consuming the idols, whereby the increasing involvement of the idols in the fictive world presents economic profitability, the BL community is in communication with mainstream culture.

The Arrival of BL Fandom in China: From Manga to Fiction and the Evolving Online Society

Manga appeared in the Chinese market around the mid-1990s. This acts as an originating point for fixing BL in its two-dimensional Japanese manga and print format in which the 2D image (print or screen-based) and anime are paramount. BL circulates in China in various forms including fan-made DIY slash and semi-commercial cinema on popular online streaming platforms, such as Bilibili and iQiyi (愛奇藝). BL, or danmei, in contemporary Chinese media has been examined in relation to queer and gender studies, such as a cinematic text in terms of the affective economy[67] and using a particular movie as a case study to investigate the Chinese female audience.[68] Major concerns in current literature include danmei culture as a female subculture in Chinese society,[69] investigation of danmei online platforms,[70] interpretations of individual danmei works with Chinese traditional elements,[71] and analysis of the social and cultural impact of danmei in relation to Chinese government crackdowns.[72] Drawing on the BL/yaoi aesthetic, the danmei aesthetic has been contextualized in the Chinese socio-cultural environment. There is a similar application in that most readers and writers are heterosexual females who appreciate the male body as young, slim, tall, feminine, and beautiful. Although we acknowledge that the terms "aesthetics" and "characteristics" mean different things, this chapter uses them interchangeably in the case study to draw similarities between the two-dimensional characters made for the danmei aesthetic and the male idols endowed with danmei characteristics.

Scholars are expanding on the differences or even peculiarities of Chinese danmei in their case studies—for example, Madill and Zhao state that policies of the Chinese government with regard to regulating pornographic content have determined that certain genres of danmei are more popular than others in comparison to BL in Anglophone regions.[73] While "BL explores a vast range of scenarios from the gently implicit, through to romance, the sexual explicit, BDSM themes, and 'fetishistic' niche taste,"[74] the national socio-cultural environment does not particularly encourage creations outside mainstream traditional values. The government has zero tolerance for genres such as manga and animation containing graphic sexual scenes, therefore Chinese danmei production is most commonly concentrated in the form of narrative fiction. In other words, it is relatively safer to circulate fiction on the internet, which is written in text (with symbol keys used to represent sensitive vocabularies if necessary) to avoid censorship regulations and the crackdown on internet pornography by the Chinese government; animation largely circulates through piracy, subject to official restrictions for any sexual content. In addition, mainstream discomfort with homosexuality is another reason that makes the circulation of danmei complex in China.[75] According to John Wei, along with other forms such as popular literary websites and online blogs, danmei fiction has grown into one of the major genres of cyberliterature in China, which creates incomes for writers to produce online writings and paid services for readers to view online and download content,[76] despite "a huge black market online where they can consume, exchange, and download BL texts for free."[77]

Several prominent websites dedicated to danmei fans in China have appeared over the past two decades, as acknowledged by all of our interviewees. For example, the fan-operated Lucifer Club[78] was established in 1999 and became the most influential danmei website in China until 2007. A plagiarism-related incident took place in 2007 that caused two-thirds of users to leave in protest against the way the incident was handled. Despite the significant drop in its popularity ever since, Lucifer Club is still up and running. The commercial website Jinjiang[79] has taken over the lead and has been operating since 2003. It is the largest women's literature website in China, with a permanent section featuring danmei content. Yanrui Xu and Ling Yang provide an overview of the scale of danmei products available on Jingjiang in 2012, which had about 199,100 works of BL stories, of which 145,600 were original while the rest were fanfiction.[80] Original fiction is created featuring danmei content with no reference to existing characters from other story worlds or persons in reality, whereas those with such references would be regarded as fanfiction. Xu and Yang further categorize the types of fiction written in terms of narrative content, such as abuse fiction, sweet fiction, and realistic fiction; different pairings of *seme* and *uke* characters regarding their characterization and age; and different backgrounds situated in ancient, modern, or fantasy worlds. However, what is of particular interest to us is a certain trade emerging in Chinese fanfiction in recent years that involves male idols in danmei practice, where there are two main approaches: writers creating their own original stories by using male idols in homoerotic love stories as danmei characters, or using male idols as substitutes for existing danmei characters in stories.

In our survey of self-identified danmei fans conducted in June 2020, 177 (71%) out of 249 respondents in total voted for Xiao Zhan (108 respondents or 43.4%) and Wang Yibo (sixty-nine respondents or 27.7%) as the top two idols that reflect the danmei aesthetic and are a good fit for danmei characters. The top two are featured on the current main danmei discussion platforms, namely Bai Du Tie Ba (百度貼吧), Weibo (微博), and Dou Ban (豆瓣). For example, there is a section entitled **Bo** Jun Yi **Xiao** (博君一肖) on Weibo, which contains one character from each of the two idols' names in bold. The platforms are where fan reviews/discussions and information can be found regarding online published fictions starring the two idols. The Bo Jun Yi Xiao section has 3.4 million registered danmei fans who want to see Wang Yibo and Xiao Zhan in a relationship in the fictional world, and contains over 8 million threads with over 91 billion views as of June 2021.[81] Moreover, there are other dedicated websites that publish danmei fiction which recasts and re-characterizes the two idols as a couple, as shown in Quotev that has the best known section on Bo Jun Yi Xiao,[82] and there were 573 works of fiction titled Bo Jun Yi Xiao published under the danmei section on Jinjinag as well between July 2019 and June 2021.[83] Scholars who focus on social issues, such as Elizabeth Miles, note that the desire for BL characters themed on male-to-male intimacy make us to reconsider "what sex is and how legal and social proscriptions deny sexual access and the rights of full sexual citizenship,"[84] while, for Aleardo Zanghellini, "the yaoi/BL genre caters to deeply felt needs, desires, preferences or fantasies of the subculture that consumes it."[85] We acknowledge the importance of these concerns, but would argue that the increasing involvement of male idols in danmei fandom over the past decade also reflects an attempt to profit from the subcultural fans who are consuming idols as danmei characters.

Ground Rules in the Danmei Community: Male Idols as Danmei Characters

According to our interviews with danmei fans, there are three commonly known ground rules that apply to writers and readers within the Chinese danmei community. The first is to keep a low profile and stay away from mainstream culture, which reflects Andrea Wood's argument that BL fans "often operate in contradictory tension with and against anime industries and socio-cultural values as they access, consume and create around a form of homoerotic media that they do not want to be assimilated into mainstream culture and its norms."[86] However, apart from more transnational publishers and distributors becoming involved, the internet is the most popular publishing platform that had sped up the spread of danmei material and made the boundaries between the subcultural and the mainstream become blurred.

The second rule is to provide clear tags/labels on the front page of each online production/title to indicate the level/content of the fiction in terms of its broad subgenres. This is an essential tool to direct fans to what they prefer to read and skip any content that they are not interested in or that might cause discomfort. Take for example *The Untamed* (陳情令), a 2019 Chinese TV series starring Xiao Zhan and Wang Yibo, based on the original web novel entitled *Mo Dao Zu Shi* which depicted an explicit romance between the two main male characters. There are nearly 8,000 fanfictions found under The Untamed (TV) RPF (Real Person Fiction)[87] on AO3 featuring the relationship between Xiao Zhan and Wang Yibo, with around 4,500 works written in Mandarin and the rest in English. Each of the works is labeled with several tags which are available to choose from while the website is uploading. All tags represent certain features, contents, and styles of works that authors/uploaders use to indicate the nature of their works; and they would choose one or multiple tags as appropriate.[88] Among the many categories, works must carry one or more tags in terms of warning labels, including, for example, "Underage," "Rape/Non-Con," "Major Character Death," and "Graphic Depictions of Violence." If the work is labeled "No Archive Warnings Apply," it means that all four warning labels mentioned above will apply. Similar labeling approaches are utilized in major danmei websites such as Jinjiang in which readers can use tags to find the type of works they wish to read, or avoid.

The third rule is that the recasting and recharacterizing of real idols in the fictive danmei world need to be "approved" in advance by the idols themselves. In other words, it is inappropriate to involve the idols if they are not comfortable with the danmei aesthetic. It is observed that certain male idols have millions of danmei fans and are consumed as danmei characters, while other idols with similar popularity in mainstream culture do not appear in the danmei fictive world. Danmei fans have their own way of identifying whether or not the idols would "accept" appearing in danmei fiction. As one of danmei interviewees notes:

> As I am aware, the roles Xiao Zhan played in some drama TV series have featured a danmei aesthetic, such as the widely known one titled *The Untamed* (Chen Qing Ling) in 2019, which is a film based on a danmei fiction *Mo Dao Zu Shi*. The drama is a stereotypical story featuring traditional Chinese martial arts with technology and visual effects. The interaction between the two main male actors is intimate and implies a danmei aesthetic. My danmei friends and I think that accepting the particular danmei-like character-setting in the drama is a kind of "approval" from the idol himself and that he would not be opposed to danmei culture.[89]

The case study on the AO3 incident reflects the complexities of BL idols in China when the three ground rules of the danmei community were breached and in turn caused the controversy. The event reflects the possible motivation for the potential capitalization of danmei fans.

Male Idols as Brand Ambassadors

1. The Relationship Between Brand Ambassadors and Fashion Branding

The brand has value that not only reflects the quality of the product but is recognized as having its own property.[90] Branding focuses on the connection between consumers and products through creating shared experiences and emotions in the contemporary time.[91] Therefore, brands "are about *culture* as much as they are about economics" and branding is "both reliant on, and reflective of, our most basic social and cultural relations."[92] Grant McCracken states that branding is the transfer of the culturally formed world into products,[93] which is consistent with Bernard Cova and Véronique Cova's finding that consumers pay more attention to the social contacts and cultural identities linked to and brought by the brand than the object of the products.[94] Therefore, the shared experiences and emotions, which derive from and are contextualized in the "cultural contexts for everyday living, individual identity, and affective relationships,"[95] have become the focus of the current discourse on building a long-lasting brand and customer relations.[96]

There is rich scholarship investigating emotional communication in terms of experiential marketing and branding, which is commonly approached through the design, ambience, and layouts of retail shopping areas, for example, to create multi-sensory experiences for customers in order to achieve an emotional connection to the brands.[97] Moreover, the multi-sensory experiences are enhanced by digital tools to create an emotional experience with the use of both spatial and heritage storytelling in connection with fashion brands across both online and offline retail spaces.[98]

Shaz Smilansky notes that live brand experience, which is the "brand-relevant, two-way communications between consumers and brands, [and which] can be delivered face to face or remotely," promotes brand personality,[99] and that the ambassador is "the only human interface between the Brand personality and the consumer."[100] That is to say, brands can act and express feelings via brand ambassadors when interacting with customers. The brand ambassador, therefore, consolidates, or weakens, the sense of a brand, performing like a living being in the interaction with customers.

Appointing brand ambassadors is, therefore, a means to create an active emotional connection between brands and customers. The appointees are always popular cultural idols/celebrities who have fan bases or are already known to potential consumers; this has proven effective in marketing products for the brands. Using anonymous models as ambassadors is acknowledged as an alternative pathway in transferring cultural meaning to products.[101] For example, professional climbers, who are not widely known, are appointed as brand ambassadors to sell climbing gear because they are "cultural intermediaries between production and consumption infusing every facet of the everyday experience."[102] The appointed professionals are the representation of the specialized products experienced and tested through everyday practice and first-hand experience. Their endorsement of these products can be seen as a testimonial and serves as a type of warranty that is conceivable and persuasive to customers. The characteristics of the ambassadors are usually matched with the culture of the brand in promoting products to targeted customers, which is an essential part of the value of the brand. The characteristics of professional climbers, such as being persistent and dauntless in challenging rough weather and environments, are extended to the image of the brands they represent and, in turn, are so perceived by the customers.

There has been a history of luxury fashion brands appointing ambassadors as a strategy in marketing products. The purpose of ambassadors in the contemporary context is to humanize the brand and facilitate relational connections in order to provide brand meaning for consumers while consolidating the identity of the organization.[103] The selection of the ambassadors is crucial, so that the characteristics of the ambassadors match the image of the brands and is appropriate to the actual products being promoted.[104] For instance, a study conducted of two fashion brands, Levi's and Abercrombie & Fitch, found that the personality of the ambassadors can be transferred to the brands, and that the consumer's attachment and purchase intentions are influenced by brand personalities.[105] The matching between brands and ambassadors has a mutual impact which is seen as a form of co-branding strategy in recent studies, and is regarded as an interactive and reciprocal process.[106]

2. Popular Cultural Idols as Danmei Characters and Luxury Fashion Brand Endorsement

Although there is no simple or straightforward definition for luxury, Julia-Sophie Jelinek sums up the values of luxury brands, which are also seen as the characteristics of the brands,[107] and determines that the appointed ambassadors are the extension of the characteristics of the brands which are needed in order to reach the targeted customers. For example, some European luxury fashion brands wish to be perceived in terms of the values of their embodied cultural heritage. Their cultural characteristics are always accompanied with inherited history and excellent craftsmanship. Therefore, the ambassadors of these brands would provide customers with matching characteristics and values, such as having classic attributes and being elegant, well established, and so on. However, our study observes and discusses through examples that these same brands tend to appoint a particular style of male idol as brand ambassadors in China, who seem to have no direct association with the values of the brands and who would not be appointed for the European market. The particular type of male ambassador appointed in recent years appears to be young, beautiful, and feminine. These idols are made to cater to female desires and as ambassadors to reach female customers in the Chinese market.[108]

There are various collaborations between fashion brands and "little fresh meat." The latter are male idols who are millennials born in Mainland China. They have several million fans on social media, such as Weibo, which is the equivalent of Facebook. For instance, Tod's officially announced Xiao Zhan as its brand ambassador in 2021, and in the relatively short official announcement, apart from emphasizing the perfect fit of the match-up between the brand's "classic DNA" deemed as being deeply rooted in the brand's personality and Xiao's "unique charm" characteristic, where his "gentlemanship embodies the timeless and enduring Italian spirit [that the brand carries],"[109] Tod's explicitly points out that "the brand's focus [is] on the young generation in China."[110] Notwithstanding news reports that drew attention to Xiao's 30 million followers on Weibo celebrating the newly granted endorsement,[111] this was in fact Xiao's first international luxury brand collaboration since the February 2020 incident which triggered a cyberwar against Xiao's fans which led to a boycott by many of his then brand collaborators, including Cartier, Estée Lauder, and Piaget.[112]

There are many other "little fresh meat" who are brand ambassadors, as listed in Table 4.1 (below),with details of their endorsements.[113]

The "little fresh meat" are all similar in appearance: their bodies are meticulously maintained and can be described as slim, delicate, elegant, young, and beautiful, which are characteristics that are aesthetically coherent with danmei characters. As Anna Madill notes,"since about 2006, recognizably *danmei* elements involving public figures and performers are increasingly evident in ordinary media. It seems that 'homoeroticism' has considerable commercial value and that *yaoi* and *danmei* may be seeping into more hegemonic forms of popular

Table 4.1 Male popular cultural idols who are considered as 'little fresh meat' with substantial followers on social media have attracted endorsements with international luxury fashion brands

The 'little fresh meat'	Number of followers on Weibo	Fashion brands endorsed	Year of endorsement
Wang Yibo	38.5 million	Evisu and Chanel	2021
Lu Han	4.6 million	Cartier	2016
Wu Yifan	51.5 million	Burberry and Bulgari	2016
		Louis Vuitton	2018
Huang Zitao	63.8 million	Lacoste	2019
Liu Haoran (Turbo Liu)	32.2 million	Puma	2017
		Tod's	2019
Yang Yang	53.1 million	Guerlain	2016
Zhang Yixing (Lay Zhang)	50.6 million	Valentino	2017
		Chaumet	2018
		H&M	2019
Yi Yang Qian Xi (Jackson Yee)	87.9 million	Bottega Veneta	2018
		Tiffany&Co., Bulgari, and Armani	2020
Deng Lun	39.9 million	Bally	2019

culture."[114] Our survey shows that the third, fourth, and fifth among the top five idols selected by the participants reflect the danmei aesthetic and represent a good fit for danmei characters; these are Lu Han (forty-three participants, or 17.3%), Deng Lun (twenty-seven participants, or 11%), and Yi Yang Qian Xi (sixteen participants, or 6.4%). They are popular on major danmei websites too. For example, there were 225 fiction works featuring Lu Han, 191 with Yi Yang Qian Xi, and nine with Deng Lun—found by searching titles containing the idols' names in the danmei section of the Jinjiang website on June 25, 2021. However, there were relatively fewer works of fictions featuring other "little fresh meat" during the same search: there were forty-four fiction works with Wu Yifan, ten with Huang Zitao, twenty-five with Liu Haoran, forty-five with Yang Yang, and seventy-four with Zhang Yixing.

As acknowledged by our interviewees, the data reflects that in general most danmei fans have been conscious of the recasting and recharacterizing of male idols as danmei characters with respect to the community rules previously outlined, namely, that only the idols who are not opposed to danmei culture would appear in the fictive worlds. Since the community is self-regulating, concrete follow-up actions are not applied to any cases that breach the rules except when the works in question are taken down by the writers themselves. At the same time, the number of male idols who are acting as brand ambassadors has increased, as danmei characters are correspondingly being consumed by female danmei fans who feel empowered to objectify male figures by controlling the way they interpret and make meaning of the story. This has resulted in both the growing number of fans for idols and the consequent additional revenue for brands.[115] Therefore, the female danmei fans are becoming the targeted (potential) customers of the luxury fashion brands. According to our survey and interviewees, comprising danmei fans that are mainly either tertiary and postgraduate students or professionals in their early career, the large numbers of fans represent the promise of future economic returns. The appointment by the brands of male brand ambassadors with young, beautiful, and feminine bodies works in tandem with the danmei fans; even though this notion has been neither admitted nor rejected by either party, it can be interpreted as a deliberate marketing strategy to capitalize on danmei fans. When the danmei community with hundreds of millions of members becomes targeted by fashion brands seeking to increase potential revenue and make the fashion brand young again, any breaching of the rules highlights the complexity of the relationship between idols, fans, and fashion brands.

AO3 Case Study

Xiao Zhan as a Male Idol in the Chinese Fashion Market

Before the incident that we are about to consider took place in February 2020, Xiao was announced as the face of the fragrance and beauty line for Estée Lauder in September 2019, and the brand friend of Polo watch and the Possession jewelry range for Piaget in December 2019. He also shot advertisements for Cartier and Gucci in early 2020.[116]

The AO3 Incident

The fiction titled *Xia Zhui* (下坠), which means falling, was originally published on AO3 in serial form on January 30, 2020, and completed on February 24, 2020. The fiction, written in Chinese, contains thirteen chapters with a total of around 80,000 words and narrates stories between a prostitute and a high school boy, featuring Xiao Zhan and Wang Yibi as these two characters respectively. In the story, Xiao Zhan is recharacterized as a biological male who suffers from gender dysphoria and works as a female prostitute, while Wang Yibi is recharacterized as a high school boy who falls in love with Xiao Zhan. Parts of the setting of the scenario and the detailed descriptions of actions caused discomfort among some fans, where Xiao appears as a breathtakingly beautiful woman flirting with Wang who is captivated by Xiao's beauty. However, Wang later realizes Xiao's biological gender and that he is working as a female prostitute. In the writing, the real names of the two idols were retained, along with descriptions of the physical appearances of both characters, such as being young, tall, and slim, matching the two idols in reality. In short, readers could recognize the characters in the story as the two idols (see Figure 4.1).

The controversy was triggered by the uploading of the fiction on Weibo, with a link to Lofter on February 24. Later, an illustration of the fiction was created by an anonymous painter to visually present a scene of the two characters shown in the reflection of a cosmetics mirror. The illustration depicts a beautiful woman standing with one hand against the mirror table to support her body while the other hand holds a brush applying blusher on her cheek. Her face is fully exposed and highly similar to Xiao. There is a tall and slim male body standing behind the woman as the only other person in the scene, with only his back showing.[117] Xiao's mimei fans in the mainstream culture were concerned about the fiction, which was found offensive for several reasons. Firstly, Xiao Zhan was recasted

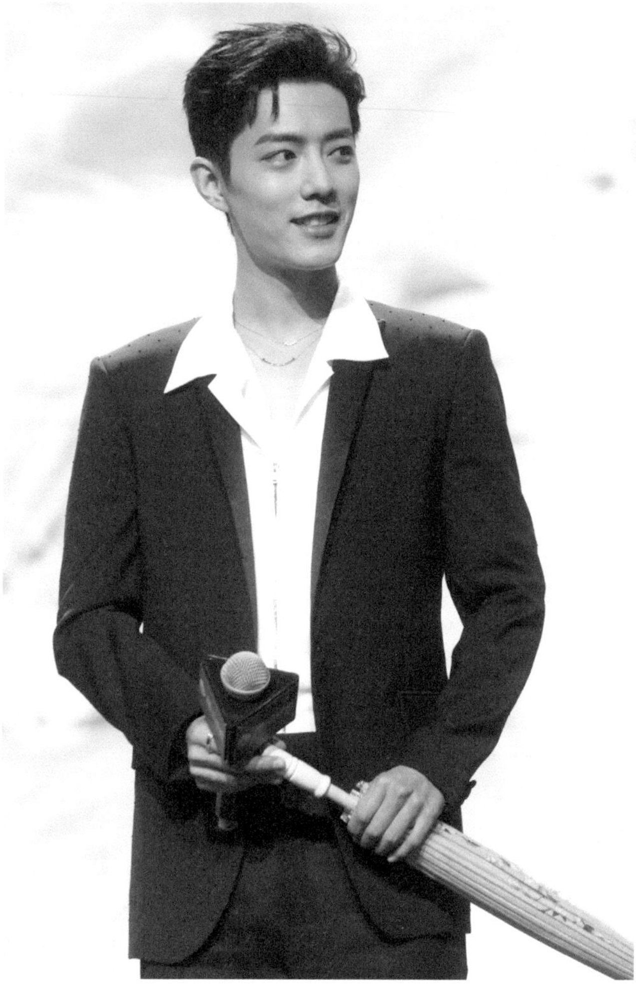

Figure 4.1 Actor Sean Xiao (aka Xiao Zhan) attends the TenCent Video 10th anniversary ceremony on June 7, 2021 in Shanghai, China. Photo by VCG/VCG via Getty Images.

and recharacterized as the "femalized" character in the story. It is worth noting that femalizing an original manga or anime male character to recreate a male-male couple is regarded as common practice in yaoi. The male is seen as being in a dominant position over the female in a patriarchal society; hence, being femalized means the loss of the dominant position in society.[118] Secondly, the fiction has pornographic content; and thirdly, the work represents a humiliation of Xiao and it is far from his image of a young and adorable male character in the cultural industry.

On February 25, Xiao's mimei fans began to report the author and the fiction to the Internet Police, a government department specializing in cybercrime that is responsible for enforcing the government's regulation and crackdown on internet pornography. On the following day, February 26, more mimei fans became involved and their reporting of the incident escalated to the extent that guidelines prepared and circulated by anonymous mimei fans were released to teach mimei fans how to report their concern to the Anti-Piracy and Pornography Committee, another government department. At the same time, some other danmei writers were targeted and bullied randomly by mimei fans online which caused those fiction works to be taken down by the uploaders, while many other danmei writers had to rename their online IDs to try to avoid the escalating online abuse from mimei fans. Apart from reporting the author and the particular work to the authorities, mimei fans extended their targets to also reporting Archive of Our Own (AO3) and Lofter (网易) as allegedly pornographic sites where the offending work was initially uploaded. Mimei fans regarded their widespread reporting behavior as exercising their personal rights and defending the dignity of their idol. The incident escalated and more parties became involved, representing different sides of the debate while and extended the debate to include broader

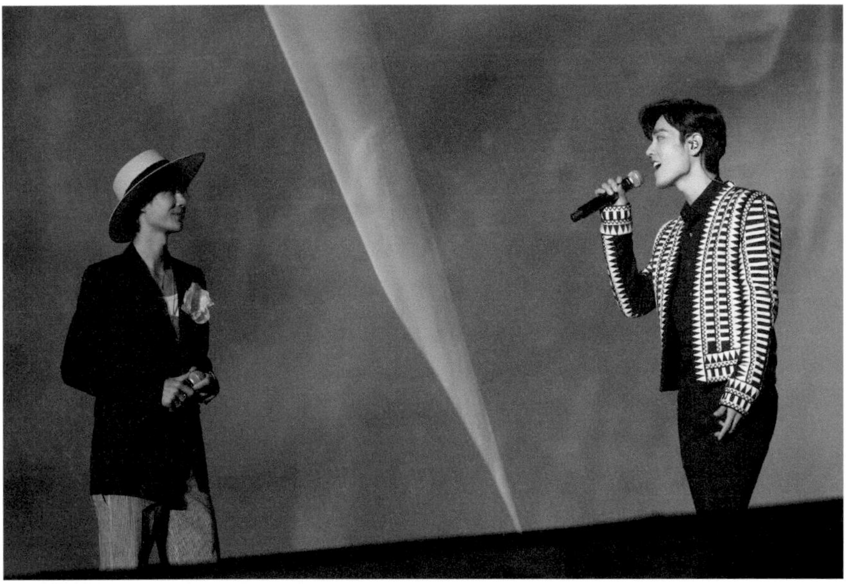

Figure 4.2 Sean Xiao Zhan (right) and Wang Yibo (left) perform on stage during The Untamed National Style Concert on November 1, 2019 in Nanjing, Jiangsu Province of China. Photo by VCG/VCG via Getty Images.

issues such as the definition and boundary of literature writing, the impact of collective social behavior, freedom of creative writing, and so on.

On the other side, the danmei community feared that such reporting, both online and offline, could attract tighter regulations from the state regulatory body that would sabotage their rights to the freedom of creation in danmei practice. Danmei users on AO3, Lofter, and other major danmei websites started voicing their opposition to Xiao's mimei fans. However, as a result of the constant reporting to the relevant authorities, danmei-like fictions were taken down on Lofter on February 27, followed by an authoritarian block that prevented Mainland Chinese users from accessing AO3 on February 29. Meanwhile, several other Chinese danmei websites were also temporarily closed, followed by the application of stricter government regulations on online danmei productions afterwards. The government crackdown had a relatively large negative impact on the broader danmei community in China, when this cultural practice became suppressed and compromised. The authoritarian actions upset the danmei community which intensified their confrontation with Xiao's mimei fans and the idol himself. The first major retaliation conducted by the danmei community was taken on February 28, when Xiao's homepage on Lofter was bombarded with junk messages. The retaliation was given the name *227 Solidarity* to mark the date of the first blockage of the danmei website as well as the solidarity and retaliation of the danmei community in defending their right to write freely. Moreover, continuing a show of resilience, the 227 Group was formed by the community soon afterwards, comprising mainly danmei writers. The group is dedicated to encouraging followers to boycott Xiao Zhan and the brands that he represents, notably Estée Lauder and Piaget,[119] and this lasted for months as a form of retaliation against his mimei fans.[120] Boycott actions included posting online messages on Weibo and other major online media platforms threatening to boycott the brands; leaving negative messages on the brands' Weibo pages; requesting hard copy invoices from the brands for products purchased;[121] requesting entertainment hosts to pixelate Xiao in popular cultural activities, films, and television programs; and deliberately low-ranking the films featuring Xiao as an actor via film reviews websites. One of our danmei interviewees interprets the community retaliation as collective action on a massive scale:

> I think there is strong retaliation and resilience against Xiao Zhan from the danmei community who are apparently not his fans because their online community is temporarily taken down or blocked for reasons that have nothing to do with them. Xiao Zhan then becomes their target to express the arguments.[122]

There are two focal points that mark the event as truly controversial, both of which concern the ground rules of the danmei community that were contravened in the case study. On the one hand, idols would not appear in danmei fiction as a recasted character if the idols show no interest in this. In the case of Xiao, however, the role he played in *The Untamed*, for example, featured a danmei aesthetic and, as such, this was interpreted by danmei fans as implying that the idol was not opposed to the subculture and that he intended to grow in influence within this field, which he did quite successfully, according to our interviewees. Hence, the appropriately labeled fiction published on AO3 is considered standard practice in the danmei community. The crackdown on danmei culture is, therefore, blamed on "over-reacting" mimei fans as well as Xiao himself who was expected to "manage and be responsible for his mimei fans including their behaviors, which he apparently failed to do in the event."[123] As one of our interviewees notes, "attracting danmei fans for greater influence and economic return without taking responsibility when things go wrong is how the event has been seen from danmei fans' perspective."[124]

On the other hand, mimei fans complained that publishing works of fiction on AO3, which is the largest specialized yaoi/danmei website in the world, is fine but not on Weibo, which is the main socio-cultural platform with hundreds of millions of mainstream users, hence the online exposure of the fiction to Xiao's mainstream mimei fans was considered inappropriate. Moreover, by reposting this content on Weibo, the work did not follow AO3 protocols and was not clearly tagged or labeled to indicate the classification of its content, which was considered "poor behavior and should have been better self-regulated"[125] by both sides. Mimei fans urged danmei writers/readers to have self-awareness about their practice and that they should only be operating and staying within their own subcultural field. The incident shows the conflict over the consumption of the male idol in both the real and fictive worlds among the different categories of his fans, which places the idol in a dilemma. The incident continues to make for a very intriguing case study, particularly in terms of testing the solidity of the brand–idol connection.

The danmei world offers a space for fans to retreat from the social reality of gender inequality while embracing gender ambiguity and sexual fluidity.[126] Danmei writers/readers tend to stay away from mainstream culture and its norms, yet the previously discussed alternative masculinity, which "attempt[s] to redraw the fixed gender boundaries and heterosexual norms"[127] in the idol-making industry, makes it possible for male idols to be consumed in the fictive world as danmei characters in China. In other words, there are shared aesthetic and social functionalities across the danmei world and real-world idol-making. As noted by Glasspool, elements of the idol-making industry in Japan have influenced Korea and China, reflected in the alternative masculinity appreciated by female fans, such as the idols being set up to be emotionally sensitive and domestic, young, and performing "male–male relationships that tread a fine line between the homosocial and what could be considered homosexual"[128] as forms of commercial activities. These elements are essential in danmei characters. For example, cuteness is always used to describe male idols' appearances, which links it to contemporary female consumption, shown in terms of slender and stylishly dressed bodies. The particular feminine look of both the idols and the danmei characters offers a sense of security, which is also reflected in the "little fresh meat" nickname, of being a manageable size, a form of fresh novelty, and meat to be eaten, thus providing a holistic sense of control over the object under the female gaze. As noted by Glasspool, the danmei type of male idol "provides a 'safer' form of masculinity"[129] for female audiences, and for such audiences, idols with feminine characteristics make them "safer objects of love."[130]

Moreover, while danmei fans can participate as both writer and reader in the story making to practice their active control over the characters, mimei fans practice their influence over their idols via their purchasing power by buying idol-related items, such as commercial films and music singles, miscellaneous products, and fashion products of the represented brands. Rather than being passive, the proactive approach of mimei fans represents a shift in how they express their care for their idols, in terms of how they adopt the maternal role, caring for their idols like their own children.[131] For example, the digital music single by Xiao Zhan, titled "Spotlight," released on April 25, 2020, marked his return from the controversial event, with over 25 million electronic copies downloaded in 24 hours, amounting to over 73 million Chinese yuan in sales (or more than US$10 million).[132] Purchasing is not just an individual action to show personal support for the idol in the fan economy but rather a collective social/cultural action organized by Xiao's mimei fans community on a massive scale. A community organization called Xiao Zhan Global Support Association purchased over 9 million e-copies of the single[133] in one day on QQ Music, one of the popular music platforms, which pushed its total sales over 1 billion Chinese yuan in four days since its initial release. The purchasing power of the fans demonstrates the commercial potential of the idol,[134] while fans in addition to their purchasing actions also consider their role to be one of nurturing the idol, which in turn helps to redeem the idol. The mothering role of mimei fans allows them to immerse themselves in the active idol–fan relationship, where the collective actions of fans are able to reshape the idols via purchasing power. Mimei fans and their idols are made into a union deeply sharing an inseparable destiny that expands the fan economy in China.

Of particular note is that mimei fans attempted to make Xiao Zhan dissociate himself from the danmei aesthetic in order to extricate the idol from male-to-male relationships, which is how he got famous in the first place. To dissociate from male-to-male relationships is to protectively distance him from being as labeled "femalized"; mimei fans wish to realize their idol as the one that occupies the dominant position over females in Chinese patriarchal society, which must be a heterosexual male, because as noted by Chizuko Ueno, being femalized means the loss of the dominant position in a patriarchal society.[135] Adhering to the idea of dominant males and subservient females is a typical patriarchal thought that also appears in danmei practice, as shown in female danmei fans' preference not to see stereotypical female characters in these fictions. For example, one of our interviewees said she prefers to see male-male relationships where the *seme* is seen as the one leading the relationship which is not only followed by the *uke* in the fictive world but also by the female readers in reality. There is no competition in fighting for the love of *seme* between the *uke* and the readers, as the readers know the *uke* is the male figure that female readers can consume and manipulate. Nevertheless, both characters, as well as supporting roles if applicable, must be males, thus resulting in the readers being the only females in this dynamic.[136] Although Zanghellini notes that female readers "find [female characters] distracting [and] interfering with the consumption of yaoi/BL [which is] essentially a voyeuristic practice where the objects of the gaze are men,"[137] this explains why there is seldom a stereotypical female character in these fiction works. Our interviews have established that female readers/writers are the stereotypical female characters themselves in the traditional patriarchal society —dominated by both the *seme* and the *uke*. In other words, the physical and emotional feminine features are shown in the *uke* characters in BL/yaoi fiction, as the female readers/writers dominate and manipulate the males in the relationship. Rather, the *uke* consolidates the role of the female in traditional society. This has been criticized by Pagliassotti as a reproduction of the patriarchal gender hierarchy.[138] Despite BL's progressiveness with regards to same-sex relations, it has also been criticized for simply perpetuating traditional and patriarchal heterosexual paradigms.[139]

Consequently, a stronger characterization of *uke* is now appearing and becoming popularized, displaying independence in terms of both behaviors and emotions. The change in the aesthetic of danmei characters is enabling more varieties and allowing flexibility in mobilizing male idols as danmei characters, such as in the case of Xiao Zhan, who is being recharacterized as both *seme* and *uke* by different writers in different works. Nevertheless, mimei fans are critical of the fluidity of his representation as either dating with *uke* in the male-to-male relationship or being the *uke* in terms of becoming the "femalized" character.[140] According to two of our interviewees, A2 and A15, they expect to see the performance of male-male relationships of their beloved idols as homosocial or even homosexual, where they can project themselves to be the *uke* but also as an independent and equal character in relation to the *seme*, while at the same time being loved by the *seme*:

> I became Xiao Zhan's fan because of *The Untamed* with its portrayal of the male-male relationship between characters played by Xiao Zhan and Wang Yibo. The ambience of the romantic male-male coupling is what I am after. I enjoy reading Xiao Zhan as a danmei character in the reliable and trustworthy relationship between two people, which is real and earnest, a form of being together. I always imagine myself to be the *uke* who is seen [as] passive on the surface but desires the *seme*'s attention and wants to be cared [for] by the *seme*. I want to see the independent character of the *uke*, someone who is able to express his feelings and emotions to request attention from the *seme*. In other words, I intentionally choose to be passive in the relationship, so I made the *seme* to be the dominant position, which makes me happy.[141]
>
> I see the *uke* character as a better shape of me who is physically more capable while maintaining the delicate feminine gesture and the level of sensitivity in feeling and emotion. The *uke* character himself in my opinion is already the full story of love, that the love takes place within himself. The character of *seme* is here to activate the love inside of the *uke*. And I, as a reader while reading the fiction, become the *uke* and witness the love unfold within my body.[142]

The Capitalization of Danmei Fans

According to the ground rules, the practice of danmei fans' writing and reading should be kept within the community to avoid unnecessary social attraction from mainstream culture. The matter of involving real-life idols in danmei fiction widely rests upon the belief that the idol himself is not against the danmei aesthetic. Notably, the idol, or rather the management company behind him, has its own agenda about what character the idol is supposed to have in order to fit in and thrive in the current cultural industry, so that particular cultural aesthetics as well as gender and age groups can be targeted to keep increasing the number of fans, which is vital for all stakeholders in the business. For example, in a parallel discussion on girl idol industries in South Korea, the corporate management system creates and controls popular cultural idols in which the body of the idol is no longer just an image to represent the heterosexual and patriarchal society, but a concrete social and cultural production where consumption takes place.[143] Similarly, the design and cultivation of male idols in China are a form of social operation/practice in which the body of the idol is a social subject. In other words, the selection, cultivation, and exhibition of male idols have been done strategically and systematically, serving the purpose of creating "a series of derivative commodities and economic values"[144] to capitalize on the fans.[145]

After the success of the character he played in The *Untamed*, Xiao Zhan has grown a large number of danmei fans. The exhibiting of a sense of male-to-male intimacy outside of the TV drama is economically beneficial—for example, the gesture and action suggesting homosexuality, such as the "affectionate display of friendship between [male] members … [and] the expression of closeness through physical touch,"[146] are intended for and made to cater to female fans; they are performative and can lead to attracting more danmei fans. There has been no statement issued from the idol himself or his representatives regarding his recasting and recharacterization in danmei fictions. However, this approach by danmei fans is largely driven by economic motivation and it is hard for his mimei fans to accept this, rejecting his femalized recharacterization and any other recreations of him that are far from his real-life character and setting.

Meanwhile, some of our interviewees (A5, A10, A11) also mentioned that they prefer not to confuse Xiao's character in the drama with his identity as a male idol. For example, A5 states:

> In fact, I do not read fiction with popular cultural idols as characters who would make me feel uncomfortable. Only if the male idols admit to being open-minded or happy to be seen as homosexual in reality. The homosexual relations represented in the drama series cannot be regarded as reflecting their personal beliefs in reality. Even if I like the idol to be in a homosexual relationship, I actually like the characters they play in the drama, not their identity as male idol in reality.[147]

By appointing idols or "little fresh meat" as brand ambassadors, instead of others who are considered to be renowned and well-established artists that match the values of the brands, luxury fashion brands have shown their clear intention to capitalize on the millions of fans of the idols in China. With Xiao and other "little fresh meat" becoming popular in the subcultural community, danmei fans can be thought of as a means to grow further profits and make additional sales. Nevertheless, it is still unclear if the danmei fans of the idols are also targeted when considering the appointment and selection of the particular type of idol to be a brand ambassador. The number of cases of "little fresh meat" idols that have been appointed as brand ambassadors has increased in recent years, while the characteristics of the selected idols overlap with the danmei aesthetic. It would be ideal for both the idol and the brands to grow fans in the danmei community; however, it requires considerate and sensitive steps to develop the relationship among the brands, the idols, and the various fans, as shown in the following comments by our interviewee A3:

> I don't like the recent dramas that came out after *The Untamed* with their studious emphasis on male-male relationships, trying to ingratiate themselves with, or stretching their aesthetic to suit the danmei community.[148]

Most of our interviews were carried out with senior danmei fans who see themselves as reasonable and who can understand both sides of the conflict when it comes to talking about issues regarding the Xiao Zhan incident and the danmei community. Our interviewees see themselves as danmei fans rather than mimei fans of any male idol (A1, A2, A3, A4, A5, A9, A10, and A12). They consume male idols as danmei characters; however, they mainly do not wish to engage with mainstream culture.[149] They are aware of the motivation of gaining profits that lies behind the luxury fashion brands' appointment of "little fresh meat" as brand ambassadors, but they are cautious about the consequences for the danmei community of capitalizing on the fans economy via idols as brand ambassadors. As A2 and A13 respectively state:

> I do purchase accessories and products from the drama to show my support of Xiao Zhan. But the deliberate capitalizing on the danmei community is abundantly clear and it makes me feel they are trying too hard.[150]
>
> I feel like brands are making quick money, via the "little fresh meat," from the danmei fans, but the brands have no interest in the subculture. It is purely a business decision and brands would act quickly to end the contract with the ambassadors if the idols are involved in social events that could impact negatively on the brands' image.[151]

While aware of this commercial aspect, our interviewees are not impulsive when it comes to purchasing idol-associated items. As A10 states:

> I don't spend money on stuff just because my idol is the ambassador of the product or the brand unless I need it [the product]. However, when I do need

> something and have to choose between two products that give similar results at the same price range, such as between Estée Lauder Advanced Night Repair Synchronized Recovery Complex and Lancôme Advanced Génifique Sensitive, I would go for the one where my idol is the brand or the product ambassador.[152]

The fans economy has been reshaping luxury fashion brands' preference for, and selection of, ambassadors in marketing cosmetics and skincare in the Chinese market in recent years. In particular, the use of male idols in cosmetic advertisements for marketing and promotion purposes has been surging, as addressed in research regarding the increased purchasing power of women in China, Japan, and Korea;[153] the impact of the cultural dimension, religion, and Korean Wave on local consumers in the Indonesian market;[154] and male idols as representative of the "consumption of sexualized men"[155] in the Chinese market through a postfeminist perspective. Growing fans/consumers is the core value of the idols and brands relationship, but, as noted by ome interviewee, "for idols, growing fans in the danmei community can be a double-edged sword;"[156] this is reflected in the AO3 incident which resulted in a difficult time for Xian Zhan as well as the brands he represented. The intention to package and promote male idols under the aesthetic of alternative masculinity has been seen to be effective and influential in terms of the large number of mimei fans that could be potentially reached. However, extending this scope to cover the subcultural domain to suit the aesthetic in the danmei community can be problematical.

Conclusion

In the past decade, China has been visibly experiencing the fans economy involving the relationship between fashion brands, male idols as ambassadors, and various fan communities. With luxury fashion brands touting the rhetoric of culture, creativity, and rich history to cast their influence on potential consumers for better economic profitability, and luxury products being designed in collaboration with internationally renowned designers and artists, the rising crop of "little fresh meat" as brand ambassadors seems to herald the diversification of the Chinese fashion market, enmeshed in the profit-driven marketing of cosmetics, skin care, and accessories in particular. Despite outwardly resembling the Western aesthetic and often branded to embrace the intangible cultural heritage attached to Western luxury brands, the conceptions and commercial practices of the brands continue to adjust, adapt, and apply in relation to the fans economy in China, stretching from the mainstream cultural domain to the subcultural aesthetic. Male idols who are consumed as "little fresh meat" and objectified under the gaze of female consumers deserve attention beyond the economic scope. Given the historical, geo-cultural, political, and economic contexts of the nation in which these "little fresh meat" are localized, and their Japanese and Korean counterparts in the idol-making industry from which the idols often learn and to which they aspire, their very specificities are worthy of interrogation in the subcultural context. The AO3 incident examined as a case study shows the peculiarities of the danmei subculture in relation to the mainstream in the hierarchical society in China. The "alternative" masculinity represented by the aesthetic of "little fresh meat," alongside the practice of hegemonic masculinity in Chinese society, could potentially move this society towards the pluralization of masculinity and support the development of a multicultural economy. By this, we mean that the social impact of the practices of "little fresh meat" as brand ambassadors, apart from their commercial values, probes the boundary between cultures as well as various groups in terms of ages, genders, and aesthetics.

5

A Comparative Perspective: The Culture of Korean K-Pop Idols as Brand Ambassadors

Amanda Sikarskie

Big Bang, BTS, EXO, GD x Taeyang, Got7, Holland, Infinite, JYJ, Kim Sungjoo, NCT-127, NEXT, Pentagon, Rain, Stray Kids, Super Junior, SHINee, UNIQ, WOODZ—these are some of the most influential male K-Pop (and K-Pop/C-Pop hybrid) groups and solo artists of the 2010s and early 2020s, in South Korea (hereafter simply, "Korea"), throughout East Asia—including China, and globally. There are several terms for the influence of Korean idol culture in China—Korea Craze, Korean Wave, *hallyu*, *ha han*—and Korea's influence on China's youth culture and fashion in the twenty-first century is undeniable. Korea's consumption of idols as brand ambassadors leads the world, and this influence on marketing in China is palpable as well. Kim Suk-Young, author of "Beauty and the Waste: Fashioning Idols and the Ethics of Recycling in Korean Pop Music Videos," explains the far-reaching impact of Korean idols on Chinese consumers:

> K-pop idols' effect on the fashion industry became even more significant with the explosive growth of the Chinese consumerist market. K-pop stars who rise to the status of highly visible celebrity on the Chinese entertainment scene exert enormous fashion influence on the world's fastest-growing consumer group. In the eyes of the global fashion brands, K-pop stars are more influential than Hollywood celebrities for their marketing campaigns in Asia. No wonder many fashion labels have been passionately courting K-pop's shiniest stars to boost their brand recognition in Asia. K-pop stars have come to be not only front-row fixtures at haute couture fashion shows but also mighty ambassadors by sporting sponsors' goods in their music videos and Instagram postings. The relationship between K-pop and the fashion industry reached an even deeper collaborative stage when K-pop's most prominent fashion icon, G-Dragon, composed runway music for Nicola Formichetti (Lady Gaga's stylist, who works as creative director of Mugler) in 2013 and for Alexander Wang's fashion show in 2016.[1]

According to an article in *SeoulBeats* from 2012, commercials featuring celebrities occur (out of the percentage of total TV and web commercials) at rates of 15% across all Western countries (except Brazil—in which celebrities appear in 25% of commercials), 25% for China and Hong Kong, 25% for Malaysia, and a whopping 65% for South Korea.[2]

In South Korea, more than one in two products promoted in a commercial is promoted by a celebrity, and this is most often a K-Pop idol. One could argue that what is true for Korea in this case is not necessarily true for China, but one must consider the long-standing historical trade triangle in luxury goods—including cosmetics and skincare—between China, Korea, and Japan. Valérie Gelézeau writes:

> As for body care and aesthetics, here again the practices of the pre-modern aristocracy expressed the sophistication and the taste for luxury that we find in China and Japan in similar guises (Bouissou *et al.* 2013). The circulation of luxury products in East Asia, from China to Japan and vice-versa, passing through Korea, which provided a natural bridge for this movement, was a fundamental element of economic trade in this part of the world, regulated by the Chinese. Indeed, tributary trade, a characteristic of the relations between Korea and China, was founded on commercial/diplomatic delegations, where luxury items were important tributes according to a system that consisted of giving and receiving gifts, China had to give back to Korea more than it had received.[3]

Thus, the precedent for the consumption of Korean (and Japanese) luxury goods in China (and vice versa) is a long-standing phenomenon. The consumption of Korean popular audio-visual media culture is, by technological necessity, a more recent phenomenon, though perhaps already an even more deep-seated one.

Korean Brand Ambassadors in Global Markets

K-Pop groups are a well-known commodity in the United States. A few years ago it was Big Bang; in 2020, BTS, EXO, and Got7 were all nominated for Best Social Artist at the Billboard Music Awards (BTS won). In October 2020, the Korea Society announced on Twitter that, "South Korean K-pop boy band BTS won the 2020 #VanFleetAward for its contribution to strengthening ties between South Korea and the United States."[4] The award is named after US General James A. Van Fleet, one of the founders of the Korea Society in New York City in 1957. (Upon leaving Korea after the war, Van Fleet famously said, "I shall come back.

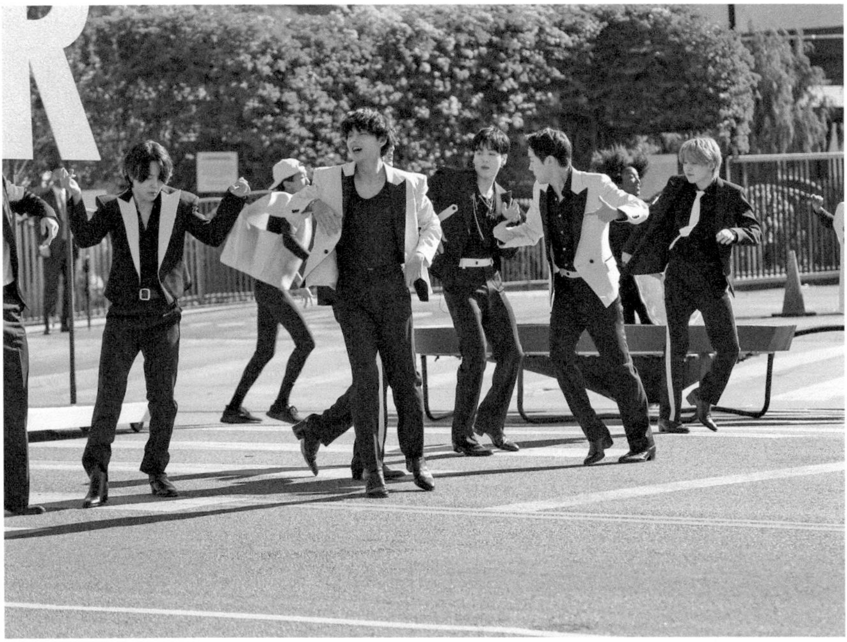

Figure 5.1 Jimin, V, Jungkook, J-Hope and Suga of the K-Pop band BTS are seen filming for the *The Late Late Show With James Corden* on November 23, 2021 in Los Angeles, California. Photo by Bellocqimages/Bauer-Griffin/GC Images.

You have made me a part of you. I know you are a part of me. I shall not ask you to give me back my heart. I leave it with you."[5]) BTS performed on the *Late Show* with Jimmy Fallon after their song "Dynamite" topped the Billboard Hot 100 chart. (In 2019, they performed their song "Black Swan" on *The Late Late Show With James Corden*, a show that EXO, Got7, and Jackson Wang—as a solo artist—have done as well.) And in 2021, BTS became the first K-Pop group to be nominated for a Grammy Award (see Figure 5.1).

C-Pop, or Mandopop (and Cantopop), artists are less well known in the US, although there are of course Chinese artists in Korean groups (Lay and Z.Tao, EXO; Jackson, Got7):

> The answer to why the need for a star-struck advertising industry exists is simple at a first glance. The viewers establish a connection with their favorite idols. When they appear on a show, you watch your bias, often separating her/him from the rest: you know what's *yours* and what's not. This simple association of one's individual choices with a public person's actions makes the fans more prone to pay attention when the object/subject of their affection shows up. Besides, most commercials use celebrities as role-models: they are successful,

> beautiful and desirable. By linking their products with their achievements, ads insinuate the average citizen can take a shortcut and look just as good by simply using their merchandise. But these reasons are general and fail to explain regional differences. So why such a huge rate in South Korea? Without doubt, the Korean entertainment industry plays a huge role in the South Korean socio-economical equation, which influences the way enterprises prefer to sell their products. The ubiquitous K-pop idols have gathered around themselves a mass of dedicated fans who support them to worrying extents sometimes. These entertainers and their companies have shaped throughout the years the music scene we love today, which welcomes devout and trustworthy individuals as main buyers. Taking into account the audience we're talking about is also the main target of many of the marketers, it makes more sense to pay an idol for a promotion.[6]

C-Pop artists are, however, known very well to fashion houses, and rightly so, as China's economy is not only poised to be the world's largest, but also now because Chinese luxury consumers were quickest globally to recover their spending after the Coronavirus pandemic hit, due in part to the PRC's strict quarantine measures.

Korean and Chinese Artists as Global Brand Ambassadors

South Korean rapper, producer, and fashion designer G-Dragon (b. 1988) has been dubbed the "millennial Michael Jackson" and represents the potential of a K-Pop (or C-Pop or J-Pop) idol to become a global phenomenon. In Asia, G-Dragon has been hugely successful as a brand ambassador, collaborating with fashion labels from Nike to Chanel, wearing the latter in anime form for the special edition book that accompanied the single "Good Boy" (see Figure 5.2). In "Beauty and the Waste: Fashioning Idols and the Ethics of Recycling in Korean Pop Music Videos," Kim Suk-Young describes G-Dragon's importance to the fashion industry:

> There are many instances of G-Dragon influencing sales of fashion items. When a picture of G-Dragon sporting a limited edition of MCM's backpack in 2011 surfaced in online communities, the company received overwhelming inquiries about the product and the item was sold out in an hour in Korea, prompting MCM to manufacture more of its "special edition"; in 2010, when G-Dragon was frequently spotted wearing Chrome Hearts accessories, the brand's kz bracelet was completely sold out in South Korea, Hong Kong, and Japan, so that buyers had to order it at Chrome Hearts' headquarters in New York City and wait three

> months to receive their merchandise. His influence on consumers was such that in 2012 Givenchy sponsored BIGBANG's Alive Galaxy Tour (2012–2013). In 2015, he attended Chanel's F/W haute couture show as the only Asian invitee. Since then, he's been spotted annually in the front rows of Chanel, Saint Laurent, and Thom Browne runway shows.[7]

G-Dragon's Big Bang bandmate Taeyang (Dong Young-bae) has also transformed success in Big Bang and after into brand agreements with global reach (see Figure 5.3). Taeyang has been Lexus's Korean brand ambassador since 2017 and has collaborated with Fendi to create the "Fendi for Taeyang" capsule collection of streetwear featuring his group's iconic daisy motif and uplifting words such as

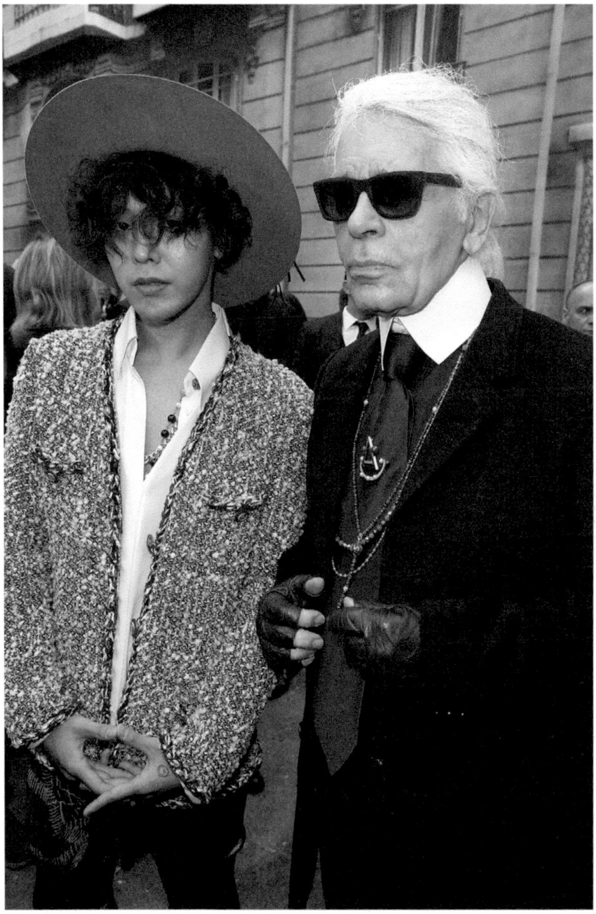

Figure 5.2 G-Dragon and Karl Lagerfeld attend the Chanel show as part of the Paris Fashion Week Womenswear Spring/Summer 2015 on September 30, 2014 in Paris. Photo by Rindoff/Dufour/French Select/Getty Images.

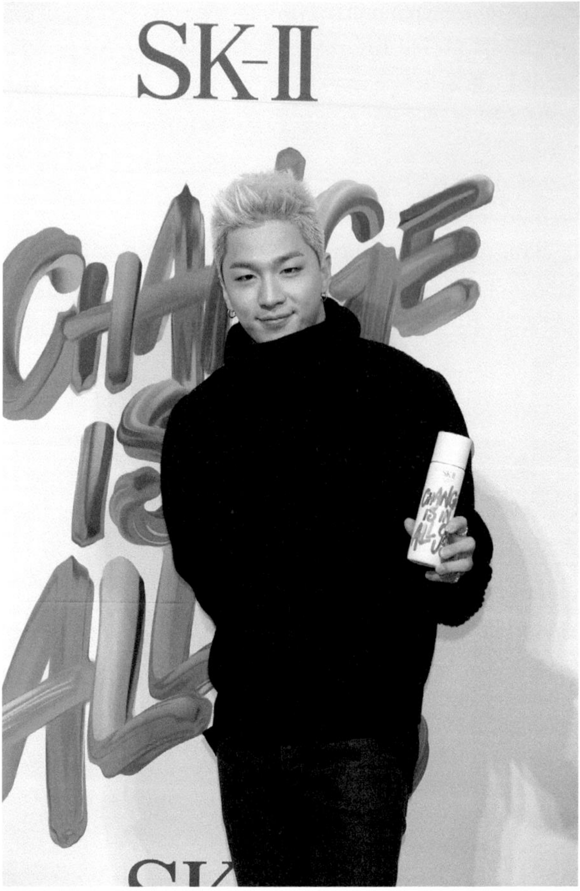

Figure 5.3 Singer and songwriter Taeyang of Big Bang attends the SK-II Pitera Pop Up Store Opening on December 1, 2017 in Seoul, South Korea. Photo by Han Myung-Gu/WireImage.

"Faith," "Grace," "Passion," and "Saved." Fendi for Taeyang debuted in Hong Kong on July 27, 2017, priced at $447–$9,490.[8]

G-Dragon himself has done multiple capsule collections, including one for Giuseppe Zanotti footwear in 2015, glittery, 1980s-inspired unisex styles for both men and women, stating that "it's not just girls or women who get excited and worked up over pretty shoes ... Guys can feel that way, too."[9] G-Dragon exemplifies the gender-fluid approach to dress that typifies Millennial and Gen Z (Post-95) consumers, as evidenced by headlines like "BlackPink's Jennie and G-Dragon Wear the Same Chanel Jacket."[10] Zanotti himself said of his encounter with G-Dragon, "I am used to working with celebrities around the globe, and my collaboration with G-Dragon is something that we wanted to do as he is currently one of the biggest stars in Korea with a huge following in Asia . . . He has a unique style in playing his music. I find it really impressive, and our cooperation means a thrilling challenge to me. I love to work with other artists and brainstorm on the creative process."[11] In terms of brand collaborations, G-Dragon is surely best known for his "Para-noise" Air Force 1 shoes for Nike, however, shoes that Nike has called "an ode to G-Dragon's 'self-actualization.'"[12]

"Peace Minus One": Selling Love and Peace

G-Dragon's logo, which has appeared on his brand collaboration merchandise since 2013, is known as "Peace Minus One." The symbol, a peace sign missing the lower right-hand descending line, comes from the placement of his stage name's initials, G and D, in adjacent proximity. The meaning of the symbol is much more than a simple visual pun, however; G-Dragon vehemently wishes for world peace, and believes that it will one day be achieved, though probably not, he thinks, in his own lifetime. Something, or someone, in this worldview is still missing, and their absence prevents us from finally making lasting peace with each other. Is G-Dragon waiting for some sort of messiah figure? Perhaps. He certainly does not envision himself as such, but rather as an ambassador of future world peace (in addition to being an ambassador for Chanel and Nike.) For his Nike Para-noise Air Force 1 collaboration, G-Dragon used a hybrid of his own Peace Minus One logo with his former band Big Bang's daisy logo, featuring a daisy missing one petal. This new hybrid logo advertises both world peace and G-Dragon and Big Bang, and for Nike customers represents an opportunity to consume a product both associated with a popular idol, and, through its connection to aspirations for world peace, to consume a product that functions as conspicuous virtue signaling, which can be defined as the intentional flaunting of one's moral virtue, either through one's dress or through posts made or liked on social media, for the purpose of advancing one's social status amongst like-minded individuals.

G-Dragon's obsession with world peace is hardly unique to him, and this yearning for peace writ large is essential for understanding the young East Asian consumer. Globally, Millennials (G-Dragon's generation) have been dubbed the "social justice warrior" generation. This interest in social justice did not diminish with Gen Z. *Trigun*, a Japanese manga and anime of the late 1990s popular with both of these generations, which is set in the distant future, after humanity has destroyed the Earth's climate to the point that the planet is unlivable and as a result has colonized other planets, including the dusty desert world in which this

Table 5.1 Celebrities and athletes who wear G-Dragon's "Para-noise" Air Force 1s

Country	Celebrities
Brazil	Neymar
China	Jay Chou Wang Yibo[14] Justin Huang G.E.M. Karry Wang Zhou Jieqiong Trendy Wubi
Colombia	J Balvin
France	Kylian Mbappé Oleg Moscal (CHANEL designer)
Indonesia	RiaSW YB Najwa Shihab
Japan	Ryosuke Yamamoto Dori Sakurada P THE WAVY Yuko Og Akira Leica
Mexico	Jaime Camil
Philippines	Thirdy Ravena Julius Babao Vice Ganda Inigo Dôminic Pascual
South Korea	Park Shin Hye Lee Si Young Lee Chung Ah Song Haena Lee Da-hee Ki Eun-Se Han Ye-seul Yoo Ah Joo Won Jung Il Woo Lee Jae-Wook Park Jae Min Giriboy Simon Dominic The Quiett Punchnello Paloalto Hangzoo REDDY

Country	Celebrities
	Kid Milli pH-1 Ravi Elly Ahn Chanhyuk Dara Kim Hyoyeon Jeon Somi Gray DK Soyou Suho Chanyeol Jung Eun-ji Heo Young-ji Jang Woo Hyuk Kino Hyeri Han Noma Ha Neul Irene Kim Hyunho Kim Sunghee DJ Glory Park Na Rae Jo Se-ho Lee Young-Kyoon Choi Kanghyuk Lia Kim
Taiwan	Nick Wang Alec Su
Thailand	Bie Thassapak Hsu Jaylerr Pok Chirathivat Oabnithi Wiwattanawarang Mark Siwat Joss Way-ar Sangngern Phiravich Attachitsataporn Teeradon "James" Supapunpinyo Ploi Horwang URBOYTJ
United States	Trinidad James Priscilla Ono Steven Yeun

(*Continued*)

Table 5.1 Continued.

Country	Celebrities
Vietnam	Phuong Nguyen Cao Ky Duyen Phat To Nguyễn Văn Toàn Lou Hoang OnlyC

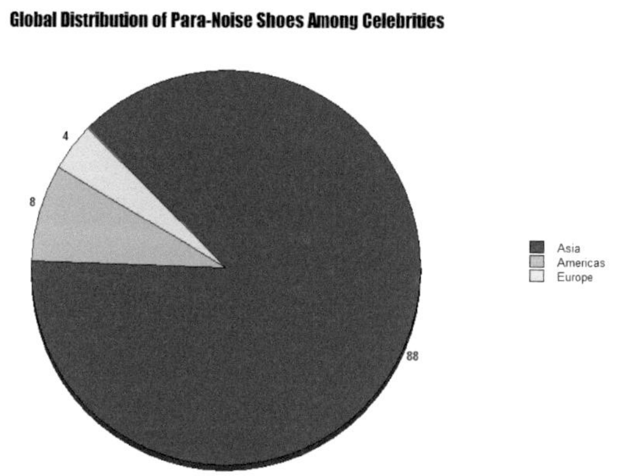

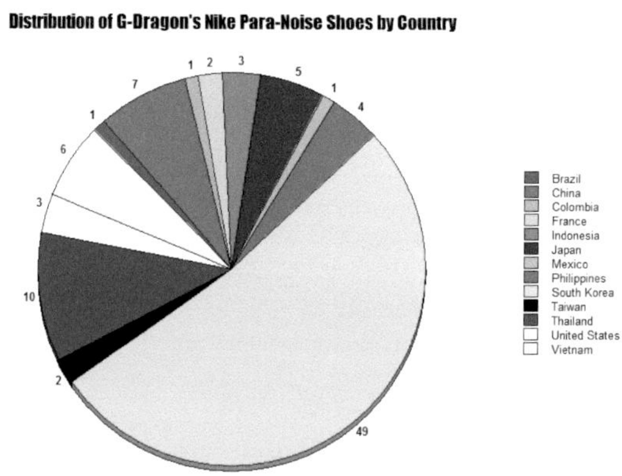

Figures 5.4 and 5.5 Pie charts showing the distribution of Nike Air Force 1 Para-noise shoes globally and by country. Created by Amanda Sikarskie.

story takes place. The series features a godlike, non-human protagonist, Vash the Stampede, a pacifist gunslinger who loves humanity—indeed, his motto is "love and peace"—but who is cursed with catastrophic power that he cannot control. His inability to control the enormous amount of stored energy in his angel arm leads to an atomic bomb blast-like destruction of the city of July, and even puts a hole in one of the planet's moons. The story is a parable of what twenty-first-century social justice must be, putting aside the traumas of the past (horrific atomic bomb detonations in Japan, brutal Japanese occupation of China during World War II, a Korean War that never really ended, war in Vietnam, genocide in Cambodia, authoritarianism in Myanmar) to focus on loving each other and stabilizing the climate before it is too late. This aside about Vash the Stampede is not merely an aside, but rather illustrates that this sensibility about love and peace is not only virtue signaling for these consumers (though that likely factors in many consumers' decisions), but is also a product of a deep-seated reaction to historical trauma in the region and a recognition that the planet is in great peril. Has this need for love and peace been mobilized by G-Dragon and Nike to sell a lot of daisy-embellished shoes? Absolutely.

The table below features a list of ninety-four global celebrities and athletes who wear G-Dragon's "Para-noise" Air Force 1s with the iconic Peace Minus One daisy:[13]

From the graphs below, one can see that, among celebrity wearers, 88% hail from Asia, 8% from the Americas, and 4% from Europe (see Figure 5.4). When the distribution is broken down by country, the South Korean market represents 49% of celebrity Para-noise wearers, and 51% represents the international market, including 10% from Thailand and 7% from mainland China (see Figure 5.5). This data shows that while the shoes are making inroads among elites internationally outside Asia, the Para-noise shoes remain largely a pan-Asian phenomenon.

Western Influencers and Asian KOLs

In comparison, it is useful to consider celebrity endorsement in the West. In *Fashion Promotion*, her helpful guide for fashion students, Gwyneth Moore explains that:

> Brands that have a level of notoriety or appeal to the general public can be catapulted into mass-consumer awareness through the endorsement or support of a particular high-profile celebrity or influencer. This has been shown through partnerships such as Cardi B's collection created for Fashion Nova, and the Rihanna Manolo Blahnik collection. The resulting collections were highly

> coveted and sought out by high-street shoppers keen to own an item associated with a high-profile figure . . . Whether a celebrity is actually significantly involved in the design of a collection is not necessarily of key importance—the consumer is more interested in the notional association with the style or image of the celebrity or influencer.[15]

This willingness on the part of the consumer to overlook whether or not their idol was actually involved in the design process also exists in Asia, though, as we have seen with G-Dragon and the Peace Minus One logo and the Para-noise shoe, some idols are heavily involved and emotionally invested in the design process. In the West, as in Asia, of paramount interest to brands is not necessarily whether the celebrity or KOL (key opinion leader, an acronym used widely in East Asia to describe someone who would be called an "influencer" in the West) helps to design the clothing, accessories, or cosmetics, but that they been photographed in public *wearing* them. Moore continues, "PR agencies/consultants and in-house teams work hard to encourage celebrities, influencers and those with a high profile to wear clothes by the designers they represent in the hope that they will be photographed in them. Influencer or celebrity endorsement can make items appear much more desirable to the consumer."[16] Do Gen Z idols such as Wang Yibo have increased potential as brand ambassadors to tap into luxury markets outside Asia? I believe so, and in the case study chapter earlier in this book on Wang, I made the case that the time for idols as global brand ambassadors has truly come.

Korean idols are indeed making inroads as global, not just Pan-Asian, influencers. EXO's management in particular has been particularly successful in securing high-profile brand agreements for its members in 2020. The following are some of the top global fashion endorsements for male Millennial and Gen Z ambassadors from Korean idol groups in 2020: G-Dragon of Big Bang for Chanel (since 2016); Oh Sehun (b. 1994) of EXO for MZ Generation x Cartier and Zegna; Suho (Kim Junmyeon, b. 1991) from EXO for Bvlgari; Jackson Wang[17] (b. 1994) of Got7 for Armani, Pasha de Cartier, and Fendi (as well as Beats by Dr. Dre); Lay Zhang (b. 1991) of EXO for Converse (see Figure 5.6); Z.Tao (Huang Zitao, b. 1993) of EXO for YSL Beauty; and Kai (Kim Jong-in, b. 1994) from EXO for Gucci.[18] Pieces in Kai's 2021 KAIxGucci collection feature a signature print of a vintage-looking teddy bear wearing a blue bow tie and debuted in South Korea before becoming available at GucciPins pop-up stores in Mainland China, Hong Kong, Singapore, Thailand, and Vietnam.[19] And as of April 2021, all of BTS are ambassadors for Louis Vuitton. According to *The Fashion Law:*

> The move by Louis Vuitton to put RM, Jin, SUGA, j-hope, Jimin, V and Jung Kook at the front of its menswear division is the latest—and certainly, the most momentous—example of a Western giant looking to tap into the increasingly globalized appeal of K-Pop and its mega-stars. Worth an estimated $6 billion, K-Pop as an industry has become a global phenomenon, with brands both in and outside of Korea looking to the hyper-influential segment as a way to reach a pool of hyper-engaged fans. Chanel, for instance, has been tapping into Korean demand by way of former boy-bander G-Dragon, who has served as an ambassador to the French fashion house for several years. Speaking about the decision to enlist G-Dragon, Bruno Pavlovsky, Chanel's president of fashion, stated back in 2017 that "today, South Korea is the most influential country in Asia, with its energy and creativity, its youth culture and the pop music and TV celebrities, who have become incredibly powerful, even in China and Japan."[20]

This idea that—in popular culture, and specifically in its idol culture—South Korea is now seen from the West as the most powerful country in Asia is an incredibly compelling one for fashion houses looking to bet on fresh new faces as ambassadors.

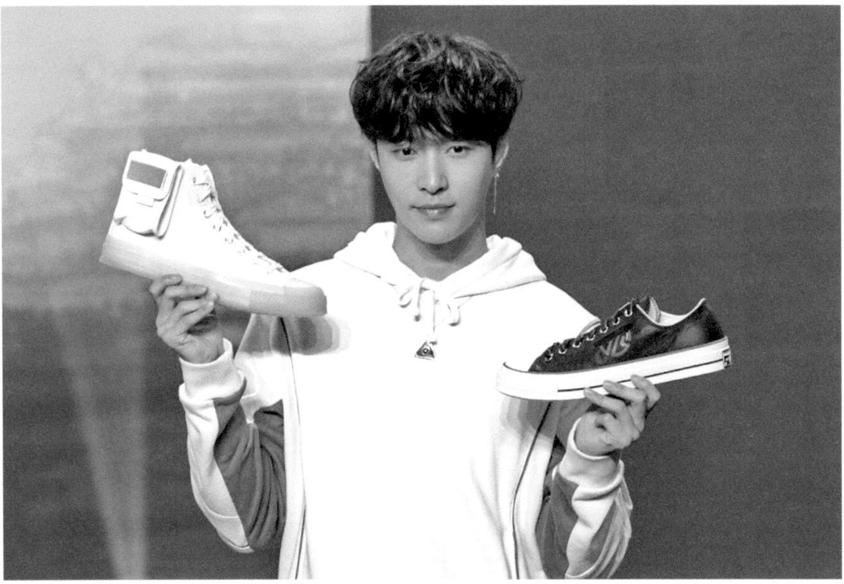

Figure 5.6 Singer Lay Zhang Yixing attends the Converse new products launch event on October 19, 2019 in Beijing, China. Photo by VCG/VCG via Getty Images.

A View from Thailand

It is worth noting that many other K-Pop idols hold multiple product endorsements outside the realm of fashion and cosmetics and skincare. For example, BamBam (Kunpimook Bhuwakul, b. 1997), member of Got7 and nicknamed the "Prince of Thailand," is YSL Beauty's official Thailand Muse, but also has endorsements for AIS 5G, Vivo VP, and Yamaha in his native Thailand (see Figures 5.7 and 5.8).[21] Earlier in this chapter, we saw that commercials featuring celebrities occur (out of the percentage of total TV and web commercials) at rates of 25% for China and Hong Kong, 25% for Malaysia, and

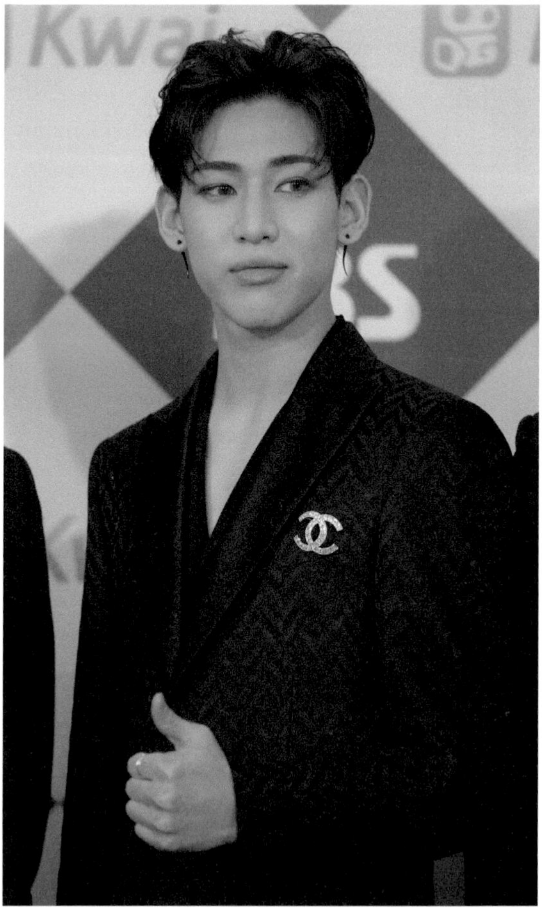

Figure 5.7 Two different looks for BamBam, the "Prince of Thailand." BamBam of GOT7 attends the 2017 SBS Gayo Daejeon at Gocheok Sky Dome on December 25, 2017 in Seoul, South Korea. Photo by The Chosunilbo JNS/Imazins via Getty Images.

a whopping 65% for South Korea.[22] Smaller countries in Southeast Asia, such as Thailand and Vietnam, are major consumers of K-Pop and C-Pop, but data for these countries is spottier. How important are idols in the branding and marketing of products in Thailand? In their essay "Brand Endorsement by Celebrity in Thailand: 7Ps of Marketing Mix and the Impact of Brand Alliance" for the *International Journal of Trade, Economics and Finance*, Whachiraporn Boonpradub and Pusanisa Thechatakerng observe that, "While in Thailand, [a] brand which is endorsed by celebrity is still a new marketing strategy, especially celebrities as designers."[23] In a survey of 400 Thai respondents with an interest in fashion, Boonpradub and Thechatakerng found that 72% believe the

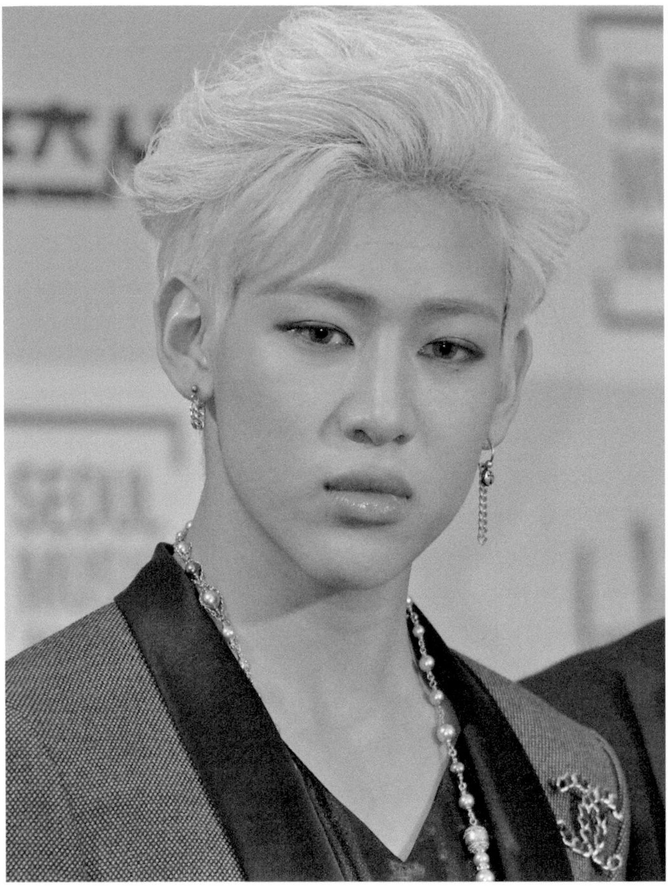

Figure 5.8 BamBam of GOT7 attends the 26th High1 Seoul Music Awards at Jamsil Arena on January 19, 2017 in Seoul, South Korea. Photo by The Chosunilbo JNS/ Imazins via Getty Images.

celebrity-product fit is important in marketing. They also found that respondents were aware of an idol's brand endorsements prior to the survey. When asked about female idol Chermarn Bunyasak and her collaboration with Thai fashion brand CPS: Chaps, "28% of customers [were] aware [of] their brand alliance via magazine, 19% via entertainment news, in addition 14% via friends and retail's staffs, respectively."[24] Further, the respondents had a very high opinion of the idol, with 31% calling her cute, 26% trendy, 16% sexy, and 12% gorgeous.[25] In summary, as in Korea, fashion consumers in Thailand are concerned that the right celebrity be matched with the right product, are aware of the idol's brand endorsements through magazines, entertainment news media, friends, and the staff of retail establishments, and generally have high opinions of the idols' physical attributes and personal style.

It would be remiss in a discussion of men, fashion, and cosmetics in Thailand not to mention Thailand's third gender, the *kathoeys* (known pejoratively in the West as "ladyboys"). The kathoeys are perhaps best known in the West today through the 1980s Murray Head hit "One Night in Bangkok," with its line, "and if you're lucky, then the god's a she." Kathoeys have existed in Thailand for generations, and are women who were assigned the male gender at birth. Today, they may or may not choose to have gender reassignment surgery, opting instead to remain a third gender. As David Yi writes in his book, *Pretty Boys*, "Probably the most recognized third gender people are from Thailand. Called *kathoey*, they have been vital members of Thai society for hundreds of years. Thailand, a predominantly Buddhist country, has had much more of an embrace of fluid gender identity compared to other Asian countries, perhaps because it is the only one in the region to have remained relatively free from Western cultural influence."[26] In more conservative Korea and China, kathoeys have never become idols, but kathoeys are major consumers of K-Pop and C-Pop culture. While kathoeys lack respect in East Asia and are something of a punchline, they are actively exploited by Western tourists. Yi continues, "Fully integrated into culture, the kathoey are represented in a variety of industries, and are known for their beauty. With their faces full of the best cosmetic techniques and their lush hair, many have gone on to become national celebrities. But in spite of how normalized they are in Thailand, the country has failed to protect everyday kathoey citizens from being exploited by Westerners for entertainment or sex, so much so that it's said that the 200,000 sex workers produce up to $4.5 billion GDP a year, roughly 1 percent of Thailand's entire economy."[27] While the discussion of Western tourists and kathoeys centers primarily on the male gaze, the Western female gaze may also be problematic in its consumption of Asian male idols.

Global Ambassadors and Optical Colonialism

As the global market for East Asian idols (and the products that they endorse) is poised for growth, it is worthwhile to consider the white female gaze and how this problematizes the study of idol culture. Vänskä describes the "optical colonialism" of the now-infamous *Vogue Bambini* photoshoot (1996): "In colonialist thinking, the Orient, that is, the Far East, was considered a feminine continent. This is evident, for instance, in the fact that in Western representations, Asian men are feminized and stereotypically shown as delicate, passive creatures—in contrast with Africans, for example, whose dominant characteristic was oversexualization. The Orientalist tradition is also visible in the visual and textual rhetoric of the Vogue Bambini fashion editorial ... In the report, 'Asianness' is forced into the mold of certain fetishized and generalized properties: feminine, passive, and delicate."[28] While it remains unclear to what extent white female (and male) consumers perpetuate these old, colonial ideas of Asian masculinity, and exactly how this is complicated by the *xiao xian rou* and *jingzhunan* stereotypes which already exist in China among Chinese fans, the events of 2020 and 2021—including the politicized rhetoric of the so-called "China virus" and the racially-motivated murders of Asian women in the Atlanta, Georgia area—demonstrate that stereotypes against Asian people still thrive in the West.

Writing a book about Chinese idols, Chinese luxury consumption, and Pan-Asian popular culture during not only the Covid-19 pandemic but also during a period of rampant violence against Asian Americans in the United States has been rather surreal at times. Charles Yu's novel, *Interior Chinatown*, was published in 2020 and made for excellent pandemic reading, as both an escape from and a reinforcement of current events. Its protagonist, Willis Wu, is a Hollywood actor dealing with the stereotypes he (and his actor father) face as Asian Americans in the entertainment industry:

> You have done this before, all of it. Have done your best to become Americans. Watched the shows, listened to the tapes, eliminated your accents. Dressed right, did your hair, took golf lessons. Encouraged English at home, even. You did everything that was asked of you and more ... Everything is going well. Until it's not. Until your father realizes that, despite it all, the bigger check, the honourable title, the status in the show. Who he is. Fu Manchu. Yellow Man. Everything has changed, nothing has changed. Yes, yes, your kung fu is perfect. Immaculate, pristine, Platonically Ideal Kung Fu from the highest plane of martial arts. But, and we hate to ask this—can you still do the accent? They ask him to put on silly

> hats. To cook chop suey, jump-kick vegetables into a thousand pieces. He hears a gong wherever he goes. He is told: you are a legend.[29]

And then, on a date with an Asian American woman in the industry, Wu narrates, "More coffee, more cold desserts. Talking. Some kissing happens. More talking. You play games. Would you rather. Would you rather: be Handsome Dead Asian with no lines or Silly Oriental who says silly things?"[30] Yu paints Hollywood as a culture in which Asian actors are marginalized—stereotypes, punchlines, silly Kung Fu masters and nothing more. In Korea, by contrast, some idols and K-drama actors are respected as aristocrats.

A Connection to Aristocracy: The Persistence of the Yangban in Korean Social Aspirations

Many people in Korea can claim *yangban* (traditional gentry) ancestry, including some of those with the surnames Byun, Han, Hong, Jeong, Kang, Kim, Kwon, Lee, Min, Na, Park, Seok, Seong, Song, and Yoon.[31] Echoing the continuing importance of the *yangban* to middle class-aesthetics and consumer behavior in Korea, Valérie Gelézeau writes:

> This increasing infatuation with aesthetics is linked to the dynamics of the creation of the middle classes in Korea and the ways in which they differentiate themselves. Economic growth has had the effect, on the one hand, of hugely expanding the great mass of the middle classes in South Korea, while at the same time bringing about the emergence of an urban bourgeoisie with its own social habitus: endogamy, frequenting certain places (grand hotels and clubs; see Gelézeau 2003b), choosing certain ways of living (in collective buildings of high standing), certain types of behaviour (a passion for luxury), education in the top universities, etc. And so, in a society where, ever since the 1990s financial crisis, the middle classes have been worrying about their position and have been fearful of a reduction of their status, being able to imitate the higher social categories has become a prime objective. To some extent, this infatuation with aesthetics (whether in the form of ostentatious acquisition of luxury items or massive recourse to plastic surgery) is, indeed, an indication of this desire to maintain or increase one's social status in the hope of acquiring social distinction. In fact, it is the same impetus as that which motivates people to invest massively in private tutoring for their children. Education is an essential element of social distinction in Korea, a fact which finds its roots in the long history of a society dominated by the lettered aristocracy, the *yangban*.[32]

Ishani Sarkar states that there are at least six Korean idols who have publicly claimed yangban ancestry, including Jin, Suga, and V of BTS, Sunny of SNSD, and Donghae and Eunhyuk of Super Junior.[33] Suga (born Min Yoongi) is widely rumored to be descended from Queen Myeongseong, the last empress of Korea, after he said as much during a livestream. According to celebrity blogger Ishani Sarkar, "Suga or Min Yoongi is a member of the Yeoheung Min Clan (驪興 閔氏/ 여흥 민씨), a very powerful clan during [the] Joseon dynasty. During a V-Live episode, Suga himself confirmed the fact and also added that his family belonged to a high ranking within the clan [see Figure 5.9]. Queen Inhyeon of King Sukjong, Queen Wongyeong of King Taejong, the last empress of Korea—Empress Myeongseong and Empress Sunmyeong all were from this clan."[34]

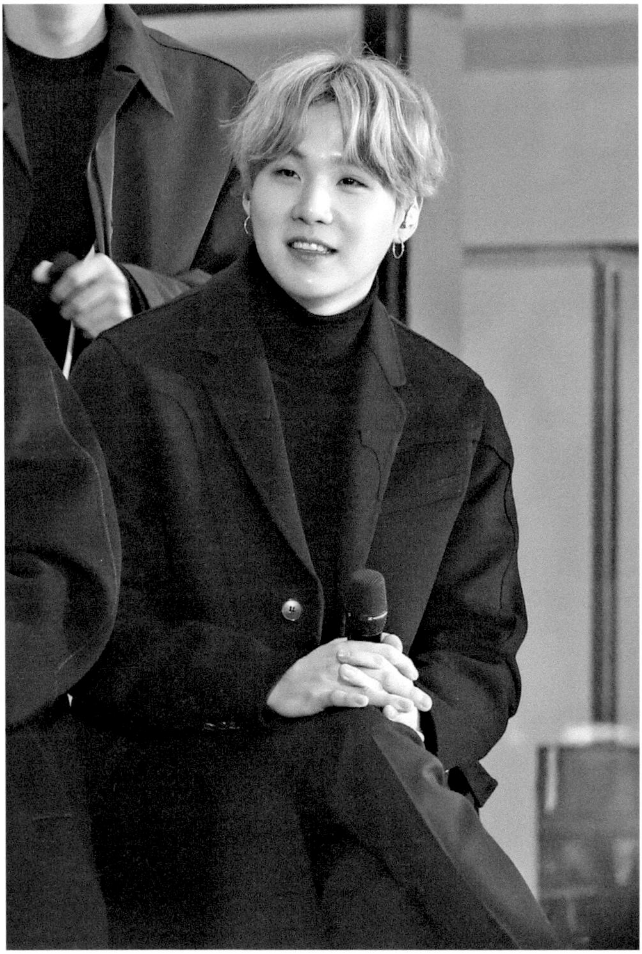

Figure 5.9 Suga of the K-Pop boy band BTS visits the Today Show at Rockefeller Plaza on February 21, 2020 in New York City. Photo by Cindy Ord/WireImage.

Queen Myeongseong has become something of a fixture in Korean pop culture, having been portrayed in historical dramas in Korea at least six times between 1988 and 2013.[35]

Holland for Byredo (and LBGTQ+)

Another Korean idol who has a certain caché with Gen Z, but because of his openness on topics still considered taboo in that country rather than his aristocratic lineage, is Holland (Go Taeseob). Holland, the first openly gay K-Pop idol, is brand spokesperson for Byredo lipsticks, and is a brand friend of Burberry,[36] Chanel (Boy de Chanel foundation base),[37] and Christian Louboutin.[38] He went to New York at the age of nineteen to launch his career (as an "out" K-Pop star is still considered too controversial for entertainment companies in Korea). Holland debuted in 2018 at the age of twenty-one with his single "Neverland" (the music video for which has a 19+ rating and cannot be shown on television in Korea as Holland French-kisses another man in the video).[39] Like Chinese idol Xiao Zhan, Holland did not go through idol school as a teenager and initially went to college to study art. Holland came out in middle school when he confessed to a crush, ushering in several years of bullying and subsequent mental illness. In *Queer Korea*, Todd A. Henry, citing Song Pae Cho, describes that, as late as the 1980s,[40] South Korea was still a "hypermasculine" dictatorship in which gays did not feel at home:

> Articulating his ethnography of male homosexuality in terms of successive normativities, John (Song Pae) Cho argues that two contradictory forces of capitalist development have shaped the subjectivities of South Korean gay men since the 1970s: biopolitical familialism and neoliberal individualism. According to this historical account, the heterosexual, nuclear family, a shifting but enshrined pillar of national life, played an important role in circumscribing how men could express same-sex desires and forge non-normative intimacies. Characterizing the 1970s and 1980s as late developmentalist, Cho reveals the centrality of a hypermasculine ideology of capitalist growth during an extended period of military dictatorship. He argues that South Korea's authoritarian development expressed itself in chrononormative terms, prescribing "proper" life courses for citizens based on a dimorphic notion of biological sex. Highly gendered in its assumptions, this Cold War ideology not only demanded that men contribute to the national economy through industrial labor and military service, but also beseeched them to abide by its heteropatriarchal strictures. As a result, men who

> harbored attractions for one another were ultimately forced to marry women and produce male heirs to carry on family lines. Discouraged from forming long-lasting relationships and homosexual identities, most postwar gays managed to engage only in fleeting practices of "skinship" in military barracks, male dormitories, and movie theaters, public sites that they transformed into temporary cruising grounds.[41]

While the situation for gay youth in Korea (and across East Asia) has improved since the 1980s, Confucian biopolitics, with its emphasis on respect for ancestors, parents, and the family line, means that there is still enormous pressure on gay youth to fit into the traditional heteropatriarchal structure that simply does not exist to that extent in the West. Holland, a believer in the strength of intersectionalism, has also been outspoken on Instagram in support of social causes not directly his own, such as the Black Lives Matter movement. As a product of this cognitive dissonance between Confucist upbringing and personal happiness, Holland hopes that his openness about his own personal experiences can inspire and give comfort to other gay youth in Asia, letting them know that they are not alone. There are currently no openly gay Mandopop idols, and as we will see, while Korean idols and idol culture have been hugely popular in China, there has been a movement within the Chinese government to dissociate from K-culture.

The Korea Craze and the Hallyu Ban in China

Historically, the Korea craze in China has as its precedent both Korean-language radio programming in China—"The Korea craze initially grew out of a Korean pop music fad. Korean pop songs were introduced to Chinese in major cities through a popular FM radio program called 'Seoul Music Hall' in 1997,"[42]—and the Japan craze of the early 2000s: "In the 2000s, a few years after the Japan craze gained popularity, the Korea craze emerged. Termed *ha han* (*han* being the Chinese character for Korea), both the Korean and Japan crazes had a strong impact on contemporary Chinese fashion at roughly the same time."[43] As JuanJuan Wu writes in *Chinese Fashion from Mao to Now*, "The emergence of the Korea craze brought a set of new ideas, cultural associations and meanings, and exotic styles to a new generation of Chinese. However, in one sense, the Korea craze was just a repetition of what had happened twenty years earlier [with the Japan craze]: it reconnected China with its past ... The Korea wave brought Chinese 'packaged,' modernized Oriental culture, containing the right mix of Euro-American and Asian cultures. Thus the fashion elements displayed in

Korean culture seemed so familiar to Chinese through the linkage to the West."[44] The importance of K-Drama and its influence on Chinese drama, particularly the *xianxia* genre, cannot be overstated: "Post-Mao Chinese pop culture had always yearned for China's glorious past. TV channels were filled with dramas set in ancient times."[45] As Zoe Suen notes, "South Korean TV shows are providing brands with a much-needed boost and an anchor for Asia marketing strategies as the region recovers faster from Covid-19 than western counterparts."[46] Historical K-Drama, and its use of idols as actors, set a precedent for idols breaking into acting in C-Dramas, such as *The Untamed*. The Chinese government has distanced itself from the Korean Wave, or *hallyu*, however, going so far as to ban Korean media for several months in 2016 over a dispute about American missile defense in Korea,[47] a ban which had disastrous consequences for the idol group UNIQ, comprised of both Korean and Chinese members.

Wang Yibo's South Korean bandmates from UNIQ, Cho Seungyoun (Cao Chengyan in Mandarin) and Kim Sungjoo[48] (Jin Shengzhu in Mandarin), have found varying levels of solo success after the hallyu ban put group activities on a (seemingly permanent) hiatus. Kim Sungjoo found work as an actor in K-Drama, best known for the role of the lead singer of rock band Crude Play in *The Liar and His Lover* (2017)—based on the popular Japanese manga of the same name (see Figure 5.10).[49] Cho Seungyoun is currently known as the solo artist "Woodz," whose single "Love Me Harder" was released in 2020.

Though Friedrich Nietzsche referred to a very different kind of idol in his *Twilight of the Idols* (1912) from contemporary K-Pop idols, a line from the work nonetheless rings true for today's star, who are taught in idol school that they must remain smiling when on camera, above all else, no matter what their physical, mental, or emotional circumstances: "Maintaining cheerfulness in the midst of a gloomy affair, fraught with immeasurable responsibility, is no small feat; and yet what is needed more than cheerfulness?"[50] WOODZ, the stage name of Cho Seungyoun, is a Korean rapper, singer, and music producer, a member of UNIQ and known for solo singles "Baby Ride," "Pool," and "Love Me Harder." WOODZ has also become known for his unusual (for Korea) openness about his struggles with poor mental health. He associates the color blue with the "Cosmic" version of his album, *Equal*. In the lyrics to the song "Love Me Harder," WOODZ equates the color red with traditional love affairs, but wants a blue-colored love with his new partner, imploring her to love him harder, that is, even more bluely. He has also said in interviews that he associates the color blue with the love he receives from his fans,[51] of course, wanting them to "love him harder" as well.

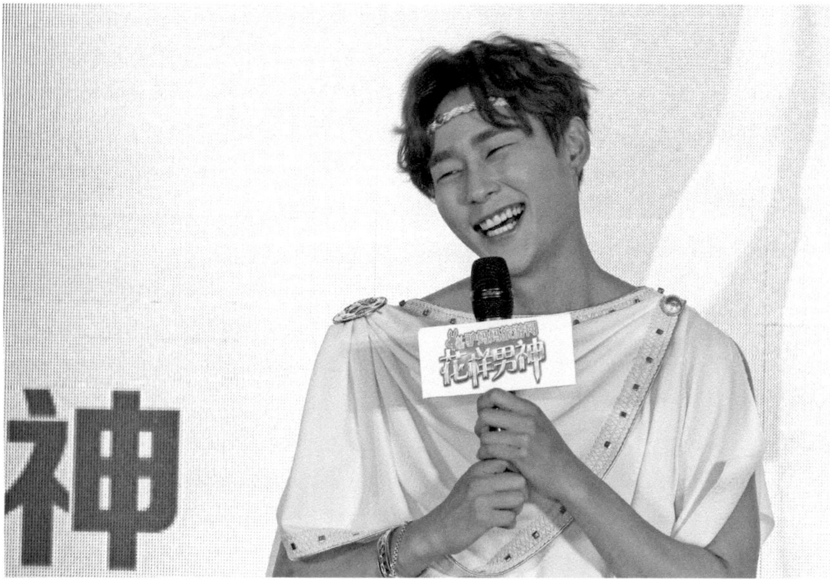

Figure 5.10 South Korean singer Kim Sungjoo of Chinese-South Korean boy group Uniq attends the press conference for a Chinese television traveling program on May 25, 2016 in Shanghai, China. Photo by Visual China Group via Getty Images/Visual China Group via Getty Images.

"Love Me Harder:" A Blue Love with Fans

In the West, blue has been used in Egypt in jewelry and the decorative arts in the forms of lapis and faience and was a preferred color in medieval stained glass and illuminated manuscripts.[52] Bringing this history of the color blue into the twentieth century, paintings created during Picasso's Blue Period "reflect death, poverty, age and loneliness."[53] To be blue is a synonym for depression in the West, for example as in singing the blues, or the Elvis song, "Blue Christmas." Michel Pastoureau's book, *Blue: The History of a Color*,[54] describes not only the historical usage of the color in art and the derivation of the color from various natural sources, but also what Giovanna Constantini calls a phenomenological method of inquiry into the meaning of the color blue:

"'Sapphire is a truly celestial stone,'" writes Michel Pastoureau in *Blue: The History of a Color.* "It is often compared to the color of the sky and is said to have healing powers." Pastoureau 's fifth book in a series that includes Black, Green, Red and Yellow draws together another stunning collection of artworks whose resplendent color has long captivated artists and viewers alike. While acknowledging scientific analyses of color composition, visual perception, human psychology, subjectivity and linguistic relativity, Pastoureau's study is premised on the conviction that a history of color is a social history in which color's meanings and conventions, known historically as iconography, require a phenomenological method of inquiry relative to the group to which it is assigned.[55] As a research method, phenomenology is non-positivist and interpretive, a good approach to take to a work like "Love Me Harder."

Like Pablo Picasso, who dealt with severe depressive episodes during his Blue Period, Cho Seungyoun dealt with major depression and suicidal ideation following the cessation of UNIQ group activities due to the hallyu ban. Cho even penned his suicide notes.[56] Suicide is still a taboo subject of conversation in both South Korea and China, but this is changing, if at times slowly and subtly. BamBam of Got7, for instance, appeared lying in a swimming pool in the guise of Sir John Everett Millais's Pre-Raphaelite painting of Shakespeare's Ophelia, Hamlet's sister who commits suicide by drowning, for *Allure* magazine Korea in summer 2021.[57] Meanwhile, other K-Pop idols have dealt with suicidal thoughts—with tragic outcomes. Kim Jonghyun, lead singer of the globally successful group SHINee, for example, committed suicide by carbon monoxide poisoning at the age of twenty-seven (see Figures 5.11 and 5.12).[58] Female idol Jang Jayeon, mentioned in the introduction of this book, is another statistic in the tally of idol suicides.[59] In an exposé on idol suicides for the *New York Times* in 2019, Choe Sang-Hun and S-Hyun Lee observed:

> Even after they make the cut to become K-pop idols, their star status rarely lasts long, as younger stars with cuter looks and fancier dance moves replace them. K-pop stars in their late 20s are already considered old, and these fading idols often try to carve out new roles in acting or as solo singers or talk-show regulars—a difficult transition that is often not successful … The K-pop phenomenon gets disseminated largely through YouTube, Instagram, Twitter and other social media channels, where its stars are exposed to both a flood of fan letters and hateful comments and cyberbullying on everything from their looks to their singing skills to their private lives. "From an early age, they live a mechanical life, going through a spartan training regimen," said Lee Hark-joon, a South Korean journalist who has produced a TV documentary on the making of a K-pop girl group and co-wrote the book "K-pop Idols: Popular Culture and the Emergence of the Korean Music Industry." "They seldom have a chance to develop a normal school life or normal social relationships as their peers do." … "Their fall can be as sudden and as dramatic as their rise to the height of fame," and all at a young age, Mr. Lee added. "Theirs is a profession especially vulnerable to psychological distress—they are scrutinized on social media around the clock, and fake news about their private lives is spread instantly."[60]

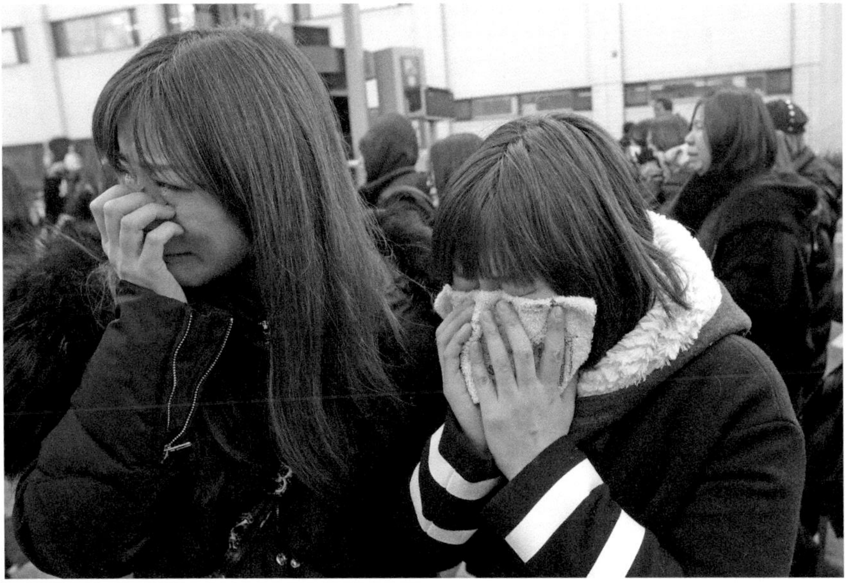

Figure 5.11 Fans who had been waiting outside the hospital for news react to the death of idol Jonghyun of SHINee at the hospital on December 21, 2017 in Seoul, South Korea. The lead vocalist of the K-pop group was found dead, in what is believed to have been a suicide at his apartment on December 18. Photo by Chung Sung-Jun/Getty Images.

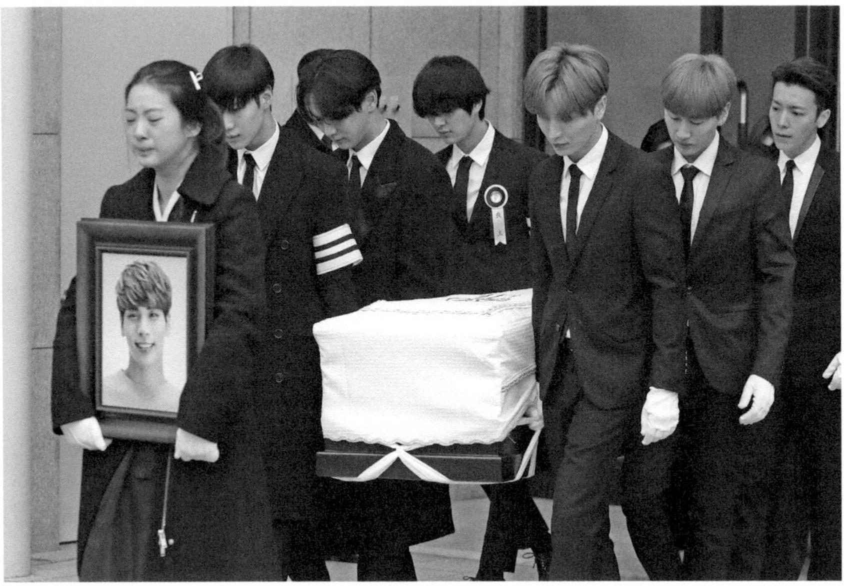

Figure 5.12 Members of pop Idol SHINee and Super Junior carry the coffin containing the body of Jonghyun of SHINee during the funeral at the hospital on December 21, 2017 in Seoul, South Korea. Photo by Chung Sung-Jun/Getty Images.

Cho received the help he needed, and now smiley face and frowny face tattoos above his wrist are his and his fans' constant reminder to take care of one's mental health.

What does it mean for fans to have a blue love for their biases? Words describing blue in the passages above include sacred, cosmic, celestial, and lonely. In ancient Chinese cosmology, both blue and green were associated with the season of spring—a time of new beginnings, the Azure Dragon (one of the directional animals) and the eastern direction, and the element of wood.[61] Interestingly, water, which is closely associated with the color blue in the West, is associated with the color black in traditional East Asia. The pseudonym WOODZ, which sounds to a Westerner like it would logically be associated with the color green, may be associated with either blue or green in the East Asian understanding of the five elements. A blue love could, therefore, refer to a love for WOODZ in particular, rather than idol biases in general.

WOODZ for Cledbel

WOODZ is brand ambassador for Cledbel, a Korean skincare brand known for lifting serums, masks, moisturizers, and eye creams, as well as cosmetics. WOODZ was both the first male idol to serve as brand spokesperson—Cledbel is already endorsed by female ambassadors Kim Hee Ae and Ko So Young—and the first Cledbel ambassador in their twenties.[62] Cledbel is relying on Cho Seungyoun to increase their visibility and popularity with Gen Z consumers. Music tie-in products and packaging are targeted at Gen Z consumers and seen as a means by which to capitalize on the popularity of idols and their songs. A 2021 Cledbel boxed set reads, "Love Me Harder," in reference to the 2020 WOODZ track, and is packaged to resemble a riotously colorful film camera. In the March 2021 promotional film for Cledbel, WOODZ wears a variety of unisex looks, popular with younger consumers, including an ensemble dripping in various Chanel brooches. (WOODZ has also been photographed in 2021 wearing clothes from Celine Menswear's "The Dancing Kid" line, a collection that suggests youthfulness by its very name.) Cledbel's similarly youthfully-styled WOODZ skincare edition boxed set comes in an orange, blue, and white box with Cho Seungyoun depicted on the cover and reads, "Protect Your Skin With CSY [Cho Seungyoun]." The set comes with a cleanser, moisture soothing cream, and a photocard of Cho Seungyoun. Cho also features in the Cledbel "Chak Chak Lip Balm" boxed set, which features five lip balms—all with a different image of Cho on the tube—and a photocard. Christmas is a major holiday in South Korea, and Cho also starred in Cledbel's 2020 "Cledbelmas" Christmas campaign. Cho's twenty-fifth birthday was in August of 2021, when the brand planned to feature twenty-fifth-birthday limited edition boxed sets in their ambassador's honor.

Generation Z grew up in a media-saturated environment, and this is particularly true in Korea. According to Juha Park and Jaehoon Chun, "Korea is the market with the highest rate of YouTube content consumption (Byun, 2018). The main concerns of Generation Z are related to appearance management issues, such as fashion and beauty, as well as leisure activities such as gaming, films and shopping (Lee, 2019b) . . . Although Generation Z is skilled at non-face-to-face interactions where they share information and opinions with others online, they do not see themselves as simple viewers or consumers who just browse for product information. They instead demand a real emotional link or attachment with the brand or influencer (Muret, 2019)."[63] Joanna Elfving-Hwang echoes this sensibility about an emotional tie between fan and idol, writing that fans see themselves as "parasocial kin" of these pop idols: "I argue that the position that the celebrity (and the manufactured idol in particular) occupies in the contemporary Korean mediascape makes them an object of both consumption and parasocial interaction in ways that construct the celebrity as an imagined 'parasocial kin'. In other words, rather than simply functioning as an 'idealised other' to simply imitate or copy, the position of the celebrity idol constructs her or him simultaneously as an object of adulation and familial affection."[64] Social media messenger app KaKaoTalk is how idols communicate with their Korean fans, and vice versa, satisfying this need for affective connection and (the perception of) real communication between fan-consumers and idols. KaKaoTalk is also, quite simply, how selling is done in South Korea nowadays, used by brands such as Cledbel, Chanel, Dior, Estée Lauder, and Saint Laurent.

> Industry insiders expressed expectations that makeup items would be least affected by the rapid increase in people shopping online because consumers have to test cosmetic products in person. But COVID-19 has made it almost imperative for the French fashion house to introduce its beauty products on Kakao Talk, where luxury brand sales have nearly doubled in the first half of this year compared to 2019. Since last month, Chanel has been selling 22 cosmetic products including lipsticks, perfumes and hand creams. It is the first time for Chanel to start selling products on any online retail platform apart from its official website. One of the benefits of selling through Kakao Talk is that the messenger application is used by 93 percent of smartphone users in Korea. Starting in August last year, it has been selling beauty products of 66 luxury

> brands including Dior, Yves Saint Laurent and Estee Lauder in its e-commerce category . . . Also, a lot of young customers don't find it necessary to visit stores to buy their makeup items anymore.[65]

WOODZ's Global Video Call with fans in August 2020 and Global Online Fansign in December 2020, for example, were available to Koreans through KaKaoTalk, to Chinese fans through WeChat, and globally on Skype.[66] [67] In Cledbel video advertisements posted to KaKaoTalk featuring WOODZ, his song "Love Me Harder" plays in the background, and in the ads, one can also see Cho's tattoos well, indicating that the brand supports Cho's openness about mental health, a factor that certainly appeals to Gen Z consumers who make up the brand's major demographic.

Avatars as Brand Ambassadors in Pokémon Go

Kim Sungjoo has also appeared in several promotional films under the UNIQ banner even after the group effectively ceased activities—such as the "Sungjoomongo" promotional video for Pokémon Go when the mobile game first debuted in 2016. Since then, Pokémon Go has been no stranger to fashion, engaging in collaborations with luxury brands to promote merchandise in the brick-and-mortar world by promoting digital versions of the products in-game for wear by player avatars. Players see high-level player avatars wearing exclusive logo merchandise, and theoretically, will want to purchase the products themselves. In this way, high-level players, rather than celebrity idols, become the brand ambassadors. An advertisement for Pokémon Go Fashion Week (yes, that is a thing) read, "Dress up for fashion week—in person and in-game! Be sure to head to the shop for a free Longchamp avatar item in Pokémon GO. Then, you can match with your Trainer avatar by picking up the same Longchamp item in stores."[68] This marketing was mirrored on the Longchamp website: "Pikachu, the mascot of the Pokémon brand, electrifies the Le Pliage®, the Maison Longchamp classic. This blend of French elegance and Japanese kawaii leaves nothing to chance."[69] My avatar in Pokémon Go, RyohgaHibiki, wears the in-game Longchamp Le Pliage bag (see Figures 5.13 and 5.14).

It is noteworthy in the context of this larger study on male idols that while I am a woman, my avatar is male. As Martti Lahti writes in "As We Become Machines: Corporealized Pleasures in Video Games," "They [game menus] suggest that cyborgization is partially driven by a desire to try on different bodies, to trespass or toy with racial and sexual boundaries, underlining psychic

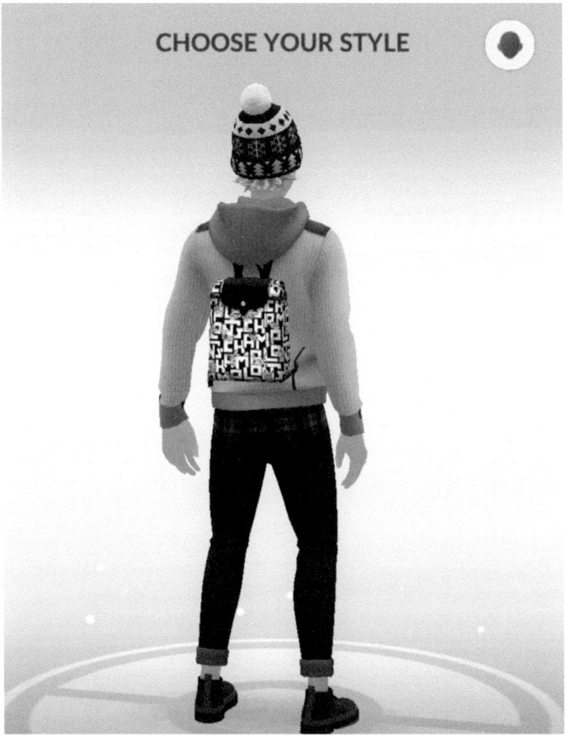

Figure 5.13 Avatar RyohgaHibiki models the Longchamp Le Pliage backpack in Pokemon Go. In-game screenshot.

and social structures motivating racial and sexual cross-dressing."[70] Male avatars may represent female-identifying players, and female avatars may represent male-identifying players. In-game, women who idolize fashionable males may, inadvertently and unbeknownst to them, actually be idolizing fashionable females. Such a contingency is also quite possible in the brick-and-mortar world, though there are currently no openly transgender idols. Just as I play a male avatar in some games, it is likely that male idols playing the game incognito may adopt a female avatar. Lahti reminds the reader that, "It is crucial to recognize, in this regard, that the entire range of characters offered by such games share a single dominant quality, that is, the mastery in their field. If femininity for men has been associated with passivity and weakness [in the West], for instance, 'trying on' femininity within the context of such games nonetheless remains a kick-ass experience."[71] Players may feel jealous of avatars—their own or the avatars of others—because of their ability to perform a different gender, or

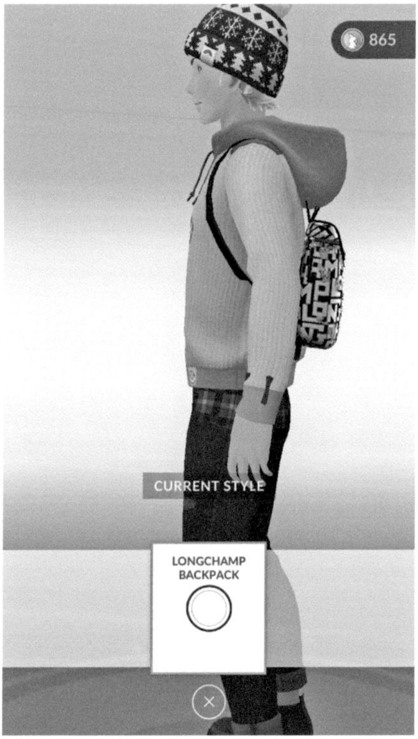

Figure 5.14 Avatar RyohgaHibiki models the Longchamp Le Pliage backpack in Pokemon Go. In-game screenshot.

simply their ability to obtain a Longchamp bag for free: "Allucquère Rosanne Stone has labeled this kind of 'cybernetic interaction,' in which our pleasure is based on being in a loop with the computer, as 'cyborg envy.'"[72] I developed a serious case of cyborg envy, for example, when I saw the avatar of an in-game friend wearing the entire new North Face x Gucci collection for Pokémon Go, a collection that, because of travel restrictions during the Covid-19 pandemic, was impossible for me to attain. (It is worth noting that the digital fashion objects created by Longchamp and North Face x Gucci described in this chapter, while desirable for players, are not unique NFTs with personalized blockchains, but massively multiple objects, the number of which is only limited by the number of in-game users who collect them.)[73]

My German friend's avatar, Inselpapst, wears the North Face x Gucci collaboration t-shirt, boater hat, and bag (see Figure 5.13). The level cap was only raised above 40 in late 2020, so when this in-game screenshot was taken, level 41 players were still rarely seen in the game world in early January 2021. Being level

41 afforded an avatar in this moment a certain cache within the game, and this status is emphasized by wearing the somewhat difficult to acquire North Face x Gucci collection. Interestingly, in the context of the game, the fact that the items could only be added to one's account by spinning a Poké stop at a Gucci store probably enhanced the items' luxury status as much as the Gucci brand. Between January 4, 2021 and January 11, 2021, players had to physically visit the Gucci Poké stop in one of the following cities[74] to acquire the collection:

Europe, the Middle East, and Africa

- ☐ Milan
- ☐ Florence
- ☐ Rome
- ☐ Paris
- ☐ Cannes
- ☐ Madrid
- ☐ London
- ☐ Moscow
- ☐ Vienna
- ☐ Brussels
- ☐ Berlin
- ☐ Frankfurt
- ☐ Munich
- ☐ Kuwait City
- ☐ Monaco
- ☐ Amsterdam
- ☐ Doha
- ☐ Cape Town
- ☐ Johannesburg
- ☐ Barcelona
- ☐ Geneva
- ☐ Istanbul
- ☐ Dubai
- ☐ Abu Dhabi

North America

- ☐ Toronto
- ☐ Vancouver
- ☐ New York City
- ☐ Los Angeles

- ☐ Chicago
- ☐ San Francisco
- ☐ Atlanta
- ☐ King of Prussia
- ☐ Palm Desert
- ☐ Scottsdale
- ☐ Houston
- ☐ Honolulu
- ☐ Orlando
- ☐ Paramus
- ☐ Manhasset
- ☐ Las Vegas
- ☐ Beverly Hills
- ☐ Miami
- ☐ Tysons
- ☐ Boston
- ☐ Troy
- ☐ Costa Mesa
- ☐ San Diego
- ☐ Seattle
- ☐ Dallas
- ☐ Washington DC
- ☐ Nashville

Latin America

- ☐ Sao Paulo
- ☐ Santiago
- ☐ Monterrey
- ☐ Mexico City

Asia[75]

- ☐ Bangkok
- ☐ Hong Kong
- ☐ Singapore
- ☐ Osaka
- ☐ Tokyo
- ☐ Macau
- ☐ Kanazawa
- ☐ Nagoya

- ☐ Fukuoka
- ☐ Sendai
- ☐ Yokohama
- ☐ Kobe
- ☐ Sapporo
- ☐ Hiroshima
- ☐ Kyoto
- ☐ Taipei
- ☐ Taichung

Australia

- ☐ Sydney
- ☐ Melbourne

According to Lahti, "Games commodify our desires, our will to merge with and become technology. To be able to earn a more spectacular outfit, the player

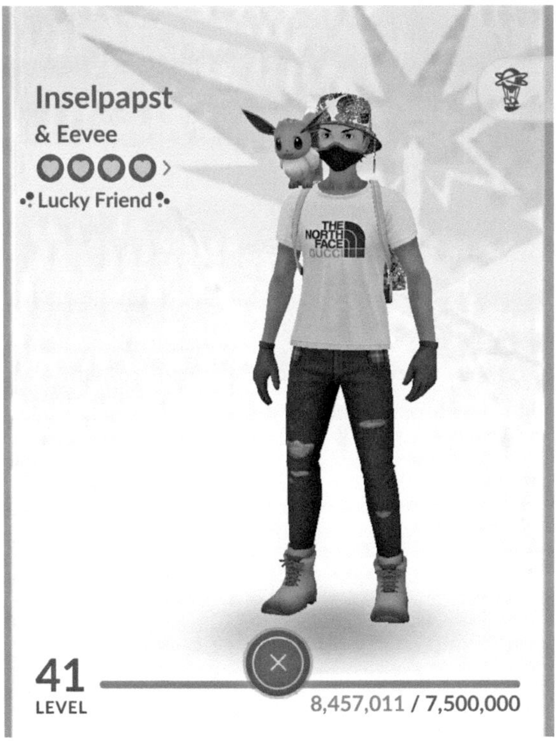

Figure 5.15 Avatar Inselpapst wearing North Face x Gucci t-shirt, boater hat, and bag. In-game screenshot.

is invited to learn repetitive bodily movements and reactions [such as fast button combinations for martial arts or aiming for shooting games]."[76] Or, in the case of Pokémon Go, which is an augmented-reality game rooted in the exploration of the physical, brick-and-mortar world, the desire for a spectacular outfit compelled players to seek out Gucci stores. On January 11, on account of the global pandemic and the undesirability of unnecessary travel, Gucci relented on the exploration requirement and made the collection available to players worldwide using a code. During the initial launch of the collection in Pokémon Go, the products were also unavailable to players in Hong Kong, although they were available at Poké stops in Macau.

The Matter of Military Service

Being three years older than bandmate Cho Seungyeon, Kim Sungjoo's career has already been interrupted by compulsory military service.[77] One of the elements that makes a study of male K-Pop idols really compelling is the matter of mandatory military service in South Korea, a legacy of the Korean War which spilt the Korean peninsula and never technically ended. Like other young men, these idols can defer until they are twenty-eight years old, but no male South Korean citizen gets out of it (except for medical reasons). G-Dragon had to enlist in the military, for example, and he is worth over $30million USD. Enlistment is hugely traumatic for many of these idols, whose training hitherto has prepared them for the physical demands of service but not for the spartan lifestyle or lack of emotional support from fellow group members, management, and fans. And all of this is to say nothing of the monetary loss to the Korean economy. These idols are on top of the entertainment industry one moment, and the next get an unfashionable haircut and effectively disappear from the planet for eighteen months.

Big Bang Enlists

There is a considerable controversy in South Korea as of the autumn of 2020 in which management, fans, and commercial interests are trying to get the group BTS out of compulsory military service, though it is also a possibility that they will all be sent to enlist together at the same time to minimize downtime (and financial losses) for the group. Idols from the same group are not kept together during military service, even if they enlist at the same time, however. Big Bang's

G-Dragon and Taeyang both enlisted in 2018, but G-Dragon was sent to the 3rd Infantry Division, while Taeyang was sent to the 6th Infantry Division (see Figure 5.16).[78] A long, though by no means comprehensive, list of K-Pop idol enlistment and military discharge dates can be found on the K-Pop Database.[79]

The Enlistment of Kim Sungjoo

Idols often wait until the last moment to announce their enlistment to fans, as was the case when Kim Sungjoo enlisted in March 2020. In an English-language letter posted to Instagram, Kim wrote:

> Hello Unicorns ! This is Sungjoo
> How are you all doing these days?
> I wasn't able to tell fans ahead of time, so I am leaving a letter like this.
> I am enlisting in the military! March 9.
> Our Unicorn fans who have always loved our UNIQ from beginning to end!
> Unicorn who always gives us strength to be courageous like a ray of light whenever we are having hard times, I love you.
> Each of us are doing our best in our individual positions.
> Please watch over us and show support!
> Be well while I am in the military!
> I will also be well until I return!
> Everyone be healthy and happy while I am in the military.
> I will also be healthy and happy until I return!
> The next time we meet, I will return as even more of a man!
> —From Sungjoo[80]

This heartbreaking letter to fans reveals emotion, but also the masculine pride inherent in military service ("I will return as even more of a man").

Korean Idols and the "Feminization" of Male Youth in China

In 2021, the PRC announced "The Proposal to Prevent the Feminization of Male Adolescents,"[81] arguing that male youths had become too feminine due to the popularity of Korean and Korean-trained idols and their penchant for cosmetics and earrings. Kerry Allen, a BBC China correspondent reported, "A notice from China's education ministry has caused a stir after it suggested young Chinese men had become too 'feminine.' The message has been criticised as sexist by many online users—but some say China's male celebrities are partly to blame,"[82] and noted that, "Si Zefu [a top delegate of China's Advisory Body] said the home

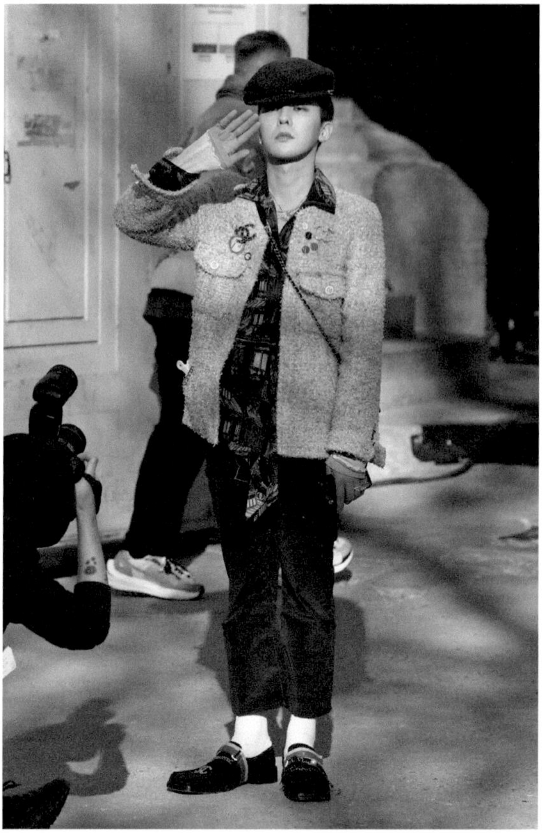

Figure 5.16 G-Dragon attends the Chanel Haute Couture Spring/Summer 2020 show as part of Paris Fashion Week on January 21, 2020 in Paris, France. Photo by Jacopo Raule/GC Images.

environment was partly to blame, with most Chinese boys being raised by their mothers or grandmothers. He also noted that the growing appeal of certain male celebrities meant that many children 'did not want to be 'army heroes' anymore.'"[83] Disregarding for a moment the absurdly sexist nature of the notion that China's male youth have somehow become too feminine, it is useful to consider the historical Confucist and Western patriarchal thought that has led to such a belief in the twenty-first century. Joseph Bazil Manietta addresses the matter in "Transnational Masculinities: The Distributive Performativity of Gender in Korean Boy Bands":

> The concept of patriarchal authoritarian masculinity, for example, stems from the household structure of the aristocracy in the Joseon Dynasty (1392–1910)[84]

> in which men were considered the heads of the family and primary providers. This Confucian patriarchal ideology created a "gendered division of labor:" the realm of the home and household work was relegated to women, and men were expected to work outside of the home (Jung 2011:26). As this system of Confucian patriarchy became industrialized patriarchy in the second half of the 20th century, "the normative gender constructs of the male-as-provider and the female-as-dependent-housewife persisted."[85]
>
> (ibid.:26)

If it is army heroes that make good role models for youth, one needs look no further than Korean idols who, as we have seen, must complete compulsory military service regardless of their idol status. Tellingly, in his goodbye letter to fans, Kim Sungjoo assured Unicorns that he would return from military service "as even more of a man." These Korean idols are not (only) "little fresh meats,"[86] but also the army heroes the PRC actually hopes to cultivate.

Korean Idols, Military Service, and Brand Agreements

Unsurprisingly, idol enlistment wreaks havoc with brand ambassadorial agreements. A typical brand ambassadorial agreement is structured as follows:

> This Brand Ambassador Agreement (this "Agreement"), beginning today, is entered into between yourself ("______________________________") and ______________________________ hereafter ("Company"). The parties agree as follows:
>
> 1. Services.
> 2. Compensation.
> 3. Ownership Rights.
> 4. Use of Likeness.
> 5. No Right of Approval.
> 6. Confidentiality.
> 7. Representations and Warranties.
> 8. Independent Contractor.
> 9. Termination of Agreement.
>
> Brand Ambassador ______________________________
> Date ____________
> Company Representative ______________________________
> Date ____________

Korean War Commemoration and Idol Boycotts

Another way in which the militaries of both South Korea and the People's Republic of China can indirectly interfere with brand ambassadors' campaigns for products is by an idol's own nationalism and love of country during periods of tension between the two Asian neighbors. October 23, 2020 marked the seventieth anniversary of the beginning of the Korean War, a war that never officially ended, and which for South Korea was the beginning of a seven-decades-long civil war turned national nightmare. But for China, historian Zhao Ma believes the Korean War was a sort of "war to end all wars," a war that marked the beginning of the end of what they saw as Western imperial incursion and hegemony in East Asia.[87]

Several Chinese idols, including Wang Yibo, Xiao Zhan, Lay Zhang, Cheng Xiao, Diliraba, Leo Luo, Meng Meiqi, Yang Yang, and Yang Zi, reblogged a post made on Weibo by the CCTV News (China's state-run media) account. The post read, "At this moment, let's all post on Weibo together! For each volunteer soldier! Pay tribute to heroes! Today, 1.4 billion people will jointly commemorate the 70th anniversary of the Chinese People's Volunteer Army leaving the country to fight the war to 'Resist the US, Aid North Korea,' remembering the great victory! The country will always remember the brave volunteer soldiers."[88] While the post was commemorative in nature, it dredged up both past and continuing tensions between the two nations and fomented outrage at the "Resist the US, Aid North Korea" posts, leading South Korean netizens to make calls on social media to boycott the aforementioned Chinese idols and the products that they endorsed. Interestingly, a similar controversy resulted in calls on Chinese social media to boycott K-Pop group and Louis Vuitton global brand ambassadors BTS (whose leader, Kim Namjoon, better known as RM, had spoken of a history of "shared pain" between the United States and South Korea over the Korean War (see Figure 5.17)).[89] Chinese and South Korean netizens also responded to posts by those of the other nationality, standing up for their idols and groups. Entertainment blogger 38jiejie noted that one Chinese blogger responded to a South Korean post by writing, "If your idol doesn't even love their own country, would you like them?"[90] Clearly, both sides were caught up in their own patriotic fervor. The salient question for brands is, would this fervor last, or were these crises of patriotism simply fleeting externalities? One year later, in 2021, BTS was indeed still facing boycotts in China. Casey Hall observed in the *Business of Fashion*:

> Then, last month, ten BTS fan group accounts, some of which had over a million followers, were banned from Chinese social media platform Sina Weibo for a

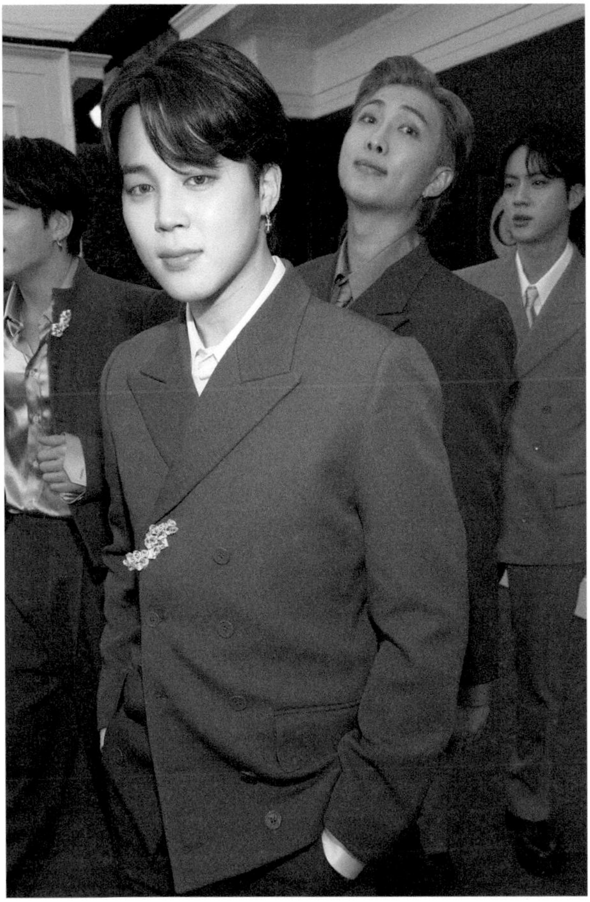

Figure 5.17 Jimin and RM of BTS, wearing Louis Vuitton, attend the 64th Annual GRAMMY Awards at MGM Grand Garden Arena on April 3, 2022 in Las Vegas, Nevada. Photo by Kevin Mazur/Getty Images for The Recording Academy.

> period of 30 days, ostensibly as part of the Cyberspace Administration of China's "Clear and Bright" campaign, which aims to combat the negative influence of "idol culture" and the "fan economy" on Chinese youth. The band members' status as persona non grata was revealed most recently when the Friends reunion special aired in China, where the original sitcom enjoys huge popularity. The guest appearance of BTS on the TV show had been cut from the version shown to Chinese audiences. It's unknown whether the censorship was an official government directive, or pre-emptively undertaken by local broadcasters to avoid angering the authorities.[91]

In China, where sales in the luxury sector are driven a whopping 80% by celebrity endorsements and Key Opinion Leaders (KOLs),[92] Louis Vuitton can ill afford

BTS's continuing unpopularity, especially when rival brands have popular Chinese idols as ambassadors, such as Wang Yibo (Chanel), Xiao Zhan (Gucci), and Cai Xukun (Prada).

Idols must also pay attention to China's history and politics with regards to Japan and conduct themselves accordingly. Chinese actor Zhang Zhehan, for example, lost several endorsements in 2021—including Pandora jewelers and Coca-Cola—after photos appeared online of him having visited the Yasukuni Shrine in Japan, a place of great pain to the Chinese people. The Yasukuni Shrine honors Japanese war dead, but specifically includes monuments to fourteen military leaders of World War II convicted as war criminals by the Allied Tribunal, some of whom participated in the Rape of Nanjing in the late 1930s.[93]

Conclusion: Successful Idols, Successful Nation

Korea is a culture deeply grounded in its history—both ancient and twentieth century—in which the modern middle class still strives to embody the old yangban aristocratic ideals, the unlikely bedfellows of Confucist biopolitics and Western-style authoritarianism color views about masculinity in general and homosexuality in particular, and as no Korean in their twenties can forget, a nation perpetually at war. Valérie Gelézeau writes:

> The South Korean infatuation or aesthetics must be understood within the framework of certain important explanatory factors, i.e. the complex combinations of transformational processes that occurred throughout the twentieth century: there was, on the one hand, the construction of a modern nation by a powerful State and, on the other hand, the emergence of the middle classes, with their strategies for social distinction inspired by the traditions of aristocratic culture (a result of the elevation of this culture in the nationalist dialogue). Thus, for the South Koreans, bodily beauty symbolises a successful nation (Leem Seo Yeon 2014, Epstein and Joo8, DiMoia, etc.), while behaviour relating to the body contributes both to the conspicuous consumerism and a sort of "Roaring Twenties" syndrome. (We must not forget that Korea is permanently at war.)[94]

Idols and the beauty products that they hawk as brand ambassadors, while their soft masculinity is at times at odds with socio-political expectations, are symbols of Korean power and economic prowess. That both China and Japan look to Korea for beauty products and now for popular culture is a testament to the country's resilience in the face of seventy years of division and war.

Epilogue: Xinjiang Cotton

Amanda Sikarskie[1]

In March 2020, Wang Yibo became the first Nike Official Partner in Mainland China. With his passion for skateboarding and the fact that his own idol—the Korean rapper G-Dragon—has been an ambassador for Nike for years, not to mention his popularity, Wang's collaboration with Nike simply made sense for both parties. In the spring of 2021, however, just as manuscript of this book was being completed for publication, there were growing calls in Europe and North America for brands to voluntarily stop sourcing cotton—"some of the best fabric in the world"[2]—from China's Xinjiang Province (the point of origin of 20% of global and 84% of Chinese cotton),[3] amidst global media reports of the alleged forced labor of more than a half a million persons,[4] re-education camps, and other human rights violations of the Uyghur Turkic Muslim population there,[5] as well as sanctions against four PRC officials by Britain, the European Union, the United States, and Canada announced on March 22, 2021.[6] Whereas many luxury brands have historically sourced their cotton elsewhere, thereby sidestepping the growing controversy over Xinjiang—Dior, Gucci, and Prada, for example, use cotton grown in California,[7] and Chanel sources Australian, Egyptian, and Texan cotton[8]—these reports and sanctions led Nike, along with other athletic and fast fashion brands[9] like Adidas, Calvin Klein, Converse, GAP, H&M, New Balance, Puma, Tommy Hilfiger, and Uniqlo, as well as British luxury paragon Burberry,[10] to announce the suspension of their use of Xinjiang cotton. Nike's official statement on the matter read in part:

> Nike is committed to ethical and responsible manufacturing and we uphold international labor standards. We are concerned about reports of forced labor in, and connected to, the *Xinjiang Uyghur Autonomous Region (XUAR)*. Nike does not source products from the XUAR and we have confirmed with our contract suppliers that they are not using textiles or spun yarn from the region . . . While Nike does not directly source cotton, or other raw materials, traceability at the

> raw materials level is an area of ongoing focus. We are working closely with our suppliers, industry associations, brands and other stakeholders to pilot traceability approaches and map material sources so we can have confidence the materials in our products are responsibly produced.[11]

Store.nike.com was unavailable in Mainland China as of March 24, 2021. These moves angered both the Chinese press and Chinese netizens, who took to social platforms such as Weibo on March 24, 2021 to announce their own boycotts of brands like H&M (which quickly led to the disappearance of H&M products on shopping websites Alibaba and Taobao and the removal of H&M store locations from mapping apps), as well as to urge Chinese idols to cancel their brand agreements with brands that had suspended sourcing cotton from Xinjiang.[12] Idols did so en masse, and even those without contracts with any of the involved brands (more than fifty actors and musicians in total as of March 25),[13] such as Xiao Zhan, posted in support of domestically-produced Xinjiang cotton using the hashtag #isupportxinjiangcotton. Athletics teams also stood in favor of Xinjiang cotton, with teams such as Shanghai Shenhua (The Flower of Shanghai), a Chinese Super League football team, announcing the removal of the Nike logo from its strips.

On March 25, 2021, Wang Yibo announced that he and Yuehua Entertainment were terminating their contract with Nike, after a night of receiving hate posts online from nationalistic (or patriotic) Chinese netizens. An excerpt of Wang's official statement was quoted in the British newspaper the *Guardian*, emphasizing that he opposed "any act to smear China."[14] A fuller version of Wang's statement on the matter was reproduced in English on the Asian entertainment website DramaPanda: "Our company [Yuehua Entertainment] and Mr. Wang Yibo firmly objects to any remarks and actions that stigmatise China. The dignity of the country cannot be violated and we resolutely safeguard the interests of the mother land."[15] DramaPanda reported that as of March 25, 2021, the following brands and ambassadors had parted ways over the Xinjiang cotton boycotts:

> Adidas/Adidas Originals: Jackson Yee, Crystal Liu Yifei, Yang Mi, Dilraba Dilmurat, Deng Lun, Angelababy, Eddie Peng, Janine Chang, Eason Chan, Chen Linong, Jackson Wang, Peng Yuchang, Cecilia Boey (Song Yanfei), Ryan Ding Yuxi, Zhao Lusi, Gina Jin Chen, and Qiu Tian;
> Burberry: Zhou Dongyu;[16]
> Calvin Klein: Lay Zhang Yixing, Liu Yuxin, and Greg Hsu;
> Converse (Nike subsidiary): Lay Zhang Yixing, Bai Jingting, and Ouyang Nana;

H&M: Huang Xuan and Victoria Song;
New Balance: Meng Meiqi and Wendy Zhang Zifeng;
Nike: Wang Yibo and Tan Songyun;
Puma: Li Xian, Yang Yang, Liu Haoran, Guli Nazha, and Greg Hsu;
Tommy Hilfiger: William Chan and Li Zhenning;
Uniqlo: Jing Boran, Lei Jiayin, Ni Ni, and Roy Wang Yuan,[17]

Notably, Dilraba Dilmurat (Mandarin name Diliraba), who ended a contract with Adidas, is herself of Uyghur ethnicity. Wang Yibo was among the last of the celebrities in China to announce separation from a brand over the Xinjiang cotton boycotts (most celebrities announced this the same day, on March 24). It took nearly a full twenty-four-hour news cycle for Wang and Yuehua to do this, not because he had considered staying with Nike but then been swayed by angry fans, but rather because Nike left it for Wang to cancel his contract, rather than being let go by the brand. While many stars in China are really only popular domestically, Wang is popular across Asia and helped to sell Nikes in Korea and Japan and in Southeast Asian markets like Cambodia, Laos, Singapore, Thailand, and Vietnam. "Does Wang Yibo have no shoes?" became something of an internet joke in China in the days that followed, but on March 28, 2021, Wang Yibo was photographed leaving the Changsha airport for a taping of *Day Day Up* wearing white Chanel SS/20 low-top sneakers rather than his usual Nikes, and the Chanel shoes went viral, with one blogger commenting, "Pure white shoes. As plain and white as cotton in Xinjiang. The child's pure heart."[18] For those who had seen global media reports on the humanitarian situation in Xinjiang, such comments may well have been distasteful, but one must realize that those in Mainland China receive and consume very different news. Regarding Wang's shoes, the reality is, ironically, that the Chanel shoes described as by a Chinese blogger as "plain and white as cotton in Xinjiang" likely contain no cotton from the province, as Chanel sources cotton from Australia, Egypt, and Texas.[19]

On April 11, 2021 Wang Yibo (modeling Anta Kids) announced a new partnership with Anta Sports, a brand that gained popularity in China in the spring of 2021 on account of their continued reliance on Xinjiang cotton. The move was a logical one, considering that Wang is the Goodwill Ambassador of the Beijing 2022 Winter Olympic & Paralympic Games and Anta is an official clothing partner of the games (see Figure 6.1). Interestingly, Wang's Untamed/CQL co-star Xiao Zhan was also reported to be the new ambassador for Li Ning, another Chinese sportswear company and Anta's domestic rival, a move that gained much attention for the brand. Chinese popular culture blog *Sip of Tea*

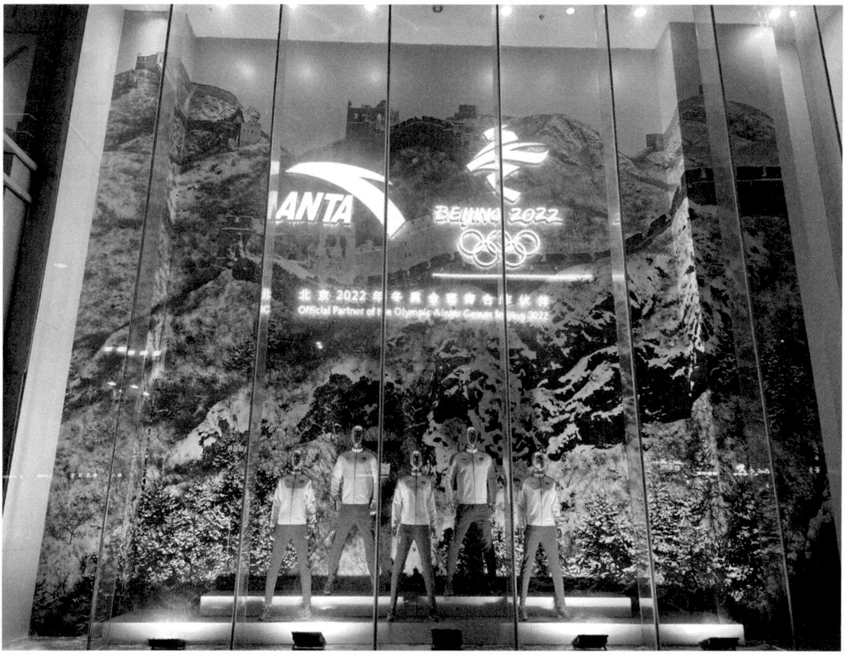

Figure 6.1 Logos of Anta and the Beijing 2022 Winter Olympics are seen at an Anta store on February 18, 2021 in Putian, Fujian Province of China. Photo by Chen Xiaoke/VCG via Getty Images.

reported that, "The wave of domestic brand support (probably) hit the peak when popular domestic sportswear brand Li Ning officially announced Xiao Zhan as its global spokesperson on March 26. The news immediately reached the top of the hot search list with an 'Exploded' remark and the hashtag #LiNingofficiallyannouncesXiaoZhan gained over 1 billion views. The Li Ning series of products endorsed by Xiao Zhan was quickly sold out after they were put on the shelves."[20] And in June 2021, Goldman Sachs rated Anta at "buy" following the acquisition of Wang Yibo as brand ambassador. Goldman Sachs also forecast positive sales of Wang Yibo-endorsed Anta merchandise for the 6.18 Shopping Festival.[21] Regardless of which idol is more successful as ambassador, both Anta and Li Ning benefitted tremendously from the Xinjiang cotton controversy. As of March 24, 2021, Anta Sports had gained nearly 8.5 percent to 121.30 Hong Kong dollars and Li Ning had climbed nearly 10.75 percent to 50 HKD on the Hong Kong Stock Exchange.[22]

It is unclear how the Xinjiang cotton boycotts will evolve, but as Brenton Johns reported for the *Business of Fashion* on March 26, 2021, "The fallout is prompting brands to take different approaches to try and limit the damage.

Some companies, including H&M and Zara owner Inditex, appear to have removed statements relating to the use of cotton from Xinjiang from their global websites, while others, including Asics and Hugo Boss have publicly vowed to continue sourcing from Xinjiang."[23] What is clear is that Chinese idols, when forced to choose between lucrative brand agreements and their popularity in the West or their own country, resoundingly put China first. *Sip of Tea* opined in March 2021 that the wave of support for domestic brands had probably reached its zenith, but so far reaching and long lasting is this national wave, or *guochao*, that *Business of Fashion* reported four months later in July 2021 that the new preference for buying Chinese brands has now even impacted the bridal market, especially among young brides, whose maximalist tastes are at odds with the current trend for minimalism in bridal gowns in the West.[24] It seems that Chinese shoppers in 2021, like their idols, are choosing to put country first in their consumer decision-making. Whether this leads Western fashion brands to work with fewer Chinese ambassadors in the future, or whether the Chinese consumer is simply too important for brands to ignore, remains to be seen.

Postscript: China Bans *Xiao Xian Rou*

Amanda Sikarskie

On September 2, 2021, global media outlets reported that the Chinese government had banned effeminate men on television. President Xi Jinping called for a "national rejuvenation" and the National Radio and Television Administration (NRTA)[1] called on television and satellite broadcasters to "resolutely put an end to sissy men and other abnormal esthetics."[2] The Associated Press noted that the regulatory authority used "an insulting slang term for effeminate men—*niang pao*, or literally 'girlie guns.' That reflects official concern that Chinese pop stars, influenced by the sleek, girlish look of some South Korean and Japanese singers and actors, are failing to encourage young men to be masculine enough."[3] In reality, many of these young men are *liuliang*, or traffic celebrities, with rabid fanbases so powerful that they influence not only the purchasing of endorsed brands, but also the news cycle and *chaohua*, or super topics, on social media. Given their power over their fans, and particularly youth, the Chinese government feels compelled to regulate these male celebrities. But this move is disturbing in its lack of respect for these young men, as well as its failure to appreciate individuality, aesthetic diversity, and the pervasiveness of gender-fluidity in youth culture in China today, and for brands and retailers, leaves many unanswered questions regarding the viability of the idols discussed in this book as brand ambassadors in China going forward.

It may well be that this book on male idols as brand ambassadors is, quite unintentionally, something of a historical piece, a document of idol culture as it existed in China from the 2010s to 2021, piled up on the "scrap heap of history"[4] rather than a work of use to students and scholars of luxury fashion management and related disciplines. It is my sincere hope that Wang Yibo, Xiao Zhan, and the other idols included herein will continue to be able to participate, and indeed thrive, in the entertainment and fashion industries. Wang Yibo adapted well to the Chinese government's *hallyu* ban in 2016 and may be expected to adapt again to the cultural rejuvenation. As an athlete—a professional motorcycle racer, a snowboarder and ambassador of the Beijing 2022 Olympic and Paralympic Games, and a skateboarder and hopeful for the Paris 2024 Games, Wang is uniquely poised to weather this storm. Across the industry, it may well be that the gender presentation of the idols presented in this book is about to get a great deal more butch. How fans, consumers, and brands will respond is, at the moment, anyone's guess.

Glossary

5.20: May 20th, Chinese Valentine's Day.
520: Chinese texting slang: "I love you" ("*wo ai ni*").
530: Chinese texting slang: "I miss you."
6.18 Festival: The mid-year shopping festival in China and an unofficial e-commerce holiday.
1314: Chinese texting slang: "Forever."
5201314: Chinese texting slang: "I will love you forever."
aegyo: Korean term for a display of cuteness, such as pointing to one's dimples, expected to be produced on command by both female and male idols.
anti-fan: Haters of a particular idol who act out on social media.
artificial sugar: The performance of a "couple pairing" (CP—see below) in public by idols who actually feel nothing for each other romantically. Artificial sugar is done to attract fans, but is looked down upon within the industry.
Baidu: A search engine website in China, sometimes referred to as the Chinese "Google."
bias: A fan's favorite member within an idol group. For example, "Zhou Yixuan is my bias."
BL: Boy's love. A genre of media in East Asia in which two male protagonists have romantic feelings for each other. BL is generally marketed toward women.
candies: Supposed hints left by idols to the fans of their couple pairing that the CP really does exist. Many candies are considered to simply be "artificial sugar" (see above.)
chaohua: Also known as "super topics." Chaohua are a particular kind of hashtag on the Chinese social media platform Weibo reserved for very popular topics, and especially celebrities. They are not only the preserve of idols, however, as many minor celebrities and up-and-comers have chaohua as well. For example, choreographer Ma Xiaolong discussed his chaohua in a livestream.[1]
comeback: A single or album released after an idol's debut period. So, the second, third, and all subsequent albums are comebacks. (The term is used much differently in the West, where comeback connotes a return to recording after taking much time away from the industry.)
CP: Couple pairing. Widely used term in China for two co-stars or bandmates who are imagined to be a romantic couple by fans. CPs generally, but not always, have little to no basis in reality.
C-Pop: Chinese pop music, which encompasses Mandopop (Mandarin-language pop), Cantopop (Cantonese-language pop), and other variants.

danmei: A Chinese term for yaoi, which generally may be more sexually explicit than BL.
donghua: Chinese animation; the Chinese equivalent of the Japanese term anime.
expression management: The discipline in which idols school their facial expressions to appear serene, benign, or otherworldly on camera. For idols, expression management may require concealing physical or emotional pain or controlling one's laughter.
fanfiction: Often referred to simply as "fanfic," this is fiction written by fans using popular film or television characters, or real celebrities, such as idols, as protagonists. Frequently, two male characters are shipped (see below) into a romantic or sexual relationship, though such a relationship does not exist in canon or in real life.
finger heart: A heart made with the thumb and forefinger. The gesture was popularized by East Asian pop artists and is used by both idols and ordinary people (often young people) when being photographed.
fudanshi: A Japanese term, literally "rotten boy," for men and boys who like (BL) boy's love anime and manga, or BL fanfiction.
fujoshi: A Japanese term, literally "rotten girl," for women and girls who like (BL) boy's love anime and manga, or BL fanfiction.
guochao: National wave, a Chinese trend for buying domestic Chinese brands rather than Western, Japanese, or Korean ones
hallyu: Korean wave in entertainment. K-Drama, K-Pop, etc.
hallyu ban: China's ban on Korean wave which went into effect in 2016 and lasted for nearly two years.
hikikomori: A Japanese term for young people who practice social isolation, who largely become shut-ins. They may or may not be otaku or hardcore fans of a particular fandom.
idol: In East Asia, a star; specifically, anyone who has made their formal debut with a K-Pop, C-Pop or J-Pop group.
jingzhunan: Translated in English as "luxury pig men," this Chinese term refers to men who enjoy wearing makeup; related to the term *xiao xian rou*, or "little fresh meat."
J-Pop: Japanese pop.
K-Pop: Korean pop, a genre of music which combines pop music and rap, along with dancing, fashion, makeup, and cuteness.
KOL (key opinion leader): Acronym used in China meaning a social media influencer.
liuliang: Traffic celebrities—celebrities powerful enough to drive traffic on social media and news websites by such simple actions as, say, dyeing their hair a different color.
luxury pig men: English translation of the Chinese term *jingzhunan*, meaning makeup-loving men
maknae: In Korea, the youngest member of a group of friends, or of an idol group.
Mandopop: Another term for C-Pop; specifically, Mandarin-language pop.
metaverse: An aggregation of three-dimensional virtual worlds experienced by virtual reality or augmented reality. In 2021, it was hypothesized that the internet will eventually become the metaverse.

mimei: A fandom subgroup of individuals who feel a motherly relationship with their idol(s).

NFT: Non-fungible token. An often valuable digital object, with one-of-a-kind uniqueness made possible through blockchain technology.

niang pao: Literally, "girlie guns," a pejorative term for men who could be considered effeminate. Often translated as "sissy."

otaku: Japanese term for an obsessive fan of a particular media genre or sport, such as "BL otaku" or "figure skating otaku."

Post-95 Generation: Roughly the equivalent of Generation Z in the West.

shipping: The practice of creating a CP for the purpose of writing fanfiction. Shippers are people who ship, that is, who write CP fanfiction.

Singles Day: A major Chinese shopping holiday on November 11, targeted toward single people buying themselves gifts. The date 11/11 is said to resemble a group of sticks, or single people.

skinship: A portmanteau of "skin" and "kinship." Platonic or romantic physical affection displayed between idols in the same group, widely tolerated within the industry due to the ban on idols dating, especially during their trainee and debut phases, and (often boisterously) encouraged by fans at fanmeetings and concerts.

soft masculinity: A masculine ideal based on an aesthetic of male beauty, the K-Pop look, with its use of cosmetics and relatively long hair, coupled with a gentleness of temperament. Soft masculinity is considered the ideal by many East Asian women, both for idols and in looking for their own romantic partner.

stan: Fan, and may either be used as a noun or a verb. For example, one might say that "I stan UNIQ," meaning that "I am a fan of UNIQ," or "I'm a K-Pop stan," meaning that "I'm a K-Pop fan." Often misspelled as stand with a "d" by Westerners outside the K-Pop culture.

standard smile: A K-Pop trainee's usual public smile, often practiced in front of a mirror many times until perfected.

super topics: *See* chaohua

traffic celebrities: *See* liuliang

trainee: An enrollee in an idol school who has not yet formally debuted with a group.

Turtles: Fans of the Yizhan (Wang Yibo and Xiao Zhan) CP.

Weibo: A highly popular social networking platform in China, sometimes called the "Chinese Facebook."

xianxia: Fantasy martial arts genre set in the distant Chinese past, and often making use of idols as actors through "wire fu," *qing gong* (a kind of parcour in which one's body is light enough to stand on the end of a tree branch, jump easily from rooftop to rooftop, or even hover in midair for short periods) produced by idols suspended on wires, rather than actual martial arts like kung fu.

xiao gege (little older brothers): Cutesy term for idols and other young men, not necessarily of small stature but always exhibiting a fashionable soft masculinity. Not quite as sexually-charged as *xiao xian rou* (see below).

xiao xian rou (little fresh meat): Sexually-objectifying Chinese term for young, male idols.

yangban: The aristocratic elite of traditional Korea.

yaoi: Another Japanese term for BL. Yaoi denotes content that is more sexually explicit than BL.

zhai nan and zhai nü: Literally "home boys" and "home girls": housebound youth. Chinese terms for hikikomori.

Join the conversation on Twitter and Instagram using the hashtag #idolsbook

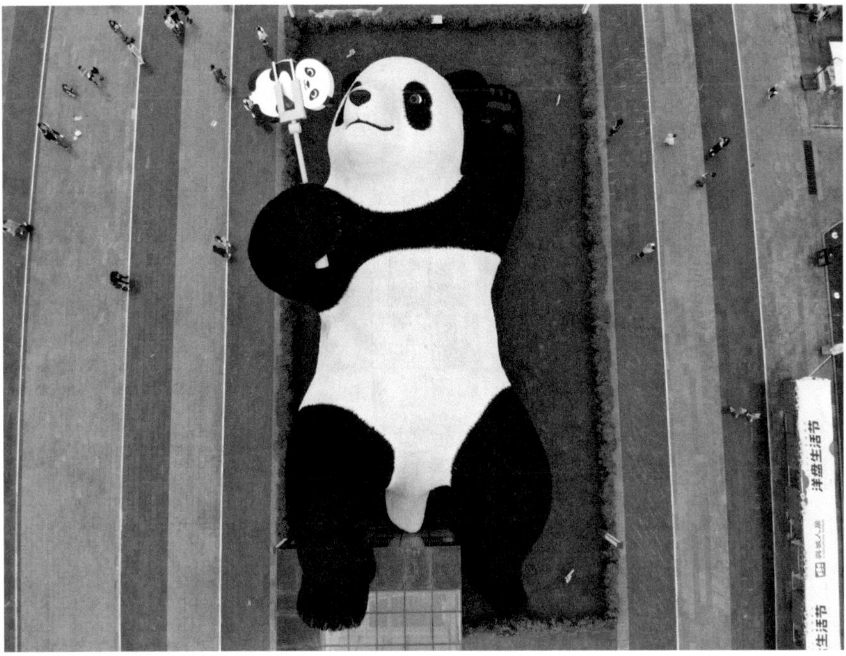

Figure 7.1 Selfie Panda—Aerial view of tourists visiting the "Selfie Panda" sculpture by Dutch artist Florentijn Hofman at the Yangtianwo square during Chinese National Day Holiday on October 4, 2021 in Dujiangyan City, Chengdu City, Sichuan Province of China. Photo by Zhang Lang/China News Service via Getty Images.

Notes

Preface: "Are you that Unicorn?"

1 Stephan Lee, *K-Pop Confidential*, New York: Point, an Imprint of Scholastic, Inc., 2020, 68.
2 Rebecca Davis, "China Bans Lip-Syncs and Mandates Patriotism in Celebrity Morality Guidelines," *Variety*, February 11, 2021, https://variety.com/2021/politics/news/china-morality-guidelines-outlaw-lip-syncing-1234905700/.
3 Lee, *K-Pop Confidential*, 68.

1 Introductions—Peacocks: Male Idols and Marketing in China

1 Research for this book was concluded on August 31, 2021, and apart from Singles Day activities of contestants of *Street Dance of China 4*, any events that occurred thereafter are not included herein. As the social, political, and economic landscape in which idols work is continually—and sometimes rapidly—shifting, we recognize that the situation for idols, their fans, and brands in China has subsequently changed since the summer of 2021.
2 A note to Chinese-language readers: Amanda Sikarskie also uses the Chinese name 宋漫漫 (Song Manman).
3 *The King's Avatar*, season 1, episode 12.
4 Laurie Chen, "The real power behind China's new trend of 'sissy men' . . . is the empowered modern woman," *South China Morning Post*, September 19, 2018, https://www.scmp.com/news/china/society/article/2163748/real-power-behind-chinas-new-trend-sissy-men-empowered-modern.
5 For literary sources, see Du Fu's *Eight Immortals of the Wine Cup* (Tang Dynasty) and Murasaki Shikibu's *The Tale of Genji* (Heian period).
6 The Edo Period lasted from 1603 to 1867 and was ended by the Meiji Restoration.
7 Wang Jingxin, "The Future of Fashion Magazines in China: From Print to Douyin," Master's Thesis defense, Parsons Paris, May 12, 2021. The quotation may be slightly paraphrased as it is reproduced here from notes taken during a live talk.

8 "A rare Imperial cloisonné and champlevé enamel 'peacocks' group, Qianlong Period (1736–1795)," *Inspired Themes: a Fine Selection of Chinese Works of Art*, Auction catalog, London: Christie's, May 10, 2016.
9 Bird Ecology Study Group, "The Use of Birds in the Civil Service of Ancient China," *Bird Ecology Study Group*, October 25, 2012, https://besgroup.org/2012/10/25/the-use-of-birds-in-the-civil-service-of-ancient-china/.
10 Literally "home boys" and "home girls," housebound youth.
11 Boy's love. A genre of media in East Asia in which two male protagonists have romantic feelings for each other. BL is generally marketed towards women.
12 More names can be found at https://news.163.com/19/0921/21/EPKKQGAN0001899O.html
13 The names are further extended into categories in terms of location and product coverage, such as: global ambassadors, Asia-pacific ambassadors, great China ambassadors, and China ambassadors, that intertwined with whole series, production line series, certain product series, or specific products.
14 According to China's New Advertisement Act 2015, clause no. 38, the representatives cannot represent the product/service the representatives did not use. That is to say, male idols can represent cosmetics such as lipsticks, facial foundation, perfumes, face masks, etc. but not sanitary pads/tampons, etc.
15 Another Japanese term for BL. Yaoi may be more sexually explicit than BL.
16 "Idols and Endorsements: The More, the Merrier?" *SeoulBeats*, August 8, 2012, https://seoulbeats.com/2012/08/idols-and-endorsements-the-more-the-merrier/.
17 Julienna Law, "Will Chongqing Become China's Next Big Luxury Hub?," *Jing Daily*, February 10, 2022, https://jingdaily.com/chongqing-international-brands-million-yuan/.
18 Peter McNeil and Giorgio Riello, *Luxury: A Rich History*, Oxford: Oxford University Press, 2016, 275.
19 McNeil and Riello, *Luxury*, 275–6.
20 McNeil and Riello, *Luxury*, 278.
21 Juwon Park, "Chinese Pop Stars Publicly Back Beijing on Hong Kong," CBC News, August 19, 2019, https://www.cbc.ca/news/entertainment/chinese-stars-hk-protests-1.5252048.
22 Zoe Suen, "Where Global Brands Are Moving Their Asia-Pacific Headquarters," *Business of Fashion*, May 11, 2021, https://www.businessoffashion.com/briefings/china/why-are-brands-moving-their-asia-headquarters.
23 Eileen Jahnke Trestain, *Dating Fabrics: A Color Guide*, Paducah, KY: American Quilter's Society, 1998, 131–3.
24 Trestain, *Dating Fabrics*, 129.
25 For example, see the lyrics of Wang Yibo's 2021 songs, "Youth Comes at the Right Time" and "So Young and So Flowering," the latter of which is a patriotic pop song

released in May 2021 in commemoration of the 100th anniversary of the founding of the Communist Party of China.

26 Phyllis Tortora and Keith Eubank, *Survey of Historic Costume*, 3rd edn, New York: Fairchild Publications, 1998, 388–90.

27 Kevin Kwan, *Crazy Rich Asians*, Crow's Nest, NSW, Australia: Allen & Unwin, 2014.

28 Sara Liao, *Fashioning China: Precarious Creativity and Women Designers in Shanzhai* Culture, London: Pluto Press, 2020, 37.

29 L'Oréal Finance, https://www.loreal-finance.com/eng/news-release/first-quarter-2020-sales.

30 L'Oréal Finance .

31 "The State of Fashion 2021 Scenarios," *Business of Fashion*, October 22, 2020.

32 Liang, 37.

33 Olav Velthuis, "Damien's Dangerous Idea: Valuing Contemporary Art at Auction," in Jens Beckert and Patrick Aspers, eds., *The Worth of Goods: Valuation and Pricing in the Economy*, 190–1, Oxford: Oxford University Press, 2011.

34 Velthuis, "Damien's Dangerous Idea, 190–1.

35 Jackson Wang's Instagram, March 18, 2021.

36 Joseph Bazil Manietta, "Transnational Masculinities: The Distributive Performativity of Gender in Korean Boy Bands," Master's thesis, University of Colorado, 2015, 9.

37 James Elkins, *Pictures and Tears: A History of People Who Have Cried in Front of Paintings*, New York: Routledge, 2004, 120.

38 Martin Heidegger, *Being and Time*, Oxford: Blackwell, 1962, 398.

39 Tom Boellstorff, *Coming of Age in Second Life*, Princeton, NJ: Princeton University Press, 2008, 71.

40 Boellstorff, *Coming of Age in Second Life*, 69.

41 Boellstorff, *Coming of Age in Second Life*, 69.

42 Boellstorff, *Coming of Age in Second Life* , 82.

43 Ramendra Pratap Singh and Neelotpaul Banerjee, "Exploring the Influence of Celebrity Worship on Brand Attitude, Advertisement Attitude, and Purchase Intention," *Journal of Promotion Management* 25, no. 2 (2019): 225–51, DOI: 10.1080/10496491.2018.1443311.

44 Stephan Lee, *K-Pop Confidential*, New York: Point, an Imprint of Scholastic, Inc., 2020, 82.

45 Justin McCurry, "Spycams, sex abuse and scandal: #MeToo reaches Korean pop," *Guardian*, March 22, 2019.

46 "Christmas episode," *Idol School*, December 14, 2014.

47 "UNIQ interview," *Bang Channel*, March 7, 2015.

48 Annamari Vänskä, *Fashionable Childhood: Children in Advertising*, trans. Eva Malkki, London: Bloomsbury, 2017, 191.

49 Vänskä, *Fashionable Childhood*, 186.

50 Vänskä, *Fashionable Childhood*, 186.

51 Chen Xi, "Kris Wu May Be Sentenced to 10 Years to Life Imprisonment: Lawyer," *Global Times*, August 1, 2021, https://www.globaltimes.cn/page/202108/1230189.shtml.

52 Anne J, "Kris Wu Loses Brand Endorsements Following Du Meizhu's Latest Interview," *DramaPanda*, July 18, 2021, https://dramapanda.com/2021/07/kris-wu-loses-brand-endorsement-following-du-meizhus-latest-interview.html.

53 Saito Tamaki, *Hikikomori: Adolescence Without End*, trans. Jeffrey Angles, Minneapolis: University of Minnesota Press, 2013, 171, 183.

54 Avery Booker, "China's 'Lying Flat' Trend Meets its New Champion: The Free Idler," *Jing Daily*, March 4, 2022, https://jingdaily.com/chinas-lying-flat-trend-meets-its-new-champion-the-free-idler/.

55 Tamaki, *Hikikomori*, 183.

56 Tamaki, *Hikikomori*, 77.

57 Tamaki, *Hikikomori*, 24.

58 Tamaki, *Hikikomori*, 31.

59 Angles, in Tamaki, *Hikikomori*, xii.

60 Pinyin lyrics translated by YouTuber @rvjoy0903.

61 UNIQ being too honest.

62 O. E. Dadzie and A. Petit, "Skin bleaching: Highlighting the misuse of cutaneous depigmenting agents," *Journal of the European Academy of Dermatology and Venereology*, June 3, 2009, https://onlinelibrary.wiley.com/doi/abs/10.1111/j.1468-3083.2009.03150.x.

63 Valérie Gelézeau, "The Body, Cosmetics and Aesthetics in South Korea: The Emergence of a Field of Research," HAL SHS, 2015, 7, halshs-01211686

64 Liao, *Fashioning China*, 99.

65 Liao, *Fashioning China*, 100–1.

66 Chinese and Korean names in this book, including index terms, are given with the family name stated first.

67 Liao, *Fashioning China*, 100.

68 Liao, *Fashioning China*, 100.

69 See Fefe H, YouTube.

70 Boy's Love. Pan-Asian term referring to bromantic (in the case of *The Untamed*) or male–male homo-romantic media.

71 Fantasy martial arts genre set in the distant Chinese past, and often making use of idols as actors through "wire fu," *qing gong* (a kind of parcour in which one's body is light enough to stand on the end of a tree branch, jump easily from rooftop to rooftop, or even hover in midair for short periods), produced by idols suspended on wires, rather than actual martial arts like kung fu.

72 As of March 3, 2021, there are 20,314 unique stories featuring the ship (relationship) of Xiao and Wang. Of these stories,3,747 are rated explicit and 3,123 are rated mature.

73 For in-depth analysis of the AO3 incident, see Emily Feng, "China Blocks Website After Complaints About Fan Fiction Story on a Celebrity," *NPR*, October 28, 2020, https://www.npr.org/2020/10/28/928805796/china-blocks-website-after-complaints-about-fan-fiction-story-on-a-celebrity; Casey Hall, "Toxic Fan Culture Puts Brands at Risk in China," *Business of Fashion*, March 12, 2020, https://www.businessoffashion.com/articles/intelligence/toxic-fan-culture-puts-brands-at-risk-in-china; Jiaqi Luo, "The Dark Side of China's Idol Economies," *Jing Daily*, March 6, 2020, https://jingdaily.com/the-dark-side-of-chinas-idol-economies/; Marrian Zhou, "When China's Massive Fan Economy Goes Wrong," *Nikkei Asia*, May 6, 2020, https://asia.nikkei.com/Business/Media-Entertainment/When-China-s-massive-fan-economy-goes-wrong.

74 Zhou, "When China's Massive Fan Economy Goes Wrong."

75 Singles Day, November 11, is a major shopping holiday in China. For more on idols and Singles Day marketing, see the case study chapter on Wang Yibo.

76 Source data on lipstick sales: Feng, "China Blocks Website After Complaints About Fan Fiction Story on a Celebrity."

77 *China Star News*, November 8, 2020.

78 Amanda Sikarskie, "Idols as Brand Ambassadors in China: The Rise and Fall and Rise of Xiao Zhan: Crisis Management at Estée Lauder and Olay," in *Bloomsbury Fashion Business Cases*, London: Bloomsbury, 2022.

79 Tania de Sostoa-McCue, "Rhetorics of Resistance: Reading Taboo in Fanfiction," Master's thesis, Michigan State University, 2007, 10.

80 All of these fanfictions are available on Archive of Our Own and were published in the fall of 2020. (Search by title.) Please note that all are rated teen to explicit. Not available via a mainland Chinese IP address.

81 Jaemyun, "Yiling Poltergeist," published March 17, 2021, https://archiveofourown.org/works/29892411/chapters/73564917/.

82 JuxtaposeFantasy, *The Gege Collector*, Archive of Our Own. Please note that this is a work of fiction, depicting relationships with no basis in reality. Content is explicit and unavailable via mainland China IP address.

83 de Sostoa-McCue, "Rhetorics of Resistance," 10.

84 Xiao Zhan Fans Charity Project 2020, https://missacs.wordpress.com/2020/10/19/xiao-zhan-fans-charity-project-2020/.

85 Casey Hall, "Prada's Next Move in China," *Business of Fashion*, January 21, 2021.

86 Sikarskie, "Idols as Brand Ambassadors in China."

87 The stream is archived on YouTube at https://www.youtube.com/watch?v=l0oHCWXf6iA.

88 A program on which UNIQ member Zhou Yixuan debuted his song "Do Back."

89 Sky Canaves, "Beauty Brands Face China's 'Cancel Culture,'" *Content Commerce Insider*, March 2020, https://contentcommerceinsider.com/blog/beauty-brands-face-chinas-cancel-culture.

90 Daniel Black, "The Virtual Idol: Producing and Consuming Digital Femininity," in Patrick W. Galbraith and Jason G. Karlin, eds., *Idols and Celebrity in Japanese Media Culture*, 209–28, Basingstoke: Palgrave Macmillan, 2012.

91 Daniel Black, "Digital Bodies and Disembodied Voices: Virtual Idols and the Virtualised Body," *Fiberculture Journal* 54.9, https://nine.fibreculturejournal.org/fcj-054-digital-bodies-and-disembodied-voices-virtual-idols-and-the-virtualised-body/.

92 Kristen Bateman, "I Attended Helsinki Fashion Week as an Avatar," *Teen Vogue*, August 28, 2020.

2 Exploring the Relationship Between Fashion Brands, Culture Idols, and Fans: The Power of Naming as Market Strategy

1 Karen Page Winterich, Manish Gangwar, and Rajdeep Grewal, "When Celebrities Count: Power Distance Beliefs and Celebrity Endorsements," *Journal of Marketing* 82 (2018): 70–86.

2 Naming, like nomenclature in technical sounding, is to create and give a vocabulary to someone in the form of a name or nickname. This chapter uses "naming" as a noun and "to name" as a verb. Acknowledging "name" and "title" can be different terms: the distinction between the two and their relations to social status and power, for example, can be the interest of sociological scholars; this chapter, however, uses "name" as the general term to investigate the content of the vocabularies in the naming practices of endorsement and nicknaming giving. The naming practice of the fashion brands is communicated to fans/consumers via multimedia advertisements as well as offline activities, such as fan meeting.

3 Jie Jie Ba Gua Shuo, "Celebrity Endorsement Categorized in Hierarchy: Brand Ambassador, Brand Spokesperson, Brand Friend," *Sohu*, July 2, 2021, https://www.sohu.com/a/475277830_121030782; Maigoo, "Can You Differentiate Brand Spokesperson, Brand Friend and Brand Ambassador? A Picture to Show the Difference Between Various Celebrity Endorsements," *Maigoo*, June 22, 2020, https://m.maigoo.com/news/552734.html.

4 Ann Anagnost, "The Politicized Body," in Angela Zito and Tani E. Barlow, eds., *Body, Subject and Power in China*, 133, Chicago: University of Chicago Press, 1994.

5 Richard D. Alford, *Naming and Identity: A Cross-cultural Study of Personal Naming Practices*, New Haven, CT: HRAF Press, 1988.

6 Clare Hayes-Brady, "'I Kept Saying Her Name': Naming, Labels and Power in the Early Writing of David Foster Wallace," *Orbit: A Journal of American Literature* 5, no. 1 (2017): 23.

7 Minwoo Jung and NaYoung Lee, "Fandom Managing Stars, Entertainment Industry Managing Fandom," *Media, Gender and Culture* 12 (2009): 191–240.

8 According to the China New Advertisement Act 2015, clause no. 38, the brand ambassadors cannot represent products/services that they cannot use. That is to say, male idols can represent cosmetics, such as lipsticks, facial foundation, perfumes, face masks, etc., but not sanitary pads/tampons, etc.

9 There were three options available for that question—male, female, and non-gender; four respondents selected "non-gender."

10 Burleigh Bradford Gardner and Sidney Jay Levy, "The Product and the Brand," *Harvard Business Review* 33, no. 2 (1955): 33–59.

11 Max Blackston, "Beyond Brand Personality: Building Brand Relationships," in David Allen Aaker and Alexander L. Biel, eds., *Brand Equity and Advertising: Advertising's Role in Building Strong Brands*, Hillsdale, NJ: Laurence Erlbaum Associates, 1993, 115.

12 Martin Kornberger, *Brand Society: How Brands Transform Management and Lifestyle*, Cambridge: Cambridge University Press, 2010, 5.

13 Jennifer Lynn Aaker, "Dimensions of Brand Personality," *Journal of Marketing Research* 34, no. 3 (1997): 347–56, original italics.

14 Youngjun Sung and Jooyoung Kim, "Effects of Brand Personality on Brand Trust and Brand Affect," *Psychology and Marketing* 27, no. 7 (2010): 639–61.

15 Rodoula Tsiotsou, "Developing a Scale for Measuring the Personality of Sport Teams," *Journal of Services Marketing* 26, no. 4 (2012): 238–52.

16 Malaika Brengman and Kim Willems, "Determining Fashion Store Personality Dimensions: An Exploratory Study Based on Repertory Grid Data and Grounded Theory," *European Institute of Retailing and Services Studies* 15 (2008).

17 Audrey Azoulay and Jean Noël Kapferer, "Do Brand Personality Scale Really Measure Brand Personality?" *Journal of Brand Management* 11, no. 2 (2003): 143–55, original italics.

18 Jillian C. Sweeney and Carol Brandon, "Brand Personality: Exploring the Potential to Move from Factor Analytical to Circumplex Models," *Psychology and Marketing* 23, no. 8 (2006): 639–63, original italics.

19 For example, rich culture can be realized in human perception as a sense of pride from which a characteristic of arrogance can derive, while long history indicates one's experience of moving up and down in society which provokes a sense of toughness and is perceived by others as a core characteristic.

20 Kornberger, *Brand Society*, 13.

21 Kornberger, *Brand Society*, xi.

22 Grant McCracken, "Who is the Celebrity Endorser? Cultural Foundations of the Endorsement Process," *Journal of Consumer Research* 16, no. 3 (1989): 310–21.

23 Seong-Yeon Park and Eun Mi Lee, "Congruence Between Brand Personality and Self-Image, and the Mediating Roles of Satisfaction and Consumer–Brand Relationship on Brand Loyalty," in Yong-Uon Ha and Youjae Yi, eds., *AP–Asia Pacific Advances in Consumer Research*, Volume 6, 39–45, Duluth: Association for Consumer Research, 2005.
24 Charles Atkins and Martin Block, "Effectiveness of Celebrity Endorsers," *Journal of Advertising Research* 23, no. 1 (1983): 57–61.
25 McCracken, "Who is the Celebrity Endorser?" 310.
26 Bayram Zafer Erdogan, "Celebrity Endorsement: A Literature Review," *Journal of Marketing Management* 15, no. 4 (1999): 291–314.
27 Ronald E. Goldsmith, Barbara A. Lafferty, and Stephen J. Newell, "The Impact of Corporate Credibility and Celebrity Credibility on Consumer Reaction to Advertisements and Brands," *Journal of Advertising* 29, no. 3 (2000): 43–54.
28 Mary Walker, Lynn Langmeyer, and Daniel Langmeyer, "Celebrity Endorsers: Do You Get What You Pay For?" *Journal of Services Marketing* 6, no. 4 (1992): 35–42.
29 Erdogan, "Celebrity Endorsement," 292.
30 Bergkvist and Zhou propose an updated definition: "*a celebrity endorsement is an agreement between an individual who enjoys public recognition (a celebrity) and an entity (e.g., a brand) to use the celebrity for the purpose of promoting the entity.*" Lars Bergkvist and Kris Qiang Zhou, "Celebrity Endorsements: A Literature Review and Research Agenda," *International Journal of Advertising* 35, no. 4 (2016): 644, original italics.
31 Lynn R. Kahle and Pamela Miles Homer, "Physical Attractiveness of the Celebrity Endorser: A Social Adaptation Perspective," *Journal of Consumer Research* 11, no. 4 (1985): 954–61; E. C. Klohnen and S. Luo, "Interpersonal Attraction and Personality: What is Attractive—Self Similarity, Ideal Similarity, Complementarity, or Attachment Security?" *Journal of Personality and Social Psychology* 85, no. 4 (2003): 709–22; Matthew Tingchi Liu and James L. Brock, "Selecting a Female Athlete Endorser in China: The Effect of Attractiveness, Match-up, and Consumer Gender Difference," *European Journal of Marketing* 45, no. 7–8 (2011): 1214–35.
32 David H. Silvera and Benedikte Austad, "Factors Predicting the Effectiveness of Celebrity Endorsement Advertisements," *European Journal of Marketing* 38, no. 11–12 (2004): 1509–26; Lars Bergkvist, Hanna Hjalmarson, and Anne Magi, "A New Model of How Celebrity Endorsements Work: Attitude Toward the Endorsement as a Mediator of Celebrity Source and Endorsement Effects," *International Journal of Advertising* 35, no. 2 (2016): 171–84.
33 Sejung Marina Choi and Nora J. Rifon, "Who is the Celebrity in Advertising? Understanding Dimensions of Celebrity Images," *Journal of Popular Culture* 40, no. 2 (2007): 304–24; Sejung Marina Choi and Nora J. Rifon, "It is a Match: The Impact of Congruence Between Celebrity Image and Consumer Ideal Self on Endorsement Effectiveness," *Psychology and Marketing* 29 (September 2012): 639–50.

34 Parasocial interaction was a term coined by Donald Horton and R. Richard Wohl in the fields of psychology and media studies. Donald Horton and R. Richard Wohl, "Mass Communication and Para-Social Interaction: Observations on Intimacy at a Distance," *Psychiatry: Interpersonal and Biological Processes* 19, no. 3 (1956): 215–29.

35 Jennifer Anette Lueck, "Friend-zone with Benefits: The Parasocial Advertising of Kim Kardashian," *Journal of Marketing Communications* 21, no. 2 (2015): 91–109.

36 Tony Proctor and Philip J. Kitchen, "Celebrity Ambassador/Celebrity Endorsement—Takes a Licking but Keeps on Ticking," *Journal of Strategic Marketing* 27, no. 5 (2019): 378.

37 Jung-Gyo Lee and Esther Thorson, "The Impact of Celebrity-product Incongruence on the Effectiveness of Product Endorsement," *Journal of Advertising Research* 48 (September 2008): 433–49.

38 Alice Li has analyzed the transformation of China's men's facial skincare market during the Covid-19 pandemic. Alice Li, "China Men's Facial Skincare Market has Started Its Transformation," *Mintel Blog*, 2020, https://www.mintel.com/blog/beauty-market-news/china-mens-facial-skincare-market-has-started-its-transformation.

39 Lisa Nan, "How Brands Can Monetize Male Beauty in China," *Jing Daily: The Business of Luxury in China*, May 4, 2021, https://jingdaily.com/local-male-skincare-brands-china-shakeup/.

40 Other reports include Mintel market reports on men's personal care, *China Men's Facial Skincare Market Report*, as well as those by other consultancy companies such as Allied Market Research and NPD's *iGen Beauty Consumer* report.

41 *Report of Product & Sale Demand and Investment Forecast Analysis on China Skin Care Products Industry 2021–2026*. https://bg.qianzhan.com/report/detail/7e937889903041d8.html.

42 Adina-Laura Achim, "How Brands Can Take Advantage of the Male Beauty Boom in China," *Jing Daily: The Business of Luxury in China*, July 17, 2020, https://jingdaily.com/how-brands-can-take-advantage-of-the-male-beauty-boom-in-china/.

43 There are various approaches among scholarly discussions regarding the use of male idols to promote skincare and cosmetics products to female consumers; for instance, some studies emphasize purchase behaviors by male consumers in marketing-orientated quantitative research, and others use qualitative approaches to focus on gender role representation and entertainment theory.

44 For example, an official notification was issued on September 2, 2021, by the National Radio and Television Administration, titled "The General Office of the State Administration of Radio and Television on further strengthening the management of cultural programs and their personnel," which lists eight points, of which no. 3 refers to "resolutely put[ting] an end to 'girly' male and other abnormal aesthetics." http://www.nrta.gov.cn/art/2021/9/2/art_113_57756.html.

45 Sky Canaves, "CBI Case Study: Male Celebrities Give Beauty Marketing a Makeover," *China Film Insider: The Business of Entertainment in China*, October 15, 2019, https://chinafilminsider.com/case-study-male-celebrities-beauty/.

46 Kris Wu lost all his collaborations with national and international brands due to the sexual allegations made against him in China in 2021.

47 "Never Stop Discovering," *Origins Natural Resources*, https://www.insurgents.io/origins.

48 Michel Foucault, *Power/knowledge: Selected Interviews and Other Writings 1972–1977*, ed. Colin Gordon, New York: Pantheon, 1980; Michel Foucault, *The History of Sexuality: An Introduction*, Harmondsworth: Penguin, 1981.

49 Foucault, *Power/knowledge*; Foucault, *Sexuality*; Michel Foucault, "The Subject and Power," *Critical Inquiry* 8, no. 4 (1982): 777–95.

50 Foucault, "Subject."

51 Roger Deacon, "Truth, Power and Pedagogy: Michel Foucault on the Rise of the Disciplines," *Educational Philosophy and Theory* 34, no. 4 (2002): 437.

52 Dacher Keltner, Deborah Gruenfeld, and C. Anderson, "Power, Approach, and Inhibition," *Psychological Review* 110 (2003): 265–84.

53 Nathanael J. Fast, Nir Halevy, and Adam Daniel Galinsky, "The Destructive Nature of Power Without Status," *Journal of Experimental Social Psychology* 48, no. 1 (2012): 391–4.

54 Joe C. Magee and A. Galinsky, "Social Hierarchy: The Self-reinforcing Nature of Power and Status," *Academy of Management Annals* 2 (2008): 351–98.

55 Steven L. Blader and Ya-Ru Chen, "What's in a Name? Status, Power, and Other Forms of Social Hierarchy," in Joey T. Cheng, Jessica L. Tracy, and Cameron Anderson, eds., *The Psychology of Social Status*, 71–95, New York: Springer, 2014.

56 Eric F. Dépret and Susan Tufts Fiske, "Social Cognition and Power: Some Cognitive Consequences of Social Structure as a Source of Control Deprivation," in Gifford Weary, Faith Gleicher, and Kerry Marsh, eds., *Control Motivation and Social Cognition*, 176, New York: Springer, 1993.

57 Susan Tufts Fiske, "Interpersonal Stratification: Status, Power, and Subordination," in Susan Tufts Fiske, Daniel Todd Gilbert, and Gardner Lindzey, eds., *Handbook of Social Psychology*, 5th edn, 941–82, New York: Wiley, 2010.

58 Adam Daniel Galinsky, Deborah H. Gruenfeld, and Joe C Magee, "From Power to Action," *Journal of Personality and Social Psychology* 85 (2003): 453–66.

59 John C. Georgesen and Monica J. Harris, "The Balance of Power: Interpersonal Consequences of Differential Power and Expectancies," *Personality and Social Psychology Bulletin* 26 (2000): 1239–57.

60 Deborah H. Gruenfeld, M. Ena Inesi, Joe C. Magee, and A. D. Galinsky, "Power and the Objectification of Social Targets," *Journal of Personality and Social Psychology* 95 (2008): 111–27.

61 Peter Burke and Roy Porter, *The Social History of Language*, Cambridge: Cambridge University Press, 1987.
62 Herrlee Glessner Creel, *Shen Pu-Hai: A Chinese Political Philosopher of the Fourth Century B.C.*, Chicago: University of Chicago Press, 1974.
63 Janet Brennan Croft, "Noms de Guerre: The Power of Naming in War and Conflict in Middle-earth," *Mythlore* 34, no. 1 (2015): 105.
64 Anagnost, "The Politicized Body," 133–4.
65 Confucius, Book XIII: Zi-Lu 名不正则言不顺，言不顺则事不成. ('If names be not correct, language is not in accordance with the truth of things. If language be not in accordance with the truth of things, affairs cannot be carried on to success'), *Confucian Analects* (James Legge, 1893).
66 Jenny Edkins, "Missing Migrants and the Politics of Naming: Names Without Bodies, Bodies Without Names," *Social Research* 83, no. 2 (2016): 359–89.
67 Raymond Boyd and Richard Fardon, "Naming Powers: Hausa Tsafi and Tiv Tsav," *Journal of African Cultural Studies* 26, no. 1 (2014): 33–55.
68 Hayes-Brady, "I Kept Saying Her Name," 3–4.
69 Hayes-Brady, "I Kept Saying Her Name," 5.
70 Susan Debra Blum, "Naming Practices and the Power of Words in China," *Language in Society* 26, no. 3 (1997): 358.
71 Justina Cheang, "Choice of Foreign Names as a Strategy for Identity Management," *Intercultural Communication Studies* 17, no. 2 (2008): 197–202.
72 Peter Sercombe, Tony Young, Ming Dong, and Lin Lin, "The Adoption of Non-heritage Names Among Chinese Mainlanders," *Names: A Journal of Onomastics* 62, no. 2 (2014): 65–75.
73 Hao Wang and Mingfa Yao, "The Discursive Construction of English Naming Practice in Mainland China: A Nationalism and Authenticity Perspective," *English Today* 34, no. 2 (2018): 39–45.
74 Wided Batat, *The New Luxury Experience: Creating the Ultimate Customer Experience*, New York: Springer, 2019, vii.
75 The score is calculated using the weighted grading method.
76 The number of fans on Weibo, a Chinese social website equivalent to Facebook, is often seen as the first reference in media reports about Wang and Li. Wang Yibo has more than 39 million followers and Li Xian has around 23 million fans.
77 The purpose of the question is to seek opinions from the perspective of fans in terms of what aspects can be considered as signs of the "success" of their idols in celebrity endorsement, rather than quantify "success."
78 Estee Lauder was established in 1946 and entered the China market in 1993, which is longer and earlier than Shu Uemura, which was established in 1967 and set up business in China in 2004.

79 "Si and Hei: Reviling the Professional Industry of 'Fan Cycle Culture,'" *Fortnightly Talk*, January 10, 2020, Xinhua News Agency (Commissioned by the Propaganda Department of the Central Committee of the Communist Party of China), http://www.banyuetan.org/jrt/detail/20200110/1000200033134991578617474855451762_1.html.

80 "Notice on Launching the Special Rectification of the Network Environment for Minors in the Summer of 2020 'Qinglang,'" July 13, 2020, *Cyberspace Administration of China*, http://www.cac.gov.cn/2020-07/13/c_1596175859026231.htm.

81 "Notice on Jointly Carrying Out Special Governance Actions on the Internet Environment of Minors," August 26, 2020, *Xin Hua Web*, Ministry of Education of the People's Republic of China, National Press and Publication Administration, Cyberspace Administration of China, Ministry of Industry and Information Technology of the People's Republic of China, The Ministry of Public Security of the People's Republic of China, and State Administration for Market Regulation, http://education.news.cn/2020-08/26/c_1210771294.htm?baike.

82 "Notice on Further Strengthening the Control of Chaos in the Fan Culture," August 27, 2021, *Cyberspace Administration of China*, http://www.cac.gov.cn/2021-08/26/c_1631563902354584.htm.

83 Apart from the nicknames listed in the three categories, there are additions that can neither be fitted in, nor in which any pattern can be found, such as 老肖夏之光，军艺校草，白牡丹，来踏火盆，王一波，王耶啵，一啵，随风，博子，一博，易公子，千玺易公子，土豆，摩托车男孩，博君一笑，博君一肖. Presumably, the nicknames are quite private and relate to the respondents' own experiences.

84 Bruce Mannheim and Dennis Tedlock, "Introduction," in Dennis Tedlock and Bruce Mannheim, eds., *The Dialogic Emergence of Culture*, 8, Urbana: University of Illinois Press, 1995.

85 Including ones with the same meaning but written in different Chinese characters which happens in the case of local dialogue.

86 Ben Caplan, "Millian Descriptivism," *Philosophical Studies* 133 (2007): 182, https://doi.org/10.1007/s11098-005-4544-y.

87 George Lakoff and Mark Johnson, *Metaphors We Live By*, Chicago and London: University of Chicago Press 1980, 125, original italics.

3 Idol Case Study—Wang Yibo, Aloof White Peony of Luoyang: Subverting Celebrity Styling

1 Technically, Wang Yibo's rank on the program was that of Assistant Host. This is an important distinction in China, as full-fledged television hosts are required to take and pass a state-run exam.

2 Wang had to leave his position as a host on the show in October 2021 due to renewed enforcement of education and licensure requirements for television presenters by the government of China.

3 Often translated as "No Sense" or "No Feelings." The song marks Wang Yibo's first songwriting credit.

4 38JieJie, "Wang Yibo Closes Out 2020 with Record Breaking Single, 'The Rules of My World,'" 38jiejie.com, https://38jiejie.com/2020/12/30/wang-yibo-closes-out-2020-with-record-breaking-single-the-rules-of-my-world/.

5 Wang Yibo was with Nike until March 25, 2021. See the section on "Xinjiang cotton and Nike" later in this chapter for detailed analysis of the controversy that led Wang and Nike to split.

6 As of April 11, 2021. Owned by Chinese company Anta Sports, FILA is considered a patriotic brand within China because of their continued use of Xinjiang cotton. See "Multi-Brand Strategy," *Anta Sports*, https://ir.anta.com/en/brand.php.

7 Goldman Sachs, "Greater China Consumer Corporate Day Takeaways," June 2021, reproduced on "[王一博][分享]210615 世界顶级投行高盛研究报告谈及安踏被专业人士认可的王一博影响力," idol001.com, June 15, 2021, https://idol001.com/news/6821/detail/60c852e317f2509b3b8b4672/.

8 Nietzsche, qtd. in Susan Sontag, *On Photography*, New York: Farrar, Straus and Giroux, 1977, 184.

9 Lauren Teixeira, "K-Pop's Big China Problem," Foreignpolicy.com, July 30, 2019, https://foreignpolicy.com/2019/07/30/k-pops-big-china-problem/.

10 In a 2014 paper published in the *Proceedings of the Royal Society*, Zhou Shi Liang et al. wrote, "Cultivated tree peonies, collectively named *Paeonia suffruticosa* Andrews, were recorded in cultivation in China 1400 years ago. Because of their beauty and fragrance, cultivated tree peonies were crowned the 'king of flowers' in the Chinese Tang Dynasty, symbolizing happiness, richness and prosperity. In the Song Dynasty, nearly 203 peony cultivars were described. They are now popular in temperate gardens, and China alone has more than 1000 modern cultivars."

11 Zhou Shiliang; Zou Xinhui; Zhou Zhiqin; Liu Jing; Xu Chao; Yu Jing; Wang Qiang; Zhang Daming; Wang Xiaoquan; Ge Song; Sang Tao; Pan Kaiyu; Hong Deyuan, "Multiple Species of Wild Tree Peonies Gave Rise to the 'King of Flowers,' Paeonia suffruticosa Andrews," *Proceedings of the Royal Society* 281 (1797): 2014.

12 The stream is archived on YouTube at https://www.youtube.com/watch?v=l0oHCWXf6iA.

13 Schopenhauer, qtd. in Sontag, *On Photography*, 183–4.

14 The video may be watched with English-language subtitles at https://www.youtube.com/watch?v=zyaY5FndadA.

15 <DESIGNER: add page cross-reference here.>

16 Sara Liao, *Fashioning China: Precarious Creativity and Women Designers in Shanzhai Culture*, London: Pluto Press, 2020, 100.
17 To see Wang Yibo in these various looks, see Sekiko, "Wang Yibo's Celine Outfits Collection," https://www.youtube.com/watch?v=g8W8jS8KdBU.
18 Trigger warning: some of the comments in the birthday livestream are highly offensive and difficult to read in the context of the situation. Viewer discretion is advised.
19 Andrew Denning, *Skiing Into Modernity*, Berkeley: University of California Press, 2015, 84.
20 Denning, *Skiing Into Modernity*.
21 Siu Wang-Ngai, *Chinese Opera: The Actor's Craft*, Hong Kong: Hong Kong University Press, 2014, 24.
22 Celeste Rain Johnson, "Enemy Officer Defeated: The Dynasty Warriors Series within the Spheres of Three Kingdoms and Videogames," Masters' thesis, University of Virginia, 2020, 23–4.
23 Rain Johnson, "Enemy Officer Defeated."
24 YIZHAN-BJYX-CQL-MDZS, "Xiao Zhan's 'Venus' is Wang Yibo | The Untamed x Harper's Bazaar China Photoshoot BTS | 王一博 肖战," YouTube, https://www.youtube.com/watch?v=YgvUiDC2aq0.
25 Walter Benjamin, "The Work of Art in the Age of Mechanical Reproduction," in *Commerce and Culture: From Pre-Industrial Art to Post-Industrial Value*, London: Penshurst Press Limited, 1989, 36.
26 As of July 6, 2020.
27 To see Wang Yibo in these various looks, see Sekiko, "Wang Yibo: How could this guy look so fine in Chanel?", https://www.youtube.com/watch?v=B0TePQr_j_0.
28 Michel Pastoureau, *Blue: The History of a Color*, Princeton, NJ: Princeton University Press, 2001, 169.
29 Pastoureau, *Blue*, 175.
30 Pastoureau, *Blue*.
31 Laetitia Cénac, *Chanel: The Making of a Collection*, New York: Abrams, 2019, 238.
32 Casey Hall, "How China's New Love Affair with Perfume is Changing the Market," *Business of Fashion*, May 18, 2021, https://www.businessoffashion.com/briefings/china/how-chinas-new-love-affair-with-perfume-is-changing-the-market.
33 Hall, "How China's New Love Affair with Perfume is Changing the Market."
34 Wang Yibo Official Weibo.
35 Cénac, *Chanel*, 238.
36 *Chanel Magazine* 17 (2017): 70–1.
37 Chanel Magazine 17 (2017): 43.
38 Cénac, *Chanel*, 50.
39 Some key lines in English are: "That Great Wall is like the dawning of a dream after five thousand years of silence" / "I unseal heaven and earth, pull all the water out of

the Yangtze River" / "The people of the ancient riverbeds are transforming!" / "Return to the primeval. Go conquer! Go take control!" / "My right fist opens the heavens! Transform into the dragon!"—Jay Chou and Vincent Fang, "Dragon Fist."

40 For example, see "Wang Yibo | Dragon Fist Edits," YouTube, May 11, 2021, https://www.youtube.com/watch?v=UR20qbWWvL0.

41 L'Oréal 2019 Asia Pacific Annual Report, https://www.loreal-finance.com/en/annual-report-2019/loreal-worldwide-2-3-0/asia-pacific-2-3-3/.

42 Since 2017, Zhou Yixuan's career has made something of a comeback, with appearances on *The Rap of China* and performances at the 2020 Sohu Fashion Awards and in the thirty-year-olds plus idols supergroup Up7, along with the likes of Jamson, Owodog and Kido, and solo singles "Do Back," "Girl, Girl, Girl," "Remember That Day When We," and the aforementioned (in the Introduction to this book) "Ice Cream (My Girlfriend)." His recent acting credits include starring opposite Betty Wu in the film *Marna* (2018), *Boys to Men*, a youth fencing drama (2019), and historical costume drama *The Origin of Love* (2020).

43 Li Wenhan's career has also rebounded since 2017, and as of July 2021, he has appeared on the reality competition series *Youth and Melody* alongside Zhou Yixuan, released a solo single, "Darlin'," was doing work for the World Wildlife Fund as an ambassador raising awareness in China about cheetah conservation, and is brand ambassador for Pantene hair care.

44 A portion of the infomercial is available online at https://www.youtube.com/watch?v=0HolGpR9Nv0&feature=youtu.be, posted by Sarah Cheng as "The Heartbreaking Moment of UNIQ."

45 @qiaoxiaointl (QiaoXiao International), Instagram, November 1, 2021.

46 Even outside of the Singles Day shopping holiday, fan favorites from *Street Dance of China*, such as Huang Xiao, find work in fashion magazines. Huang, for example, was featured in *Nylon* China wearing Bottega Veneta and Givenchy. @HelloDanceHX, Instagram, February 21, 2021.

47 Qiao Zhi is also brand ambassador for his own line of pu'er tea.

48 @derek0426 (Ma Xialong), Instagram, October 12, 2021.

49 @Swarovski, Instagram, October 21, 2020.

50 Wenzhuo Wu, "Is Celebrity Endorsement Enough For Brands To Elevate Their China Approach?" *Jing Daily*, October 23, 2020, https://jingdaily.com/celebrity-endorsement-brands-china-approach-wang-yibo/.

51 Roland Barthes, "From Gemstones to Jewellery," *The Language of Fashion*, trans. Andy Stafford, London: Bloomsbury, 2013, 54.

52 Barthes, "From Gemstones to Jewellery," 57.

53 Barthes, "From Gemstones to Jewellery," 55.

54 @bjxyyizhan, Instagram, July 23, 2020.

55 Alison S. Cohn, "Fashion Goes Fluid," *Harper's Bazaar*, November 2020, 57.

56 @ensukkie_mrs.wangxian2, Instagram, July 19, 2021.
57 Specific Louboutin footwear worn by Wang and other idols may be found on Instagram by searching the hashtag #louboutinmoment.
58 "Versace on the Floor," Bruno Mars, 2016.
59 Chris Gayomali and Max Berlinger, "Bruno Mars Would Like You to Know: He's Had Sex," *GQ*, November 4, 2016.
60 Worldwide Versace Boutiques—Store Locator, Versace.com.
61 Worldwide Versace Boutiques—Store Locator .
62 Miles Socha, "Lessons from Fendi's Fashion Show on the Great Wall of China," *WWD*, September 24, 2020.
63 Divia Harilela, "Exclusive Interview with Balmain's Olivier Rousteing," *The D'Vine*, http://www.the-dvine.com/2012/11/exclusive-interview-with-balmains-olivier-rousteing/.
64 Haejin Choi, Sarah White, and Sam Nussey, "In Asia, nascent men's make-up market starts drawing big brands," Reuters.com, December 18, 2019, https://www.reuters.com/article/us-cosmetics-men-idUSKBN1OI20Y.
65 Laurie Chen, "The real power behind China's new trend of 'sissy men' . . . is the empowered modern woman," *South China Morning Post,* September 19, 2018, https://www.scmp.com/news/china/society/article/2163748/real-power-behind-chinas-new-trend-sissy-men-empowered-modern.
66 Dzireena Mahadzir, "5 Chinese male stars fronting beauty brands," Entertainment News—Asia One, October 24, 2019, https://www.asiaone.com/entertainment/5-chinese-male-stars-fronting-beauty-brands.
67 Xiaomeng Li, "How powerful is the female gaze? The implication of using male celebrities for promoting female cosmetics in China," *Global Media and China*, January 23, 2020.
68 Casey Hall, "China Exempts Almost All Imported Cosmetics From Animal Testing," *Business of Fashion*, March 5, 2021, https://www.businessoffashion.com/news/china/china-exempts-almost-all-imported-cosmetics-from-animal-testing.
69 Li, "How powerful is the female gaze?"
70 "Yizhan" is a name often used by shippers/turtles (fans of the pairing of Wang Yibo and Xiao Zhan) to refer to the pair. The term was actually coined by Wang himself on his *Day Day Up* program when he needed to come up with a team name for himself and Xiao for a game (Xiao was a guest on the show that day).
71 https://www.shuuemura-usa.com/.
72 https://www.sephora.com/ca/en/brand/shu-uemura.
73 Shu Uemura Instagram, June 18, 2020.
74 Lucia Pica, qtd. in Cénac, *Chanel*, 23.
75 @ShuUemura Instagram, June 10, 2021, https://www.instagram.com/shuuemura/.

76 Wang Yibo x Shu Uemura Eyeshadow Palette, https://www.youtube.com/watch?v=2sL7x2atGpo.

77 David Yi, *Pretty Boys,* Boston: Houghton Mifflin Harcourt, 2021, 230.

78 Shu Uemura, Instagram, October 6, 2020.

79 Stephan Lee, *K-Pop Confidential*, New York: Point, an Imprint of Scholastic, Inc., 2020, 203.

80 Shu Uemura Instagram, June 20, 2020.

81 Faith Xue, "Eye Makeup Tips for Asian Women," *Byrdie*, December 18, 2019, https://www.byrdie.com/makeup-tips-for-asian-women-346645.

82 Peggy Wang, "19 Awesome Eye Makeup Ideas for Asians," *Buzzfeed*, August 15, 2013, https://www.buzzfeed.com/peggy/awesome-makeup-ideas-for-asian-eyes.

83 Hana Hong, "9 Best Foundations for Asian Skin Tones," *Marie Claire*, February 5, 2020, https://www.marieclaire.com/beauty/g30627499/best-foundations-for-asian-skin/.

84 Sara Berry, "Be Our Brand: Fashion and Personalisation on the Web," in Stella Bruzzi and Pamela Church Gibson, eds., *Fashion Cultures: Theories, Explorations and Analysis*, 56–7, London: Routledge, 2000.

85 L'Oréal 2019 Asia Pacific Annual Report, https://www.loreal-finance.com/en/annual-report-2019/loreal-worldwide-2-3-0/asia-pacific-2-3-3/.

86 Richard Appignanesi and Chris Garratt, *Introducing Postmodernism*, London: Icon Books, 1999, 54–5.

87 Jacques Lacan, "The Agency of the Letter in the Unconscious, or Reason Since Freud," in Hazard Adams and Leroy Searle, eds., *Critical Theory Since 1965*, 740, Tallahassee: University of Florida Press, 1986.

88 Lacan, "The Agency of the Letter in the Unconscious," 741.

89 Although readers who find the distinction between the genders to be arbitrary will likely disagree, a consequence that Lacan certainly did not intend in employing this example.

90 Jacques Derrida, "Of Grammatology," in Hazard Adams and Leroy Searle, eds., *Critical Theory Since 1965*, 97, Tallahassee: University of Florida Press, 1986.

91 Mary Bergstrom, *All Eyes East: Lessons from the Front Lines of Marketing to China's Youth*, Basingstoke: Palgrave Macmillan, 2012, 41.

92 Chen Xi, "Hashtag Lay Zhang's agency recruits third gender trainees trends on Chinese social media," *Global Times*, March 16, 2021, https://www.globaltimes.cn/page/202103/1218521.shtml.

93 Dong-Yeun Lee, "Who's afraid of Korean idols? Five keywords for understanding Korean idol pop," in *Made in Korea*, ch. 14, New York: Routledge, 2016.

94 Adapted from Stephan Lee, *K-Pop Confidential*, New York: Point, an Imprint of Scholastic, Inc., 2020, 82, 94–5.

95 Audrey Yeung, qtd. in Amalissa Hall, "Top 10: If you could swap lives with someone for a day, who would you choose and what would you do?," *South China Morning*

Post, January 26, 2021, https://www.scmp.com/yp/discover/your-voice/article/3119309/top-10-if-you-could-swap-lives-someone-day-who-would-you.

4 Capitalizing Yaoi/Danmei Fans: Fashion Brands and Male Popular Culture Idols as Brand Ambassadors in the Chinese Fashion Market

1 Patrick Galbraith, "Moe: Exploring Virtual Potential in Post-Millennial Japan," *Electronic Journal of Contemporary Japanese Studies* (2009).

2 Kazumi Nagaike, "Perverse Sexualities, Perversive Desires: Representations of Female Fantasies and Yaoi Manga as Pornography Directed at Women," *U.S.-Japan Women's Journal* 25 (2003): 76–103.

3 Mark McLelland, *Male Homosexuality in Modern Japan: Cultural Myths and Social Realities*, Abingdon: Routledge Curzon, 2000.

4 Kazumi Nagaike, "Do Heterosexual Men Dream of Homosexual Men? BL *Fudanshi* and Discourse on Male Feminization," in Mark McLelland, Kazumi Nagaike, Katsuhiko Suganuma, and James Welker, eds., *Boys Love Manga and Beyond: History, Culture, and Community in Japan*, 189–209, Jackson: University Press of Mississippi, 2015; Akiko Mizoguchi, "Male–male Romance by and for Women in Japan: A History and the Subgenres of Yaoi Fictions," *U.S.-Japan Women's Journal* 25 (2003): 49–75; James Welker, "Lilies of the Margin: Beautiful Boys and Queer Female Identities in Japan," in Fran Martin, Peter A. Jackson, Mark McLelland, and Audrey Yue, eds., *AsiapacifiQUEER: Rethinking Genders and Sexualities*, 46–66, Chicago: University of Illinois Press, 2008.

5 Andrea Wood, "'Straight' Women, Queer Texts: Boy-Love Manga and the Rise of a Global Counterpublic," *Women's Studies Quarterly* 34, nos. 1–2 (2006): 394–414.

6 Dru Pagliassotti, "Reading Boys' Love in the West," *Participations* 5, no. 2 (2008); A. Levi, "North American Reactions to Yaoi," in Mark I. West, ed., *The Japanification of Children's Popular Culture: From Godzilla to Miyazaki*, 147–174, Lanham, MD: Scarecrow Press, 2009.

7 Aleardo Zanghellini, "Underage Sex and Romance in Japanese Homoerotic Manga and Anime," *Social & Legal Studies* 18 (2009): 159–77; Mark McLelland, "Thought Policing or the Protection of Youth? Debate in Japan over the 'Non-Existent Youth Bill,'" *International Journal of Comic Art* 13, no. 1 (2011): 348–67.

8 Aleardo Zanghellini, "'Boys Love' in Anime and Manga: Japanese Subcultural Production and Its End Users," *Continuum: Journal of Media & Cultural Studies* 23, no. 3 (2009): 279–94.

9 Mark McLelland, "The World of Yaoi: The Internet, Censorship and the Global 'Boys' Love' Fandom," *Australian Feminist Law Journal* 23 (2005): 61–77.

10 Alvin K. Wong, "Towards a Queer Affective Economy of Boys' Love in Contemporary Chinese Media," *Continuum* 34, no. 4 (2020): 500–13.

11 James Welker, "A Brief History of Shōnen'ai, Yaoi, and Boys Love," in Mark McLelland, Kazumi Nagaike, Katsuhiko Suganuma, and James Welker, eds., *Boys Love Manga and Beyond: History, Culture, and Community in Japan*, 47, Jackson: University Press of Mississippi, 2015.

12 James Welker, "Beautiful, Borrowed, and Bent: 'Boys' Love' as Girls' Love in Shôjo Manga," *Signs: Journal of Women in Culture and Society* 31, no. 3 (2006): 841–70.

13 Rachel Thorn, "Girls And Women Getting Out Of Hand: The Pleasure And Politics Of Japan's Amateur Comics Community," in William W. Kelly, ed., *Fanning the Flames: Fans and Consumer Culture in Contemporary Japan*, 170, Albany: State University of New York Press, 2004.

14 Other comparable terms commonly used in Japanese society include Douginshi, Fanzine, and Tanbi, for example.

15 Welker, "A Brief History"; Kazuko Suzuki, "What can We Learn from Japanese Professional BL Writers? A Sociological Analysis of Yaoi/BL Terminology and Classifications," in Mark McLelland, Kazumi Nagaike, Katsuhiko Suganuma, and James Welker, eds., *Boys Love Manga and Beyond: History, Culture, and Community in Japan*, 93–118, Jackson: University Press of Mississippi, 2015; Kazumi Nagaike, "Perverse Sexualities, Perversive Desires: Representations of Female Fantasies and Yaoi Manga as Pornography Directed at Women," *U.S.-Japan Women's Journal* 25 (2003): 76–103; Tomoko Aoyama, "Queering the Cooking Man: Food and Gender in Yoshinaga Fumi's (BL) Manga," in Mark McLelland, Kazumi Nagaike, Katsuhiko Suganuma, and James Welker, eds., *Boys Love Manga and Beyond: History, Culture, and Community in* Japan, 233–52, Jackson: University Press of Mississippi, 2015.

16 Suzuki, "What can We Learn from Japanese Professional BL Writers?" 109.

17 Chunyu Zhang, "Loving Boys Twice as Much: Chinese Women's Paradoxical Fandom of 'Boy's Love' Fiction," *Women's Studies in Communication* 39, no. 3 (2016): 249–67. The phrase "alternative masculinity" is not specific to BL studies, but used in referring to other masculinities beyond the dominant hegemonic masculinity in traditional Japanese society. For further reading, see Emma E. Cook, "Masculinity Studies in Japan," in Jennifer Coates, Lucy Fraser, and Mark Pendleton, eds., *The Routledge Companion to Gender and Japanese Culture*, 50–9, London: Routledge, 2019.

18 Zanghellini, "'Boys Love' in Anime and Manga," 289.

19 Romit Dasgupta, "Creating Corporate Warriors: The 'Salaryman' and Masculinity in Japan," in Kam Louie and Morris Low, eds., *Asian Masculinities: The Meaning and Practice of Manhood in China and Japan*, 118, London: Routledge, 2003.

20 Raewyn Connell, *Gender and Power*, Stanford, CA: Stanford University Press, 1987; Raewyn Connell, "Masculinities and Globalisation," *Men and Masculinities* 1, no. 1

(1988): 3–23; Raewyn Connell, *Masculinities*, 2nd edn, Berkeley: University of California Press, 1995/2005.

21 Michael S. Kimmel, Jeff Hearn, and Reawyn Connell, eds, *Handbook of Studies on Men and Masculinities*, Thousand Oaks, CA, London, and New Dehli: Sage, 2005; Michael Flood, ed., *International Encyclopedia of Men and Masculinities*, London: Routledge, 2007; Sabine Frühstück and Anne Walthall, eds., *Recreating Japanese Men*, Berkeley: University of California Press, 2011; James W. Messerschmidt, "Engendering Gendered Knowledge: Assessing the Academic Appropriation of Hegemonic Masculinity," *Men and Masculinities* 15, no. 1 (2012): 56–76.

22 Connell, "Masculinities and Globalisation," 12.

23 Lucy Glasspool, "From Boys Next Door to Boys' Love: Gender Performance in Japanese Male Idol Media," in Patrick W. Galbraith and Jason G. Karlin, eds., *Idols and Celebrity in Japanese Media Culture*, 117, London: Palgrave Macmillan, 2013.

24 Uli Meyer, "Hidden in Straight Sight: Transgressing Gender and Sexuality Via BL," in A. Levi, Mark McHarry, and Dru Pagliassotti, eds., *Boys' Love Manga: Essays on the Sexual Ambiguity and Cross-cultural Fandom of the Genre*, 236, Jefferson, NY: McFarland, 2010.

25 Wim Lunsing, *Beyond Common Sense: Sexuality and Gender in Contemporary Japan*, London: Kegan Paul, 2001, 321.

26 Gregory M. Pflugfelder, *Cartographies of Desire: Male-Male Sexuality in Japanese Discourse, 1600–1950*, Oakland: University of California Press, 2007, 228.

27 Celia Rose Langford, "Queered Time on the Page: The Micro-level Revolution of the Bishōnen in 21st Century Yaoi Manga," Honors thesis submission in Asian and Middle Eastern Studies, Whitman College, 2019.

28 Langford, "Queered Time on the Page," 11

29 Langford, "Queered Time on the Page," 12 (original italics).

30 Jonathan D. Mackintosh, "Itō Bungaku and the Solidarity of the Rose Tribes [Barazoku]: Stirrings of Homo Solidarity in Early 1970s Japan," *Intersections: Gender, History and Culture in the Asian Context* 12 (2006).

31 Welker, "Beautiful, Borrowed, and Bent," 852.

32 Welker, "Beautiful, Borrowed, and Bent," 842.

33 Glasspool, "From Boys Next Door to Boys' Love," 119.

34 Laura Miller and Carolyn S. Stevens, "From Beautiful to Cute: Shifting Meanings in Japanese Language and Culture," *International Journal of Language and Culture* 8, no. 1 (2021): 62.

35 Welker, "Beautiful, Borrowed, and Bent," 855.

36 Glasspool, "From Boys Next Door to Boys' Love," 120. It is acknowledged rich intellectual work has been done in gender and queer theories over the past several decades that complicate understandings of representational politics and how representations work, including appreciation of the aesthetic of alternative

masculinity as a way of exploring sexuality and gender inequality; however, this is not the focus of the chapter.

37 Anne Kustritz, "Slashing the Romance Narrative," *Journal of American Culture* 26 (2003): 371–84.

38 Pagliassotti, "Reading Boys' Love in the West," 2008.

39 Simon Turner, "Interdisciplinary Approaches to Yaoi Manga: A Review," *Journal of Graphic Novels and Comics* 9, no. 5 (2018): 469.

40 Björn-Ole Kamm, "Rotten Use Patterns: What Entertainment Theories Can Do for the Study of Boys' Love," *Transformative Works and Cultures* 12 (2013).

41 Pagliassotti, "Reading Boys' Love in the West," 2008.

42 Agnes Zsila, Dru Pagliassotti, Robert Urban, Gabor Orosz, Orsolya Kiraly, and Zsolt Demetrovics, "Loving the Love of Boys: Motives for Consuming Yaoi Media," *PLoS One* 13, no. 6 (2018), e0198895, https://doi.org/10.1371/journal.pone.0198895.

43 "AO3 Census Masterpost," https://archiveofourown.org/works/17019228.

44 Anna Madill and Yao Zhao, "Engagement with Female-oriented Male–Male Incest Erotica: A Comparison of Sinophone and Anglophone Boys' Love Fandom," *Deviant Behavior* (2021): 1–2, https://doi.org/10.1080/01639625.2021.1891845.

45 Turner, "Interdisciplinary Approaches to Yaoi Manga," 469.

46 Wim Lunsing, "Yaoi Ronso: Discussing Depictions of Male Homosexuality in Japanese Girl's Comics, Gay Comics and Gay Pornography," *Intersections: Gender, History and Culture in the Asian Context* (2006).

47 Akiko Mizoguchi, "Theorizing Comics/Manga Genre as a Productive Forum: Yaoi and Beyond," in Jaqueline Berndt, ed., *Comics Worlds and the World of Comics: Towards Scholarship on a Global Scale*, 143–68, Kyoto: International Manga Research Center, 2010.

48 Thomas Baudinette, "Japanese Gay Men's Attitudes Towards 'Gay Manga' and the Problem of Genre," *East Asian Journal of Popular Culture* 3, no. 1 (2017): 59–72.

49 Mark McLelland, "Why are Japanese Comics Full of Boys Bonking?" *Refractory: A Journal of Entertainment Media* 10 (2006/2007).

50 Fran Martin, "Girls Who Love Boy's Love: Japanese Homoerotic Manga as Transnational Taiwan Culture," *Inter-Asia Cultural Studies* 13, no. 3 (2012): 365–83.

51 Zhang, "Loving Boys Twice as Much," 254.

52 Lunsing, "Yaoi Ronso."

53 Kristine Michelle L. Santos, "The Bitches of Boys Love Comics: The Pornographic Response of Japan's Rotten Women," *Porn Studies* 7, no. 3 (2020): 282, https://doi.org/10.1080/23268743.2020.1726204.

54 Martin, "Girls Who Love Boy's Love," 368.

55 Martin, "Girls Who Love Boy's Love," 370.

56 McLelland, "The World of Yaoi."

57 Welker, "Beautiful, Borrowed, and Bent," 841.

58 Dru Pagliassotti, Kazumi Nagaike, and Mark McHarry, "Editorial: Boys' Love Manga Special Section," *Journal of Graphic Novels and Comics* 4, no. 1 (2013): 4.
59 Zanghellini, "'Boys Love' in Anime and Manga," 287.
60 Pagliassotti, Nagaike, and McHarry, "Editorial," 1.
61 Kathryn Hemmann, "Queering the Media Mix: The Female Gaze in Japanese Fan Comics," *Transformative Works and Cultures* 20 (2015).
62 Tan Bee Kee, "Rewriting Gender and Sexuality in English-language Yaoi Fandom," in A. Levi, Mark McHarry, and Dru Pagliassotti, eds., *Boys' Love Manga: Essays on the Sexual Ambiguity and Cross-cultural Fandom of the Genre*, 140, Jefferson, NY: McFarland, 2010.
63 Clay Calvert, *Voyeur Nation: Media, Privacy, and Peeping in Modern Culture*, Boulder, CO: Westview Press, 2000.
64 Jonathan Michel Metzl, "Voyeur Nation? Changing Definitions of Voyeurism, 1950–2004," *Harvard Review Psychiatry* 12 (2004): 127–31.
65 Metzl, "Voyeur Nation?" 130.
66 Zhang, "Loving Boys Twice as Much," 255.
67 Wong, "Towards a Queer Affective Economy," 500–13.
68 Kaibin Xu and Yan Tan, "The Chinese Female Spectatorship: A Study of the Network Community of the 'Boys Love' Movie 'Call Me by Your Name,'" *Feminist Media Studies* (2019), https://doi.org/10.1080/14680777.2019.1597752.
69 Ting Liu, "Conflicting Discourses on Boys' Love and Subcultural Tactics in Mainland China and Hong Kong," *Intersections: Gender and Sexuality in Asia and the Pacific* 20 (2009), http://intersections.anu.edu.au/issue20/liu.htm.
70 Jin Feng, "Addicted to Beauty: Consuming and Producing Web-Based Chinese Danmei Fiction at Jinjiang," *Modern Chinese Literature and Culture* 212 (2009): 1–41.
71 Yanrui Xu and Ling Yang, "Forbidden Love: Incest, Generational Conflict, and the Erotics of Power in Chinese BL Fiction," *Journal of Graphic Novels and Comics* 4, no. 1 (2013): 30–43.
72 Erika Junhui Yi, "Reflection on Chinese Boys' Love Fans: An Insider's View," *Transformative Works and Culture* 12 (2013), http://dx.doi.org/10.3983/twc.2013.
73 Madill and Zhao, "Engagement with Female-oriented Male–Male Incest Erotica."
74 Madill and Zhao, "Engagement with Female-oriented Male–Male Incest Erotica," 2.
75 Eve Ng and Xiaomeng Li, "A Queer 'Socialist Brotherhood': The Guardian Web Series, Boys' Love Fandom, and the Chinese State," *Feminist Media Studies* 20, no. 4 (2020): 484.
76 John Wei, "Queer Encounters Between Iron Man and Chinese Boys' Love Fandom." *Transformative Works and Cultures* 17 (2014).
77 Zhang, "Loving Boys Twice as Much," 261.
78 https://www.lucifer-club.com/login.php.
79 http://www.jjwxc.net/.

80 Xu and Yang, "Forbidden Love." The danmei section on Jinjiang has been renamed as "pure love/non couple" (純愛/無 cp). This title is irrelevant to danmei content in order to lower the profile of the website and thus avoid attracting unnecessary attention from the mainstream.

81 https://weibo.com/p/100808018738932824814924fedacaa8880454/super_index.

82 https://www.quotev.com/stories/博君一肖?lid=31.

83 https://www.jjwxc.net/search.php?kw=%B2%A9%BE%FD%D2%BB%D0%A4&t=1.

84 Elizabeth Miles, "Porn as Practice, Porn as Access: Pornography Consumption and a 'Third Sexual Orientation' in Japan," *Porn Studies* 7, no. 3 (2020): 274, https://doi.org/10.1080/23268743.2020.1726205.

85 Zanghellini, "'Boys Love' in Anime and Manga," 291.

86 Andrea Wood, "Boy's Love anime and queer desires in convergence culture: transnational fandom, censorship and resistance," *Journal of Graphic Novels and Comics* 4, no. 1 (2013): 44–63 (46).

87 In comparison with RPS (Real Person Slash).

88 AO3 calls it the "wrangled tagging structure."

89 A1, WeChat message to authors, October 3, 2020.

90 Celia Lury, *Brands: The Logos of the Global Economy*, London: Routledge, 2004.

91 Adam Arvidsson, "Brands: A Critical Perspective," *Journal of Consumer Culture* 5, no. 2 (2005): 235–58.

92 Sarah Banet-Weiser, *Authentic: The Politics of Ambivalence in a Brand Culture*, New York: New York University Press, 2012, 4 (original italics).

93 Grant McCracken, "Culture and Consumption: A Theoretical Account of the Structure and Movement of Cultural Meaning of Consumer Goods," *Journal of Consumer Research* 13, no. 1 (1986): 71–84.

94 Bernard Cova and Véronique Cova, "Tribal Marketing: The Tribalisation of Society and its impact on the conduct of Marketing," *European Journal of Marketing* 36, nos. 5–6 (2002): 595–620.

95 Banet-Weiser, *Authentic*, 4.

96 The current focus is in contrast to the traditional marketing developed in response to the Industrial Revolution, which has been described as being emotionless. Bernd Herbert Schmitt, "Experiential Marketing," *Journal of Marketing Management* 15, nos. 1–3 (1999): 53–67.

97 Les Binet and Peter Field, "Marketing in the Era of Accountability," *Journal of Direct, Data and Digital Marketing Practice* 9, no. 2 (2007): 225–8; Tim Jackson and David Shaw, *Mastering Fashion Marketing*, Basingstoke: Palgrave Macmillan, 2009; Bertil Hultén, "Sensory Marketing: The Multi-sensory Brand Experience Concept," *European Business Review* 23, no. 3 (2011): 256–73.

98 Peng Liu and Lan Lan, "Constructing an Affective Retail Space: Bodily Engagement with a Luxury Fashion Brand Through Spatial and Heritage Storytelling," in Amanda Grace Sikarskie, ed., *Storytelling in Luxury Fashion Marketing: Visual Culture and Digital Technology*), 157–73, New York and London: Routledge, 2020.

99 Shaz Smilansky, *Experiential Marketing: A Practical Guide to Interactive Brand Experiences*, Philadelphia: Kogan Page, 2009, 2.

100 Smilansky, *Experiential Marketing*, 140.

101 Grant McCracken, "Who Is the Celebrity Endorser? Cultural Foundations of the Endorsement Process," *Journal of Consumer Research* 16, no. 3 (1989): 310–21. Nevertheless, Diana Seno and Bryan A. Lukas have found that celebrity endorsement is the most effective way of promoting sales compared to other categories of endorsers such as professional experts and atypical consumers. Diana Seno and Bryan A. Lukas, "The Equity Effect of Product Endorsement by Celebrities: A Conceptual Framework from a Co-branding Perspective," *European Journal of Marketing* 41, nos. 1–2 (2007): 121–34.

102 Guillaume Dumont, "Creativity at Work: The Production of Work for Sale by Brand Ambassadors," *Journal of Cultural Economy* 11, no. 1 (2018): 69.

103 Laure Ambroise, Gaëlle Pantin-Sohier, Pierre Valette Florence, and Noel Albert, "From Endorsement to Celebrity Co-branding: Personality Transfer," *Journal of Brand Management* 21, no. 4 (2014): 273–85.

104 Bayram Zafer Erdogan, Michael James Baker, and Stephen Tagg, "Selecting Celebrity Endorsers: The Practitioner's Perspective," *Journal of Advertising Research* 3, no. 41 (2001): 39–48; Angela Carroll, "Brand Communications in Fashion Categories Using Celebrity Endorsement," *Journal of Brand Management* 17 (October–November 2009): 146–58; Dan Hamilton Rice, Katie Kelting, and Richard J. Lutz, "Multiple Endorsers and Multiple Endorsements: The Influence of Message Repetition, Source Congruence and Involvement on Brand Attitudes," *Journal of Consumer Psychology* 22, no. 2 (2011): 249–59; Jasmina Ilicic and Marie Webster, "Celebrity Co-branding Partners as Irrelevant Brand Information in Advertisements," *Journal of Business Research* 66, no. 7 (2013): 941–7.

105 Ambroise et al., "From Endorsement to Celebrity Co-branding: Personality Transfer," 274.

106 Matthew Thomson, "Human Brands: Investigating Antecedents to Consumers' Strong Attachments to Celebrities," *Journal of Marketing* 70, no. 3 (2006): 104–19; Diana Seno and Bryan A. Lukas, "The Equity Effect of Product Endorsement by Celebrities: A Conceptual Framework from a Co-branding Perspective," *European Journal of Marketing* 41, nos. 1–2 (2007): 121–34; Elina Halonen-Knight and Leila Hurmerinta, "Who Endorses Whom? Meaning Transfer in Celebrity Endorsement," *Journal of Product and Brand Management* 19, no. 6 (2010): 452–60.

107 Julia-Sophie Jelinek, "Art as Strategic Branding Tool for Luxury Fashion Brands," *Journal of Product and Brand Management* 27, no. 3 (2018): 295.

108 Female fans make up 70% of the total number of fans of idols labeled as "little fresh meat." "Fan economy as double edge sword," https://www.bbtnews.com.cn/2016/0831/159633.shtml.

109 The fit between the brand and the idol is embodied in this statement.

110 "Xiao Zhan for Tod's," Tod's, https://www.tods.com/ww-en/tods-world/XiaoZhanxTods.html.

111 "Tod's Wecomes Xiao Zhan as Brand Ambassador, *#legend*, https://hashtaglegend.com/fashion/tods-xiao-zhan-brand-ambassador/.

112 Wenzhuo Wu, "Tod's Leverages Idol Power in China to Boost Image," https://jingdaily.com/tods-leverages-idol-power-in-china-to-boost-image/.

113 Information on the number of fans was sourced from the idols' respective Weibo home pages.

114 Anna Madill, "The Yaoi/Boys' Love/Danmei Audience," in Karen Ross and Valentina Cardo, eds., *Encyclopaedia of Gender, Media and Communication*, 2, Hoboken, NJ: Wiley-Blackwells, 2020 (original italics).

115 Many entertainment companies refer to subcultural aesthetics when launching their own stars, and take the initiative to do what fans like, such as making references to Xiao Zhan and Wang Yibo, and using connotations about being a same-sex couple in advertising, which confirms the intention of entertainment companies to capitalize on danmei fans. https://www.thepaper.cn/newsDetail_forward_6368595.

116 Xiao Zhan had returned to being a top-end male idol a year after the AO3 event, as he became the ambassador of Gucci in October 2021, Zenith in July 2021, and Tod's in May 2021.

117 See the illustration at https://kuaibao.qq.com/s/20200304A0EOL600?refer=spider.

118 Chizuko Ueno, 厭女：日本的女性嫌惡. 翻譯：王嵐. 上海三聯書店, 2015 (*Mistry: Hate of Japanese Women*, trans. Lan Wang, Shanghai: Shanghai SDX Joint Publishing Company).

119 Casey Hall, "Toxic Fan Culture Puts Brands at Risk in China," *Business of Fashion*, March 12, 2020, https://www.businessoffashion.com/articles/intelligence/toxic-fan-culture-puts-brands-at-risk-in-china.

120 The boycotting by brands started on February 29 and also included Olay, Luckin Coffee, OPPO, Monmilk, Uni-President, Budweiser, Crest, and Vidal Sassoon.

121 Every sold product is supposed to come with a receipt at a store that the customer can use as proof of warranty entitlement for the purchased item. The receipt in some companies can be issued when the purchase is made at a store or claimed within a certain period after the products have been sold. Therefore, collective

actions requesting copies of the receipts of previously purchased items would increase the staff workload at retail shops.

122 A7, WeChat message to authors, October 3, 2020.

123 A11, WeChat message to authors, June 29, 2020.

124 A7, WeChat message to authors, June 29, 2020.

125 A8, WeChat message to authors, November 10, 2020.

126 Patrick W. Galbraith, "Fujoshi: Fantasy Play and Transgressive Intimacy Among 'Rotten Girls' in Contemporary Japan," *Signs* 37 (2011): 219–40.

127 Glasspool, "From Boys Next Door to Boys' Love," 117.

128 Glasspool, "From Boys Next Door to Boys' Love," 117.

129 Glasspool, "From Boys Next Door to Boys' Love," 119.

130 Rachel Karniol, "Adolescent Females' Idolization of Male Media Starts as a Transition Into Sexuality," *Sex Roles* 44, nos. 1-2 (2001): 72.

131 M. Jung and N. Lee, "Fandom Managing Stars, Entertainment Industry Managing Fandom," *Media, Gender and Culture* 12 (2009): 191–240.

132 http://www.nbd.com.cn/articles/2020-04-26/1428704.html.

133 https://www.jiemian.com/article/4302926_foxit.html.

134 Apart from breaking several records, such as the fastest-selling digital track in China recognized by the Guinness World Records, the music sales demonstrate the commercial value of Xiao that would in turn attract more investments in him. https://www.guinnessworldrecords.cn/world-records/616233-fastest-selling-digital-track-china.

135 Ueno, "厭女."

136 A17, WeChat message to authors, May 15, 2021.

137 Zanghellini, "'Boys Love' in Anime and Manga," 287.

138 Dru Pagliassotti, "Better than Romance? Japanese BL Manga and the Subgenre of Male/Male Romantic Fiction," in A. Levi, Mark McHarry, and Dru Pagliassotti, eds., *Boys' Love Manga: Essays on the Sexual Ambiguity and Cross-cultural Fandom of the Genre*, 59–83, Jefferson, NY: McFarland, 2010.

139 Pagliassotti, "Better than Romance?"

140 According to Jingjiang, as of July 6, 2021, there are 159 works of fiction featuring Xiao Zhan as the *seme* (penetrator) character and 214 with him as the *uke* (receiver) character; there are also seventy-six fiction works in which Xiao Zhan is both *seme* and *uke*, or swapping between the two roles.

141 A2, WeChat message to authors, October 3, 2020.

142 A15, WeChat message to authors, July 9, 2021.

143 S. Kim, "Spectacularization and Consumption of Girl Images," *Media, Gender and Culture* 15 (2010): 79–119; Yeran Kim, "Idol Republic: The Global Emergence of Girl Industries and the Commercialization of Girl Bodies," *Journal of Gender Studies* 20, no. 4 (2011): 333–45.

144 Kim, "Idol Republic," 338.

145 Idol-making in South Korea is sophisticated. Some Chinese idols were sent there for their initial training and debut, before returning to the market in Mainland China, such as Lu Han, Wu Yifan, etc.

146 Glasspool, "From Boys Next Door to Boys' Love," 120–1.

147 A5, WeChat message to author, October 3, 2020.

148 A3, WeChat message to authors, October 3, 2020.

149 Yet, in our interviews we found that younger danmei fans (A2 and A8) expressed a strong view that danmei culture should be seen as part of the mainstream culture.

150 A2, WeChat message to authors, October 3, 2020.

151 A13, phone interview with authors, May 15, 2021.

152 A10, WeChat message to authors, October 3, 2020.

153 Kam H. Louie, "Popular Culture and Masculinity Ideals in East Asia, with Special Reference to China," *The Journal of Asian Studies* 71, no. 4 (2012): 929–43.

154 Jaril Kim, Woonghee Han, DongTae Kim, and Widya Paramita, "Is Beauty in the Eye of the Beholder? Gender and Beauty in the Cosmetics Sector," *Marketing Intelligence and Planning* 31, no. 2 (2013): 127–40.

155 Xiaomeng Li, "How Powerful is the Female Gaze? The Implication of Using Male Celebrities for Promoting Female Cosmetics in China," *Global Media and China* 5, no. 1 (2020): 55.

156 A11, WeChat message to authors, October 4, 2020.

5 A Comparative Perspective: The Culture of Korean K-Pop Idols as Brand Ambassadors

1 Kim Suk-Young, "Beauty and the Waste: Fashioning Idols and the Ethics of Recycling in Korean Pop Music Videos," *Fashion Theory* 25, no. 1 (2021): 53–73, DOI: 10.1080/1362704X.2019.1581001.

2 "Idols and Endorsements: the More, the Merrier?," *SeoulBeats*, August 8, 2012, https://seoulbeats.com/2012/08/idols-and-endorsements-the-more-the-merrier/.

3 Valérie Gelézeau, "The Body, Cosmetics and Aesthetics in South Korea: The Emergence of a Field of Research" (2015): 7. halshs-01211686

4 The Korea Society, Twitter, October 8, 2020.

5 The Korea Society, Instagram, March 19, 2021.

6 "Idols and Endorsements."

7 Kim Suk-Young, "Beauty and the Waste."

8 Katie Skinner, "Big Bang's Taeyang Teases Photos Of New Fendi Collection (Ready To Spend $9K?)," *Billboard*, June 22, 2017, https://www.billboard.com/articles/news/

lifestyle/7841808/big-bangs-taeyang-teases-photos-of-new-fendi-collection-ready-to.

9 Alessandra Turra, "Giuseppe Zanotti, G-Dragon Collaborate on Footwear Capsule," *WWD*, September 3, 2015, https://wwd.com/fashion-news/fashion-scoops/giuseppe-zanotti-g-dragon-footwear-limited-edition-10210286/.

10 Alyssa Hardy, "Blackpink's Jennie and G-Dragon Wear the Same Chanel Jacket," *Teen Vogue*, June 27, 2017, https://www.teenvogue.com/story/blackpink-jennie-g-dragon-chanel-jacket?mbid=synd_msn_rss.

11 Zanotti, qtd. in Turra, "Giuseppe Zanotti, G-Dragon Collaborate on Footwear Capsule."

12 Gianlucca Russo, "K-Pop Star G-Dragon to Release Second 'Para-noise' Nike Air Force 1," *MSN*, November 6, 2020, https://www.msn.com/en-us/lifestyle/lifestyle-buzz/k-pop-star-g-dragon-to-release-second-%E2%80%9Cpara-noise%E2%80%9D-nike-air-force-1/ar-BB1aLBCj.

13 Source: https://zapzee.net/2019/12/19/celebrities-all-around-the-world-are-sporting-g-dragons-shoes/.

14 Xiao Zhan has also appeared in the Para-noise shoes, but turtles (Yizhan fans—see the Postscript) have pointed out online that these are the same custom pair as Wang Yibo's and thus are only counted as one pair of shoes in this metric.

15 Gwyneth Moore, *Fashion Promotion*, 2nd edn, London: Bloomsbury, 2021, 134.

16 Moore, *Fashion Promotion*, 134.

17 Jackson Wang is a Chinese citizen from Hong Kong, but a member of a Korean group, and is thus included here.

18 Eunice Dela Cruz, "These K-Pop Idols Are The Global and Korean Ambassadors of The Top 15 Luxury Brand Fashion Houses," *KpopStarz*, October 14, 2020, https://www.kpopstarz.com/articles/295224/20201014/these-k-pop-idols-are-the-global-and-korean-ambassadors-of-the-top-15-luxury-brand-fashion-houses.htm.

19 Gucci Instagram, February 28, 2021.

20 TFL, "Louis Vuitton is Betting Big on the Korean Market and the Global Fame of K-Pop Royalty BTS," *The Fashion Law*, April 23, 2021, https://www.thefashionlaw.com/louis-vuitton-is-betting-big-on-the-korean-market-and-the-global-fame-of-k-pop-royalty-bts/.

21 "BamBam," Kpop Wiki, https://kpop.fandom.com/wiki/BamBam#Endorsements.

22 "Idols and Endorsements."

23 Whachiraporn Boonpradub and Pusanisa Thechatakerng, "Brand Endorsement by Celebrity in Thailand: 7Ps of Marketing Mix and the Impact of Brand Alliance," *International Journal of Trade, Economics and Finance* 6, no. 1 (February 2015).

24 Boonpradub and Thechatakerng, "Brand Endorsement by Celebrity in Thailand," 11.

25 Boonpradub and Thechatakerng, "Brand Endorsement by Celebrity in Thailand," 11.

26 David Yi, *Pretty Boys*, Boston: Houghton Mifflin Harcourt, 2021, 91.

27 Yi, *Pretty Boys*, 91.
28 Annamari Vänskä, *Fashionable Childhood: Children in Advertising*, trans. Eva Malkki, London: Bloomsbury Academic, 2017, 104–5.
29 Charles Yu, *Interior Chinatown*, New York: Vintage Books, 2020, 159–60.
30 Yu, *Interior Chinatown*, 170.
31 Ishani Sarkar, "6 Idols who are the descendants of the Royal Yangban clans from the Joseon Dynasty," *Pink Villa*, December 3, 2020, https://www.pinkvilla.com/entertainment/6-idols-who-are-descendants-royal-yangban-clans-joseon-dynasty-579114.
32 Gelézeau, "The Body, Cosmetics and Aesthetics in South Korea," 8.
33 Gelézeau, "The Body, Cosmetics and Aesthetics in South Korea," 8.
34 Gelézeau, "The Body, Cosmetics and Aesthetics in South Korea," 8.
35 https://en.wikipedia.org/wiki/Queen_Myeongseong#In_popular_culture.
36 Zahna Eklund, "K-pop's LGBT star Holland: 10 facts about South Korea's first openly gay idol, born Go Tae-seob—from Neverland's R-rated music video to what his parents really think," October 16, 2020, https://www.scmp.com/magazines/style/celebrity/article/3105730/k-pops-lgbt-star-holland-10-facts-about-south-koreas.
37 Yi, *Pretty Boys*, 233.
38 Holland's Instagram, https://www.instagram.com/holland_vvv/.
39 Yi, *Pretty Boys*, 232.
40 South Korea officially became a democracy on June 29, 1987, just a year before the country hosted the 1988 Seoul Olympic Games, with the June 29 Proclamation and the establishment of the Sixth Republic.
41 Todd A. Henry, *Queer Korea*, Durham, NC: Duke University Press, 2020, 25.
42 JuanJuan Wu, *Chinese Fashion from Mao to Now*, New York: Berg, 2009, 98.
43 Wu, *Chinese Fashion from Mao to Now*, 99.
44 Wu, *Chinese Fashion from Mao to Now*, 101.
45 Wu, *Chinese Fashion from Mao to Now*, 100.
46 Zoe Suen, "Luxury's Bigger-Than-Ever K-Drama Opportunity," *Business of Fashion*, January 21, 2021, https://www.businessoffashion.com/articles/global-markets/luxurys-bigger-than-ever-k-drama-opportunity.
47 Daniel Sanchez, "China Bans All Korean Music and Entertainment," *Digital Music News*, November 29, 2016, https://www.digitalmusicnews.com/2016/11/29/china-bans-korean-hallyu-kpop/.
48 Not to be confused with Kim Sungjoo, b. 1956, the founder, Chairperson and Chief Visionary Officer of Sungjoo Group and owner of MCM, a German luxury fashion brand founded in Munich in 1976.
49 AKP Staff, "UNIQ's Sungjoo to work alongside Lee Hyun Woo and Joy in 'The Liar and His Lover,'" *All KPop*, https://www.allkpop.com/article/2017/01/uniqs-sungjoo-to-work-alongside-lee-hyun-woo-and-joy-in-the-liar-and-his-lover.

50 Friedrich Wilhelm Nietzsche, *Twilight of the Idols*, ed. Oscar Levy, London: Allen & Unwin, 1912 17, 88.
51 "Cho Seung Youn (WOODZ) Talks About New Album 'EQUAL,' Confusion Over Stage Name, And More," June 29, 2020, https://www.soompi.com/article/1409951wpp/cho-seung-youn-woodz-talks-about-new-album-equal-confusion-over-stage-name-and-more.
52 "Cho Seung Youn (WOODZ) Talks About New Album."
53 Corinna Czujack, "Picasso paintings at auction, 1963–1994," *Journal of Cultural Economics* 21, no. 3 (1997): 229–47.
54 Michel Pastoureau, *Blue: The History of a Color*, Princeton, NJ: Princeton University Press, 2001.
55 Giovanna Constantini, "Blue: The History of a Color by Michel Pastoureau (review)," *Leonardo*, January 30, 2021, muse.jhu.edu/article/781850.
56 Steffi Solano, "K-R&B Artist WOODZ Opens Up About Mental Health and Developing His Identity As a Soloist," *Status Magazine*, March 27, 2019.
57 *Allure* Korea, June 2021.
58 "SHINee singer Jonghyun's final message before suicide: 'the depression finally engulfed me entirely,'" *South China Morning Post*, December 19, 2017, https://www.scmp.com/news/asia/east-asia/article/2124871/shinee-singer-jonghyuns-final-message-suicide-becoming-famous.
59 Justin McCurry, "Spycams, sex abuse and scandal: #MeToo reaches Korean pop," *Guardian*, March 22, 2019.
60 Choe Sang-Hun and S-Hyun Lee, "Suicides by K-Pop Stars Prompt Soul-Searching in South Korea," *New York Times*, November 25, 2019.
61 Mary Dusenbury, ed., *Color in Ancient and Medieval East Asia*, Lawrence, KS: Spencer Museum of Art, University of Kansas and New Haven, CT: Yale University Press, 2015, 13.
62 Yann, "Cho Seung Youn is Out to Dominate the Modeling Industry as He Becomes the First Male Personality to Represent the Beauty Brand Cledbel!" *Hello Kpop*, March 13, 2020, https://www.hellokpop.com/news/cho-seung-youn-model-beauty-brand-cledbel/.
63 Juha Park and Jaehoon Chun, "How does watching YouTube fashion content impact perception of appearance: a phenomenological study of Korean women in Generation Z," *Humanities and Social Sciences Communications* 7, no. 1 (2020): 1–10.
64 Joanna Elfving-Hwang, "K-pop idols, artificial beauty and affective fan relationships in South Korea," in *Routledge Handbook of Celebrity Studies*, 190–201 (190), London: Routledge, 2018.
65 In Young Bae, "Chanel to Sell on KaKaoTalk," *Retail in Asia*, August 24, 2020, https://retailinasia.com/in-tech/chanel-to-sell-on-kakao-talk/.
66 https://www.mymusictaste.com/project/7d0700fad15611ea92400a58a9feac2a/detail/.
67 https://www.mymusictaste.com/project/22d00b26226511eb89e10a58a9feac2a/.

68 Pokemongolive.com, September 21, 2020.

69 Longchamp.com.

70 Martti Lahti, "As We Become Machines: Corporealized Pleasures in Video Games," In Mark J. P. Wolf and Bernard Perron, eds., *The Video Game Theory Reader*, 167, New York: Taylor & Francis, 2003.

71 Lahti, "As We Become Machines," 168.

72 Allucquère Rosanne Stone, qtd. in Lahti, "As We Become Machines," 165.

73 For a discussion of the role of NFTs in fashion in the metaverse, see Kristen Bateman's article: "The Fashion Metaverse is Here. Are You Ready?" *Town and Country*, February 28, 2022, https://www.townandcountrymag.com/style/fashion-trends/a39177878/metaverse-fashion-revolution/.

74 Pokémongolive.com, January 4, 2021.

75 It should be noted that Pokémon Go has been banned in Mainland China since 2017, although it is available in Hong Kong and Macau.

76 Lahti, "As We Become Machines," 166.

77 As of March 2020. Kim's scheduled release date from military service is September 16, 2021.

78 "K-Pop Enlistment and Discharge Dates," The K-Pop Database, Last Accessed October 22, 2020, https://dbkpop.com/db/k-pop-enlistment-and-discharge-dates

79 Ibid.

80 Kim Sung-joo, Instagram, March 8, 2020.

81 Kerry Allen, "China promotes education drive to make boys more 'manly,'" BBC News, February 4, 2021, https://www.bbc.com/news/world-asia-china-55926248.

82 Allen, "China promotes education drive to make boys more 'manly.'"

83 Allen, "China promotes education drive to make boys more 'manly.'"

84 In Korea, this aristocracy is known as the *yangban* (양반).

85 Joseph Bazil Manietta, "Transnational Masculinities: The Distributive Performativity of Gender in Korean Boy Bands," Master's thesis, University of Colorado, 2015, 7.

86 The Kerry Allen article mentions the "little fresh meats" moniker, writing, "On social media platform Sina Weibo, comments pointed towards China's male celebrities being to blame, largely those who are known as 'little fresh meats' (小鲜肉). This is a buzzword that refers to young, Chinese male icons who are seen as squeaky-clean, well-groomed, and with delicate features."

87 Zhao Ma, "China's Last War," talk given via Zoom at the Asian Studies Center, Michigan State University, March 18, 2021.

88 38jiejie, "K-Netz Canceling Deng Lun, Wang Yibo, and Other Chinese Celebs Over Reposting of 'Resist US, Help North Korea' Commemorative Post," October 27, 2020, https://38jiejie.com/2020/10/27/k-netz-canceling-deng-lun-wang-yibo-and-other-chinese-celebs-over-reposting-of-resist-us-help-north-korea-commemorative-post/.

89 Casey Hall, "How to Avoid Brand Ambassador Controversy in China," *Business of Fashion*, June 8, 2021, https://www.businessoffashion.com/briefings/china/how-to-avoid-brand-ambassador-controversy-in-china.
90 38jiejie, "K-Netz."
91 Hall, "How to Avoid Brand Ambassador Controversy in China."
92 Hall, "How to Avoid Brand Ambassador Controversy in China."
93 Reuters staff, "China Boycotts Actor After Photos of Visit to Japan's Yasukuni Shrine," Reuters.com, August 15, 2021, https://www.reuters.com/world/china/china-boycotts-actor-after-photos-visit-japans-yasukuni-shrine-2021-08-15/.
94 Gelézeau, "The Body, Cosmetics and Aesthetics in South Korea," 9.

Epilogue: Xinjiang Cotton

1 Please note that this Epilogue on Xinjiang cotton is solely the perspective of Amanda Sikarskie, and may not reflect the views of Peng Liu and Lan Lan, neither of whom contributed to this piece.
2 Alix Kroeger, "Xinjiang cotton: How do I know if it's in my jeans?" BBC News, March 27, 2021, https://www.bbc.com/news/world-asia-china-56535822.
3 Helen Davidson, "Xinjiang: more than half a million forced to pick cotton, report suggests," *Guardian*, December 15, 2020, https://www.theguardian.com/world/2020/dec/15/xinjiang-china-more-than-half-a-million-forced-to-pick-cotton-report-finds.
4 Davidson, "Xinjiang."
5 See the Uyghur Human Rights Project, https://uhrp.org/.
6 Patrick Wintour, "US and Canada follow EU and UK in sanctioning Chinese officials over Xinjiang," *Guardian*, March 22, 2021, https://www.theguardian.com/world/2021/mar/22/china-responds-to-eu-uk-sanctions-over-uighurs-human-rights.
7 Zachary Weiss, "The Non-Profit Cotton Company Used by Gucci, Prada and Dior," *Observer*, July 13, 2016, https://observer.com/2016/07/the-non-profit-cotton-company-used-by-gucci-prada-and-dior/.
8 "Le Coton—Extra Soft Cotton," *Chanel*, https://www.chanel.com/en_CA/fragrance-beauty/skincare/p/by-category/cleansers-_-makeup-removers/le-coton-extra-soft-cotton-p100100.html#.
9 Fila, whose parent company is Chinese sneaker giant Anta Sports, will continue to source cotton from Xinjiang.
10 Brenton Johns, "More Than 50 Chinese Celebrities End Brand Partnerships in Xinjiang Row," *Business of Fashion*, March 26, 2021, https://www.businessoffashion.com/news/china/more-than-50-chinese-celebrities-end-brand-partnerships-in-xinjiang-row?from=2021-03-25&to=2021-03-26.

11 "Nike Statement on Xinjiang," *Nike Purpose*, https://purpose.nike.com/statement-on-xinjiang.
12 Linda Lew "China presses global fashion brands to reverse Xinjiang cotton boycott," *South China Morning Post*, March 25, 2021, https://www.scmp.com/news/china/diplomacy/article/3126904/backlash-china-against-nike-adidas-and-other-global-brands.
13 Staff, "Over 50 Chinese stars show support for Xinjiang cotton products as H&M finds itself mired in controversy," *Global Times*, March 25, 2021, https://www.globaltimes.cn/page/202103/1219474.shtml.
14 Michael Standaert, "Nike and H&M face backlash in China over Xinjiang statements: Chinese social media condemns statements by the companies as celebrities cancel contracts with brands," *Guardian*, March 25, 2021, https://www.theguardian.com/world/2021/mar/25/nike-and-hm-face-backlash-in-china-over-xinjiang-statements.
15 Chase She, "Wang Yibo and Tan Songyun Cut Ties with Nike, Chinese Celebs Show Support for Xinjiang Cotton as More Brands Face Backlash," *DramaPanda*, March 25, 2021, https://dramapanda.com/2021/03/wang-yibo-and-tan-songyun-cut-ties-with-nike-chinese-celebs-show-support-for-xinjiang-cotton-as-more-brands-face-backlash.html.
16 Kroeger, "Xinjiang cotton."
17 All reported by Chase She for *DramaPanda*, March 25, 2021, except for Burberry.
18 "Wang Yibo appeared in Chanel, white shoes became the focus of attention!" YouTube, March 28, 2021, https://www.youtube.com/watch?v=EovembRpS7c.
19 "Le Coton—Extra Soft Cotton."
20 "Xinjiang Cotton Boycott Issue: Celebrities Busy Terminating Endorsement Contracts, Li Ning and Xiao Zhan's Collaboration Steals The Show," *Sip of Tea*, March 30, 2021, https://sipoftea.net/2021/03/30/xinjiang-cotton-boycott-issue-celebrities-are-busy-terminating-endorsement-contracts-li-ning-and-xiao-zhans-collaboration-steals-the-show/.
21 Goldman Sachs, "Greater China Consumer Corporate Day Takeaways," June 2021, reproduced on "[王一博][分享]210615 世界顶级投行高盛研究报告谈及安踏被专业人士认可的王一博影响力," idol001.com, June 15, 2021, https://idol001.com/news/6821/detail/60c852e317f2509b3b8b4672/.
22 Tianwei Zhang and Tiffany Ap, "Xinjiang Cotton: Li Ning, Anta Shares Surge While Nike, Adidas, Burberry Hit With Backlash," *WWD*, March 25, 2021, https://wwd.com/business-news/retail/xinjiang-cotton-ban-china-nike-uniqlo-hm-1234787090/.
23 Johns, "More Than 50 Chinese Celebrities End Brand Partnerships in Xinjiang Row."
24 Zoe Suen, "Why Chinese Brands Say Yes to the Dress," *Business of Fashion*, July 13, 2021, https://www.businessoffashion.com/briefings/china/why-chinese-brides-say-yes-to-the-dress.

Postscript: China Bans *Xiao Xian Rou*

1 Formerly the State Administration of Radio, Film, and Television (SARFT) until 2013.

2 Associated Press, "China Bans Effeminate Men from TV," *NPR*, September 2, 2021, https://www.npr.org/2021/09/02/1033687586/china-ban-effeminate-men-tv-official-morality.

3 Associated Press, "China Bans Effeminate Men from TV."

4 Walter Benjamin, "Theses on the Philosophy of History," 1940, https://www.sfu.ca/~andrewf/CONCEPT2.html.

Glossary

1 "Ma Xiaolong saying to put him as conflict in QiaoXiao fanfiction 馬曉龍直播有關瀟喬流水的話題," Qiaoxiao International, YouTube, November 3, 2021, https://www.youtube.com/watch?v=23WvlTvf0oA.

Bibliography

38jiejie. "K-Netz Canceling Deng Lun, Wang Yibo, and Other Chinese Celebs Over Reposting of 'Resist US, Help North Korea' Commemorative Post." October 27, 2020, https://38jiejie.com/2020/10/27/k-netz-canceling-deng-lun-wang-yibo-and-other-chinese-celebs-over-reposting-of-resist-us-help-north-korea-commemorative-post/.

Aaker, Jennifer Lynn. "Dimensions of Brand Personality." *Journal of Marketing Research* 34, no. 3 (1997): 347–56.

Achim, Adina-Laura. "How Brands Can Take Advantage of The Male Beauty Boom in China." *Jing Daily*, 2020, https://jingdaily.com/how-brands-can-take-advantage-of-the-male-beauty-boom-in-china/.

Alford, Richard D. *Naming and Identity: A Cross-cultural Study of Personal Naming Practices*. New Haven, CT: HRAF Press, 1988.

Allen, Kerry. "China promotes education drive to make boys more 'manly.'" BBC News, February 4, 2021, https://www.bbc.com/news/world-asia-china-55926248.

Ambroise, Laure, Gaëlle Pantin-Sohier, Pierre Valette Florence, and Noel Albert. "From Endorsement to Celebrity Co-branding: Personality Transfer." *Journal of Brand Management* 21, no. 4 (2014): 273–85.

Anagnost, Ann. "The Politicized Body." In Angela Zito and Tani E. Barlow, eds., *Body, Subject and Power in China*, 131–56. Chicago: University of Chicago Press, 1994.

Aoyama, Tomoko. "Queering the Cooking Man: Food and Gender in Yoshinaga Fumi's (BL) Manga." In Mark McLelland, Kazumi Nagaike, Katsuhiko Suganuma, and James Welker, eds., *Boys Love Manga and Beyond: History, Culture, and Community in Japan*, 233–52. Jackson: University Press of Mississippi, 2015.

Appignanesi, Richard and Chris Garratt. *Introducing Postmodernism*. London: Icon Books, 1999.

Arvidsson, Adam. "Brands: A Critical Perspective." *Journal of Consumer Culture* 5, no. 2 (2005): 235–58.

Atkins, Charles and Martin Block. "Effectiveness of Celebrity Endorsers." *Journal of Advertising Research* 23, no. 1 (1983): 57–61.

Azoulay, Audrey and Jean Noël Kapferer. "Do Brand Personality Scale Really Measure Brand Personality?" *Journal of Brand Management* 11, no. 2 (2003): 143–55.

Banet-Weiser, Sarah. *Authentic: The Politics of Ambivalence in a Brand Culture*. New York: New York University Press, 2012.

Barthes, Roland. "From Gemstones to Jewellery." *The Language of Fashion*. Translated by Andy Stafford. London: 2013, Bloomsbury.

Batat, Wided. *The New Luxury Experience: Creating the Ultimate Customer Experience*. New York: Springer, 2019.

Bateman, Kristen. "I Attended Helsinki Fashion Week as an Avatar." *Teen Vogue*, August 28, 2020.

Bateman, Kristen. "The Fashion Metaverse is Here. Are You Read?" *Town and Country*, February 28, 2022, https://www.townandcountrymag.com/style/fashion-trends/a39177878/metaverse-fashion-revolution/.

Baudinette, Thomas. "Japanese Gay Men's Attitudes Towards 'Gay Manga' and the Problem of Genre." *East Asian Journal of Popular Culture* 3, no. 1 (2017): 59–72.

Benjamin, Walter. "The Work of Art in the Age of Mechanical Reproduction." In *Commerce and Culture: From Pre-Industrial Art to Post-Industrial Value*, 34–40. London: Penshurst Press Limited, 1989.

Bergkvist, Lars, Hanna Hjalmarson, and Anne Magi. "A New Model of How Celebrity Endorsements Work: Attitude Toward the Endorsement as a Mediator of Celebrity Source and Endorsement Effects." *International Journal of Advertising* 35, no. 2 (2016): 171–84.

Bergkvist, Lars and Kris Qiang Zhou. "Celebrity Endorsements: A Literature Review and Research Agenda." *International Journal of Advertising* 35, no. 4 (2016): 642–63.

Bergstrom, Mary. *All Eyes East: Lessons from the Front Lines of Marketing to China's Youth*. Basingstoke: Palgrave Macmillan, 2012.

Berry, Sara. "Be Our Brand: Fashion and Personalisation on the Web," In Stella Bruzzi and Pamela Church Gibson. *Fashion Cultures: Theories, Explorations and Analysis*. London: Routledge, 2000.

Binet, Les, and Peter Field. "Marketing in the Era of Accountability." *Journal of Direct, Data and Digital Marketing Practice* 9, no. 2 (2007): 225–8.

Black, Daniel. "Digital Bodies and Disembodied Voices: Virtual Idols and the Virtualised Body." *Fiberculture Journal* 54, no. 9, https://nine.fibreculturejournal.org/fcj-054-digital-bodies-and-disembodied-voices-virtual-idols-and-the-virtualised-body/.

Black, Daniel. "The Virtual Idol: Producing and Consuming Digital Femininity." In Patrick W. Galbraith and Jason G. Karlin, eds., *Idols and Celebrity in Japanese Media Culture*, 209–28, Basingstoke: Palgrave Macmillan, 2012.

Blackston, Max. "Beyond Brand Personality: Building Brand Relationships." In David Allen Aaker and Alexander L. Biel, eds., *Brand Equity and Advertising: Advertising's Role in Building Strong Brands*, 113–24. Hillsdale, NJ: Laurence Erlbaum Associates, 1993.

Blader, Steven L. and Ya-Ru Chen. "What's in a Name? Status, Power, and Other Forms of Social Hierarchy." In Joey T. Cheng, Jessica L. Tracy, and Cameron Anderson, eds., *The Psychology of Social Status*, 71–95. New York: Springer, 2014.

Blum, Susan Debra. "Naming Practices and the Power of Words in China." *Language in Society* 26, no. 3 (1997): 357–79.

Boellstorff, Tom. *Coming of Age in Second Life*. Princeton, NJ: Princeton University Press, 2008.

Booker, Avery. "China's 'Lying Flat' Trend Meets its New Champion: The Free Idler." *Jing Daily*, March 4, 2022, https://jingdaily.com/chinas-lying-flat-trend-meets-its-new-champion-the-free-idler/.

Boonpradub, Whachiraporn and Pusanisa Thechatakerng. "Brand Endorsement by Celebrity in Thailand: 7Ps of Marketing Mix and the Impact of Brand Alliance." *International Journal of Trade, Economics and Finance* 6, no. 1 (February 2015).

Boyd, Raymond and Richard Fardon. "Naming Powers: Hausa Tsafi and Tiv Tsav." *Journal of African Cultural Studies* 26, no. 1 (2014): 33–55.

Brengman, Malaika and Kim Willems. "Determining Fashion Store Personality Dimensions: An Exploratory Study Based on Repertory Grid Data and Grounded Theory." *European Institute of Retailing and Services Studies* 15 (2008).

Burke, Peter and Roy Porter. *The Social History of Language*. Cambridge: Cambridge University Press, 1987.

Calvert, Clay. *Voyeur Nation: Media, Privacy, and Peeping in Modern Culture*. Boulder, CO: Westview Press, 2000.

Canaves, Sky. "Beauty Brands Face China's 'Cancel Culture.'" *Content Commerce Insider*, March 2020, https://contentcommerceinsider.com/blog/beauty-brands-face-chinas-cancel-culture.

Caplan, Ben. "Millian Descriptivism." *Philosophical Studies* 133 (2007): 181–98, https://doi.org/10.1007/s11098-005-4544-y.

Carroll, Angela. "Brand Communications in Fashion Categories Using Celebrity Endorsement." *Journal of Brand Management* 17 (October–November 2009): 146–58.

Cénac, Laetitia. *Chanel: The Making of a Collection*. New York: Abrams, 2019.

Cheang, Justina. "Choice of Foreign Names as a Strategy for Identity Management." *Intercultural Communication Studies* 17, no. 2 (2008): 197–202.

Chen, Laurie. "The real power behind China's new trend of 'sissy men' . . . is the empowered modern woman." *South China Morning Post*, September 19, 2018, https://www.scmp.com/news/china/society/article/2163748/real-power-behind-chinas-new-trend-sissy-men-empowered-modern.

Chen, Lu. *Chinese Fans of Japanese and Korean Pop Culture: Nationalistic Narratives and International Fandom*. Routledge, Taylor & Francis Group, 2018.

Chen, Xi. "Hashtag Lay Zhang's agency recruits third gender trainees trends on Chinese social media." *Global Times*, March 16, 2021, https://www.globaltimes.cn/page/202103/1218521.shtml.

Chen, Xi. "Kris Wu May Be Sentenced to 10 Years to Life Imprisonment: Lawyer." *Global Times*, August 1, 2021, https://www.globaltimes.cn/page/202108/1230189.shtml.

Choe Sang-Hun and S-Hyun Lee. "Suicides by K-Pop Stars Prompt Soul-Searching in South Korea." *New York Times*, November 25, 2019.

Choi, Haejin, Sarah White, and Sam Nussey. "In Asia, nascent men's make-up market starts drawing big brands." Reuters.com, December 18, 2019, https://www.reuters.com/article/us-cosmetics-men-idUSKBN1OI20Y

Choi, Sejung Marina and Nora J. Rifon. "Who is the Celebrity in Advertising? Understanding Dimensions of Celebrity Images." *The Journal of Popular Culture* 40, no. 2 (2007): 304–24.

Choi, Sejung Marina and Nora J. Rifon. "It is a Match: The Impact of Congruence Between Celebrity Image and Consumer Ideal Self on Endorsement Effectiveness." *Psychology and Marketing* 29 (September 2012): 639–50.

Cohn, Alison S. "Fashion Goes Fluid." *Harper's Bazaar*, November 2020.

Connell, Raewyn. *Gender and Power*. Stanford, CA: Stanford University Press, 1987.

Connell, Raewyn. "Masculinities and Globalisation." *Men and Masculinities* 1, no. 1 (1988): 3–23.

Connell, Raewyn. *Masculinities*. 2nd edition. Berkeley: University of California Press, 1995/2005.

Constantini, Giovanna. "Blue: The History of a Color by Michel Pastoureau (review)." *Leonardo*, January 30, 2021, muse.jhu.edu/article/781850.

Cook, Emma E. "Masculinity Studies in Japan". In Jennifer Coates, Lucy Fraser, and Mark Pendleton, eds., *The Routledge Companion to Gender and Japanese Culture*, 50–9. London: Routledge, 2019.

Cova, Bernard and Véronique Cova. "Tribal Marketing: The Tribalisation of Society and its Impact on the Conduct of Marketing." *European Journal of Marketing* 36, nos. 5–6 (2002): 595–620.

Creel, Herrlee Glessner. *Shen Pu-Hai: A Chinese Political Philosopher of the Fourth Century B.C.* Chicago: University of Chicago Press, 1974.

Croft, Janet Brennan. "Noms de Guerre: The Power of Naming in War and Conflict in Middle-earth." *Mythlore* 34, no. 1 (2015): 105–15.

Czujack, Corinna. "Picasso paintings at auction, 1963–1994." *Journal of Cultural Economics* 21, no. 3 (1997): 229–47.

Dadzie, O. E. and A. Petit, "Skin bleaching: Highlighting the misuse of cutaneous depigmenting agents." *Journal of the European Academy of Dermatology and Venereology*, June 3, 2009, https://onlinelibrary.wiley.com/doi/abs/10.1111/j.1468-3083.2009.03150.x.

Dasgupta, Romit. "Creating Corporate Warriors: The 'Salaryman' and Masculinity in Japan." In Kam Louie and Morris Low, eds., *Asian Masculinities: The Meaning and Practice of Manhood in China and Japan*, 118–34. London: Routledge, 2003.

Davidson, Helen. "Xinjiang: more than half a million forced to pick cotton, report suggests." *Guardian*, December 15, 2020, https://www.theguardian.com/world/2020/dec/15/xinjiang-china-more-than-half-a-million-forced-to-pick-cotton-report-finds.

Deacon, Roger. "Truth, Power and Pedagogy: Michel Foucault on the Rise of the Disciplines." *Educational Philosophy and Theory* 34, no. 4 (2002): 435–58.

Dela Cruz, Eunice. "These K-Pop Idols Are The Global and Korean Ambassadors of The Top 15 Luxury Brand Fashion Houses." *KpopStarz*, October 14, 2020, https://www.kpopstarz.com/articles/295224/20201014/these-k-pop-idols-are-the-global-and-korean-ambassadors-of-the-top-15-luxury-brand-fashion-houses.htm.

Denning, Andrew. *Skiing Into Modernity*. Berkeley: University of California Press, 2015.

Dépret, Eric F. and Susan Tufts Fiske. "Social Cognition and Power: Some Cognitive Consequences of Social Structure as a Source of Control Deprivation." In Gifford Weary, Faith Gleicher, and Kerry Marsh, eds., *Control Motivation and Social Cognition*, 176–202. New York: Springer, 1993.

Derrida, Jacques. "Of Grammatology." In Hazard Adams and Leroy Searle, eds., *Critical Theory Since 1965*. Tallahassee: University of Florida Press, 1986.

de Sostoa-McCue, Tania. "Rhetorics of Resistance: Reading Taboo in Fanfiction." Master's thesis, Michigan State University, 2007.

Dumont, Guillaume. "Creativity at Work: The Production of Work for Sale by Brand Ambassadors." *Journal of Cultural Economy* 11, no. 1 (2018): 69–82.

Dusenbury, Mary, ed. *Color in Ancient and Medieval East Asia*. Lawrence, KS: Spencer Museum of Art, University of Kansas and New Haven, CT: Yale University Press, 2015.

Eco, Umberto. *Postscript to The Name of the Rose*. New York: Harcourt, 1984.

Edkins, Jenny. "Missing Migrants and the Politics of Naming: Names Without Bodies, Bodies Without Names." *Social Research* 83, no. 2 (2016): 359–89.

Eklund, Zahna. "K-pop's LGBT star Holland: 10 facts about South Korea's first openly gay idol, born Go Tae-seob—from Neverland's R-rated music video to what his parents really think." October 16, 2020, https://www.scmp.com/magazines/style/celebrity/article/3105730/k-pops-lgbt-star-holland-10-facts-about-south-koreas.

Elfving-Hwang, Joanna. "K-pop idols, artificial beauty and affective fan relationships in South Korea." In *Routledge Handbook of Celebrity Studies*, 190–201. London: Routledge, 2018.

Elkins, James. *Pictures and Tears: A History of People Who Have Cried in Front of Paintings*. New York: Routledge, 2004.

Erdogan, Bayram Zafer. "Celebrity Endorsement: A Literature Review." *Journal of Marketing Management* 15, no. 4 (1999): 291–314.

Erdogan, Bayram Zafer, Michael James Baker, and Stephen Tagg. "Selecting Celebrity Endorsers: The Practitioner's Perspective." *Journal of Advertising Research* 3, no. 41 (2001): 39–48.

Erdogan, Bayram Zafer, Michael James Baker, and Stephen Tagg. "Selecting Celebrity Endorsers: The Practitioner's Perspective." *Journal of Advertising Research* 3, no. 41 (2001): 39–48.

Fast, Nathanael J., Nir Halevy, and Adam Daniel Galinsky. "The Destructive Nature of Power Without Status." *Journal of Experimental Social Psychology* 48, no. 1 (2012): 391–4.

Feng, Emily. "China Blocks Website After Complaints About Fan Fiction Story on a Celebrity." *NPR*, October 28, 2020, https://www.npr.org/2020/10/28/928805796/china-blocks-website-after-complaints-about-fan-fiction-story-on-a-celebrity.

Feng, Jin. "Addicted to Beauty: Consuming and Producing Web-Based Chinese Danmei Fiction at Jinjiang." *Modern Chinese Literature and Culture* 212 (2009): 1–41.

Fiske, Susan Tufts. "Interpersonal Stratification: Status, Power, and Subordination." In Susan Tufts Fiske, Daniel Todd Gilbert, and Gardner Lindzey, eds., *Handbook of Social Psychology*, 5th edn, 941–82. New York: Wiley, 2010.

Flood, Michael, ed. *International Encyclopedia of Men and Masculinities*. London: Routledge, 2007.

Foucault, Michel. *Power/knowledge: Selected Interviews and Other Writings 1972–1977*. Edited by Colin Gordon. New York: Pantheon, 1980.

Foucault, Michel. *The History of Sexuality: An Introduction*. Harmondsworth: Penguin, 1981.

Foucault, Michel. "The Subject and Power." *Critical Inquiry* 8, no. 4 (1982): 777–95.

Fournier, Susan. "The Brand-As-Relations-Hip-Partner: An Alternative View of Brand Personality." *Advances in Consumer Research* 22 (1995).

Frühstück, Sabine and Anne Walthall, eds. *Recreating Japanese Men*. Berkeley: University of California Press, 2011.

Galbraith, Patrick. "Moe: Exploring Virtual Potential in Post-Millennial Japan." *Electronic Journal of Contemporary Japanese Studies* (2009).

Galbraith, Patrick W. "Fujoshi: Fantasy Play and Transgressive Intimacy Among 'Rotten Girls' in Contemporary Japan." *Signs* 37 (2011): 219–240.

Galinsky, Adam Daniel, Deborah H. Gruenfeld, and Joe C. Magee. "From Power to Action." *Journal of Personality and Social Psychology* 85 (2003): 453–66.

Gardner, Burleigh Bradford and Sidney Jay Levy. "The Product and the Brand." *Harvard Business Review* 33, no. 2 (1955): 33–59.

Gayomali, Chris and Max Berlinger. "Bruno Mars Would Like You to Know: He's Had Sex." *GQ*, November 4, 2016.

Gelézeau, Valérie. "The Body, Cosmetics and Aesthetics in South Korea: The Emergence of a Field of Research." HAL SHS (2015), halshs-01211686.

Georgesen, John C. and Monica J. Harris. "The Balance of Power: Interpersonal Consequences of Differential Power and Expectancies." *Personality and Social Psychology Bulletin* 26 (2000): 1239–57.

Glasspool, Lucy. "From Boys Next Door to Boys' Love: Gender Performance in Japanese Male Idol Media." In Patrick W. Galbraith and Jason G. Karlin, eds., *Idols and Celebrity in Japanese Media Culture*, 113–30. London: Palgrave Macmillan, 2013.

Goldman Sachs. "Greater China Consumer Corporate Day Takeaways." June 2021. Reproduced on "[王一博] [分享]210615 世界顶级投行高盛研究报告谈及安踏被专业人士认可的王一博影响力." idol001.com, June 15, 2021, https://idol001.com/news/6821/detail/60c852e317f2509b3b8b4672/.

Goldsmith, Ronald E., Barbara A. Lafferty, and Stephen J. Newell. "The Impact of Corporate Credibility and Celebrity Credibility on Consumer Reaction to Advertisements and Brands." *Journal of Advertising* 29, no. 3 (2000): 43–54.

Groom, Gloria. "Spaces of Modernity." In Gloria Groom, ed., *Impressionism, Fashion and Modernity*. New Haven, CT: Yale University Press, 2012.

Gruenfeld, Deborah H., M. Ena Inesi, Joe C. Magee, and A. D. Galinsky. "Power and the Objectification of Social Targets." *Journal of Personality and Social Psychology* 95 (2008): 111–27.

Hall, Casey. "Toxic Fan Culture Puts Brands at Risk in China." *Business of Fashion*, March 12, 2020, https://www.businessoffashion.com/articles/intelligence/toxic-fan-culture-puts-brands-at-risk-in-china.

Hall, Casey. "China Exempts Almost All Imported Cosmetics From Animal Testing." *Business of Fashion*, March 5, 2021, https://www.businessoffashion.com/news/china/china-exempts-almost-all-imported-cosmetics-from-animal-testing.

Hall, Casey. "How China's New Love Affair with Perfume is Changing the Market." *Business of Fashion*, May 18, 2021, https://www.businessoffashion.com/briefings/china/how-chinas-new-love-affair-with-perfume-is-changing-the-market.

Hall, Casey. "How to Avoid Brand Ambassador Controversy in China." *Business of Fashion*, June 8, 2021, https://www.businessoffashion.com/briefings/china/how-to-avoid-brand-ambassador-controversy-in-china.

Halonen-Knight, Elina and Leila Hurmerinta. "Who Endorses Whom? Meaning Transfer in Celebrity Endorsement." *Journal of Product and Brand Management* 19, no. 6 (2010): 452–60.

Hardy, Alyssa, "Blackpink's Jennie and G-Dragon Wear the Same Chanel Jacket." *Teen Vogue*, June 27, 2017, https://www.teenvogue.com/story/blackpink-jennie-g-dragon-chanel-jacket?

Hayes-Brady, Clare. "'I Kept Saying Her Name:' Naming, Labels and Power in the Early Writing of David Foster Wallace." *Orbit: A Journal of American Literature* 5, no. 1 (2017): 1–26.

Heidegger, Martin. *Being and Time*, Oxford: Blackwell, 1962.

Hemmann, Kathryn. "Queering the Media Mix: The Female Gaze in Japanese Fan Comics." *Transformative Works and Cultures* 20 (2015).

Hemmings, F. W. J. *The Life and Times of Emile Zola*. New York: Charles Scriber and Sons, 1977.

Henry, Todd A. *Queer Korea*. Durham, NC: Duke University Press, 2020.

Hong, Hana. "9 Best Foundations for Asian Skin Tones." *Marie Claire*, February 5, 2020, https://www.marieclaire.com/beauty/g30627499/best-foundations-for-asian-skin/.

Horton, Donald and R. Richard Wohl. "Mass Communication and Para-Social Interaction: Observations on Intimacy at a Distance." *Psychiatry: Interpersonal and Biological Processes* 19, no. 3 (1956): 215–29.

Hultén, Bertil. "Sensory Marketing: The Multi-sensory Brand Experience Concept." *European Business Review* 23, no. 3 (2011): 256–73.

"Idols and Endorsements: the More, the Merrier?" *SeoulBeats*, August 8, 2012, https://seoulbeats.com/2012/08/idols-and-endorsements-the-more-the-merrier/.

Ilicic, Jasmina, and Marie Webster. "Celebrity Co-branding Partners as Irrelevant Brand Information in Advertisements." *Journal of Business Research* 66, no. 7 (2013): 941–7.

In Young Bae. "Chanel to Sell on KaKaoTalk." *Retail in Asia*, August 24, 2020, https://retailinasia.com/in-tech/chanel-to-sell-on-kakao-talk/

J, Anne. "Kris Wu Loses Brand Endorsements Following Du Meizhu's Latest Interview." *DramaPanda*, July 18, 2021, https://dramapanda.com/2021/07/kris-wu-loses-brand-endorsement-following-du-meizhus-latest-interview.html.

Jackson, Tim and David Shaw. *Mastering Fashion Marketing*. Basingstoke: Palgrave Macmillan, 2009.

Jelinek, Julia-Sophie. "Art as Strategic Branding Tool for Luxury Fashion Brands." *Journal of Product and Brand Management* 27, no. 3 (2018): 294–307.

Jin, Dal Yong and Lee Harkjoon. *K-Pop Idols: Popular Culture and the Emergence of the Korean Music Industry*. Lanham, MD: Lexington Books, 2019.

Johns, Brenton. "More Than 50 Chinese Celebrities End Brand Partnerships in Xinjiang Row." *Business of Fashion*, March 26, 2021, https://www.businessoffashion.com/news/china/more-than-50-chinese-celebrities-end-brand-partnerships-in-xinjiang-row?

Johnson, M. J. "A Brief History of Yaoi." *Sequential Tart* (2002), http://www.sequentialtart.com/archive/may02/ao_0502_4.shtml.

Jung, Minwoo and NaYoung Lee. "Fandom Managing Stars, Entertainment Industry Managing Fandom." *Media, Gender and Culture* 12 (2009): 191–240.

Kahle, Lynn R. and Pamela Miles Homer. "Physical Attractiveness of the Celebrity Endorser: A Social Adaptation Perspective." *Journal of Consumer Research* 11, no. 4 (1985): 954–61.

Kamm, Björn-Ole. "Rotten Use Patterns: What Entertainment Theories Can Do for the Study of Boys' Love." *Transformative Works and Cultures* 12 (2013).

Karniol, Rachel. "Adolescent Females' Idolization of Male Media Starts as a Transition Into Sexuality." *Sex Roles* 44, nos. 1–2 (2001): 61–77.

Kee, Tan Bee. "Rewriting Gender and Sexuality in English-language Yaoi Fandom." In A. Levi, Mark McHarry, and Dru Pagliassotti, eds., *Boys' Love Manga: Essays on the Sexual Ambiguity and Cross- cultural Fandom of the Genre*, 126–56. Jefferson, NY: McFarland, 2010.

Keltner, Dacher, Deborah Gruenfeld, and C. Anderson. "Power, Approach, and Inhibition." *Psychological Review* 110 (2003): 265–84.

Kim, Jaril, Woonghee Han, DongTae Kim, and Widya Paramita. "Is Beauty in the Eye of the Beholder? Gender and Beauty in the Cosmetics Sector." *Marketing Intelligence and Planning* 31, no. 2 (2013): 127–40.

Kim, S. "Spectacularization and Consumption of Girl Images." *Media, Gender and Culture* 15 (2010): 79–119.

Kim, Suk-Young. "Beauty and the Waste: Fashioning Idols and the Ethics of Recycling in Korean Pop Music Videos." *Fashion Theory* 25, no. 1 (2021): 53–73, DOI: 10.1080/1362704X.2019.1581001

Kim, Yeran. "Idol Republic: The Global Emergence of Girl Industries and the Commercialization of Girl Bodies." *Journal of Gender Studies* 20, no. 4 (2011): 333–45.

Kimmel, Michael S., Jeff Hearn, and Reawyn Connell, eds. *Handbook of Studies on Men and Masculinities*. Thousand Oaks, CA, London, and New Dehli: Sage, 2005.
Klohnen, E. C. and S. Luo. "Interpersonal Attraction and Personality: What is Attractive—Self Similarity, Ideal Similarity, Complementarity, or Attachment Security?" *Journal of Personality and Social Psychology* 85, no. 4 (2003): 709–22.
Korea Herald. ed. *Korean Wave*. Insight into Korea Series, vol. 5. Gyeonggi-do, Korea: Jimoondang, 2008.
Kornberger, Martin. *Brand Society: How Brands Transform Management and Lifestyle*. Cambridge: Cambridge University Press, 2010.
Kroeger, Alix. "Xinjiang cotton: How do I know if it's in my jeans?" BBC News, March 27, 2021, https://www.bbc.com/news/world-asia-china-56535822.
Kustritz, Anne. "Slashing the Romance Narrative." *Journal of American Culture* 26 (2003): 371–84.
Kwan, Kevin. *Crazy Rich Asians*. Crow's Nest, NSW, Australia: Allen & Unwin, 2014.
Lacan, Jacques. "The Agency of the Letter in the Unconscious, or Reason Since Freud." In Hazard Adams and Leroy Searle, eds., *Critical Theory Since 1965*. Tallahassee: University of Florida Press, 1986.
Lahti, Martti. "As We Become Machines: Corporealized Pleasures in Video Games." In Mark J. P. Wolf and Bernard Perron, eds., *The Video Game Theory Reader*. New York: Taylor & Frances, 2003.
Lakoff, George and Mark Johnson. *Metaphors We Live By*. Chicago and London: University of Chicago Press, 1980.
Langford, Celia R., "Queered Time on the Page: The Micro-level Revolution of the Bishōnen in 21st Century Yaoi Manga." Honors thesis submission in Asian and Middle Eastern Studies, Whitman College, 2019.
Law, Julienna. "Will Chongqing Become China's Next Big Luxury Hub?" *Jing Daily*, February 10, 2022, https://jingdaily.com/chongqing-international-brands-million-yuan/.
Lee, Dong-Yeun. "Who's afraid of Korean idols? Five keywords for understanding Korean idol pop." In *Made in Korea*, ch. 14. New York: Routledge, 2016.
Lee, Jung-Gyo and Esther Thorson. "The Impact of Celebrity-product Incongruence on the Effectiveness of Product Endorsement." *Journal of Advertising Research* 48 (September 2008): 433–49.
Lee, Sangjoon and Markus Nornes, eds. *Hallyu 2.0: The Korean Wave in the Age of Social Media*. Ann Arbor: University of Michigan Press, 2015.
Lee, Stephan. *K-Pop Confidential*. New York: Point, an Imprint of Scholastic, Inc., 2020.
Levi, A. "North American Reactions to Yaoi." In Mark I. West, ed., *The Japanification of Children's Popular Culture: From Godzilla to Miyazaki*, 147–74. Lanham, MD: Scarecrow Press, 2009.
Lew, Linda. "China presses global fashion brands to reverse Xinjiang cotton boycott." *South China Morning Post*, March 25, 2021, https://www.scmp.com/news/china/diplomacy/article/3126904/backlash-china-against-nike-adidas-and-other-global-brands.

Li, Alice. "China Men's Facial Skincare Market has Started Its Transformation." MINTEL Blog, 2020, https://www.mintel.com/blog/beauty-market-news/china-mens-facial-skincare-market-has-started-its-transformation.

Li, Xiaomeng. "How powerful is the female gaze? The implication of using male celebrities for promoting female cosmetics in China." *Global Media and China* 5, no. 1 (2020): 55–68.

Liao, Sara. *Fashioning China: Precarious Creativity and Women Designers in Shanzhai Culture*. London: Pluto Press, 2020.

Liu, Matthew Tingchi and James L. Brock. "Selecting a Female Athlete Endorser in China: The Effect of Attractiveness, Match-up, and Consumer Gender Difference." *European Journal of Marketing* 45, no. 7–8 (2011): 1214–35.

Liu, Peng. "Walking in the Forbidden City: Embodied Encounters in Narrative Geography." *Visual Studies* 33, no. 2 (2018): 144–60.

Liu, Peng. "Body in the Forbidden City: embodied sensibilities and lived experience in the affective architecture." In Jacque Micieli-Voutsinas and Angela M. Person, eds., *Affective Architectures: More-than-representational Approaches to Heritage*, 120–39. London and New York: Routledge, 2020.

Liu, Peng, and Lan Lan. "Constructing an Affective Retail Space: Bodily Engagement with a Luxury Fashion Brand Through Spatial and Heritage Storytelling." In Amanda Grace Sikarskie, ed., *Storytelling in Luxury Fashion Marketing: Visual Culture and Digital Technology*, 157–73. New York and London: Routledge, 2020.

Liu, Peng, and Lan Lan. "Museum as Multisensorial Site: Story Co-making and the Affective Interrelationship Between Museum Visitors, Heritage Space, and Digital Storytelling." *Museum Management and Curatorship* 36, no. 4 (2021): 403–26.

Liu, Ting. "Conflicting Discourses on Boys' Love and Subcultural Tactics in Mainland China and Hong Kong." *Intersections: Gender and Sexuality in Asia and the Pacific* 20 (2009), http://intersections.anu.edu.au/issue20/liu.htm.

Louie, Kam H. "Popular Culture and Masculinity Ideals in East Asia, with Special Reference to China." *Journal of Asian Studies* 71, no. 4 (2012): 929–43.

Lueck, Jennifer Anette. "Friend-zone with Benefits: The Parasocial Advertising of Kim Kardashian." *Journal of Marketing Communications* 21 no. 2 (2015): 91–109.

Lunsing, Wim. *Beyond Common Sense: Sexuality and Gender in Contemporary Japan*. London: Kegan Paul, 2001.

Lunsing, Wim. "Yaoi Ronso: Discussing Depictions of Male Homosexuality in Japanese Girl's Comics, Gay Comics and Gay Pornography." *Intersections: Gender, History and Culture in the Asian Context* 12 (2006).

Luo, Jiaqi. "The Dark Side of China's Idol Economies." *Jing Daily*, March 6, 2020, https://jingdaily.com/the-dark-side-of-chinas-idol-economies/.

Lury, Celia. *Brands: The Logos of the Global Economy*. London: Routledge, 2004.

Mackintosh, Jonathan D. "Itō Bungaku and the Solidarity of the Rose Tribes [Barazoku]: Stirrings of Homo Solidarity in Early 1970s Japan." *Intersections: Gender, History and Culture in the Asian Context* 12 (2006).

Madill, Anna. "The Yaoi/Boys' Love/Danmei Audience." In Karen Ross and Valentina Cardo, eds., *Encyclopaedia of Gender, Media and Communication*. City: Wiley-Blackwells, 2020.

Madill, Anna, and Yao Zhao. "Engagement with Female-oriented Male–Male Incest Erotica: A Comparison of Sinophone and Anglophone Boys' Love Fandom." *Deviant Behavior* (2021), https://doi.org/10.1080/01639625.2021.1891845.

Magee, Joe C. and A. Galinsky. "Social Hierarchy: The Self-reinforcing Nature of Power and Status." *Academy of Management Annals* 2 (2008): 351–98.

Mannheim, Bruce and Dennis Tedlock. "Introduction." In Dennis Tedlock and Bruce Mannheim, eds., *The Dialogic Emergence of Culture*, 1–32. Urbana: University of Illinois Press, 1995.

Manietta, Joseph Bazil. "Transnational Masculinities: The Distributive Performativity of Gender in Korean Boy Bands." Master's thesis, University of Colorado, 2015.

Mars, Bruno. "Versace on the Floor." 2016 (song).

Martin, Fran. "Girls Who Love Boy's Love: Japanese Homoerotic Manga as Trans-national Taiwan Culture." *Inter-Asia Cultural Studies* 13, no. 3 (2012): 365–83.

McCracken, Grant. "Culture and Consumption: A Theoretical Account of the Structure and Movement of Cultural Meaning of Consumer Goods." *Journal of Consumer Research* 13, no. 1 (1986): 71–84.

McCracken, Grant. "Who is the Celebrity Endorser? Cultural Foundations of the Endorsement Process." *Journal of Consumer Research* 16, no. 3 (1989): 310–21.

McCurry, Justin. "Spycams, sex abuse and scandal: #MeToo reaches Korean pop." *Guardian*, March 22, 2019.

McLelland, Mark. *Male Homosexuality in Modern Japan: Cultural Myths and Social Realities*. Abingdon: Routledge Curzon, 2000.

McLelland, Mark. "No Climax, No Point, No Meaning? Japanese Women's Boy Love Sites on the Internet." *Journal of Communication Inquiry* 24, no. 3 (2000): 274–91.

McLelland, Mark. "The World of Yaoi: The Internet, Censorship and the Global 'Boys' Love' Fandom." *Australian Feminist Law Journal* 23 (2005): 61–77.

McLelland, Mark. "Why are Japanese Comics Full of Boys Bonking?" *Refractory: A Journal of Entertainment Media* 10 (2006–2007).

McLelland, Mark. "Thought Policing or the Protection of Youth? Debate in Japan over the 'Non-Existent Youth Bill.'" *International Journal of Comic Art* 13, no. 1 (2011): 348–67.

McNeil, Peter and Giorgio Riello, *Luxury: A Rich History*, Oxford: Oxford University Press, 2016.

Messerschmidt, James W. "Engendering Gendered Knowledge: Assessing the Academic Appropriation of Hegemonic Masculinity." *Men and Masculinities* 15, no. 1 (2012): 56–76.

Metzl, Jonathan Michel. "Voyeur Nation? Changing Definitions of Voyeurism, 1950–2004." *Harvard Review Psychiatry* 12 (2004): 127–31.

Meyer, Uli. "Hidden in Straight Sight: Transgressing Gender and Sexuality Via BL." In A. Levi, Mark McHarry, and Dru Pagliassotti, eds., *Boys' Love Manga: Essays on the Sexual Ambiguity and Cross-cultural Fandom of the Genre*, 232–63. Jefferson, NY: McFarland, 2010.

Miles, Elizabeth. "Porn as Practice, Porn as Access: Pornography Consumption and a 'Third Sexual Orientation' in Japan." *Porn Studies* 7, no. 3 (2020): 269–78, https://doi.org/10.1080/23268743.2020.1726205.

Miller, Laura and Carolyn S. Stevens. "From Beautiful to Cute: Shifting Meanings in Japanese Language and Culture." *International Journal of Language and Culture* 8, no. 1 (2021): 62–83.

Mizoguchi, Akiko. "Male–male Romance by and for Women in Japan: A History and the Subgenres of Yaoi Fictions." *U.S.–Japan Women's Journal* 25 (2003): 49–75.

Mizoguchi, Akiko. "Theorizing Comics/Manga Genre as a Productive Forum: Yaoi and Beyond." In Jaqueline Berndt, ed., *Global Manga Studies*, 143–68. *Comics Worlds and the World of Comics: Towards Scholarship on a Global Scale*. Kyoto: International Manga Research Center, 2010.

Moore, Gwyneth. *Fashion Promotion*. 2nd edition. London: Bloomsbury, 2021.

Morin, Natalie. "K-Pop 101: The Terms You Need to Know Before You Stan," *Refinery 29*, June 28, 2019, https://www.refinery29.com/en-us/k-pop-music-fans-terms-meaning.

Nagaike, Kazumi. "Perverse Sexualities, Perversive Desires: Representations of Female Fantasies and Yaoi Manga as Pornography Directed at Women." *U.S.–Japan Women's Journal* 25 (2003): 76–103.

Nagaike, Kazumi. "Do Heterosexual Men Dream of Homosexual Men? BL *Fudanshi* and Discourse on Male Feminization." In Mark McLelland, Kazumi Nagaike, Katsuhiko Suganuma, and James Welker, eds., *Boys Love Manga and Beyond: History, Culture, and Community in Japan*, 189–209. Jackson: University Press of Mississippi, 2015.

Nan, Lisa. "How Brands Can Monetize Male Beauty in China." *Jing Daily*, 2021, https://jingdaily.com/local-male-skincare-brands-china-shakeup/.

Ng, Eve and Xiaomeng Li. "A Queer 'Socialist Brotherhood': The Guardian Web Series, Boys' Love Fandom, and the Chinese State." *Feminist Media Studies* 20, no. 4 (2020): 479–95.

Nietzsche, Friedrich Wilhelm. *Twilight of the Idols*. Edited by Oscar Levy. London: Allen & Unwin, 1912, 17, 88.

"Nike Statement on Xinjiang." *Nike Purpose*, https://purpose.nike.com/statement-on-xinjiang.

Pagliassotti, Dru. "Reading Boys' Love in the West." *Participations* 5, no. 2 (2008).

Pagliassotti, Dru. "Better than Romance? Japanese BL Manga and the Subgenre of Male/Male Romantic Fiction." In A. Levi, Mark McHarry, and Dru Pagliassotti, eds., *Boys' Love Manga: Essays on the Sexual Ambiguity and Cross-cultural Fandom of the Genre*, 59–83. Jefferson, NY: McFarland, 2010.

Pagliassotti, Dru, Kazumi Nagaike, and Mark McHarry. "Editorial: Boys' Love Manga Special Section." *Journal of Graphic Novels and Comics* 4, no. 1 (2013): 1–8.

Park, Juha and Jaehoon Chun. "How does watching YouTube fashion content impact perception of appearance: a phenomenological study of Korean women in Generation Z." *Humanities and Social Sciences Communications* 7, no. 1 (2020): 1–10.

Park, Juwon. "Chinese Pop Stars Publicly Back Beijing on Hong Kong." CBC News, August 19, 2019, https://www.cbc.ca/news/entertainment/chinese-stars-hk-protests-1.5252048.

Park, Seong-Yeon and Eun Mi Lee. "Congruence Between Brand Personality and Self-Image, and the Mediating Roles of Satisfaction and Consumer-Brand Relationship on Brand Loyalty." In Yong-Uon Ha and Youjae Yi, eds, *AP—Asia Pacific Advances in Consumer Research* 6, 39–45. Duluth: Association for Consumer Research, 2005.

Pastoureau, Michel. *Blue: The History of a Color*. Princeton, NJ: Princeton University Press, 2001.

Pflugfelder, Gregory M. *Cartographies of Desire: Male–Male Sexuality in Japanese Discourse, 1600–1950*. Oakland: University of California Press, 2007.

Proctor, Tony and Philip J. Kitchen. "Celebrity Ambassador/celebrity Endorsement—Takes a Licking but Keeps on Ticking." *Journal of Strategic Marketing* 27, no. 5 (2019): 373–87.

Rain Johnson, Celeste. "Enemy Officer Defeated: The Dynasty Warriors Series within the Spheres of Three Kingdoms and Videogames." Masters' thesis, University of Virginia, 2020.

Reuters staff. "China Boycotts Actor After Photos of Visit to Japan's Yasukuni Shrine." Reuters.com, August 15, 2021, https://www.reuters.com/world/china/china-boycotts-actor-after-photos-visit-japans-yasukuni-shrine-2021-08-15/.

Rice, Dan Hamilton, Katie Kelting, and Richard J. Lutz. "Multiple Endorsers and Multiple Endorsements: The Influence of Message Repetition, Source Congruence and Involvement on Brand Attitudes." *Journal of Consumer Psychology* 22, no. 2 (2011): 249–59.

Russo, Gianlucca. "K-Pop Star G-Dragon to Release Second 'Para-noise' Nike Air Force 1." *MSN*, November 6, 2020, https://www.msn.com/en-us/lifestyle/lifestyle-buzz/k-pop-star-g-dragon-to-release-second-%E2%80%9Cpara-noise%E2%80%9D-nike-air-force-1/ar-BB1aLBCj.

Sanchez, Daniel. "China Bans All Korean Music and Entertainment." *Digital Music News*, November 29, 2016, https://www.digitalmusicnews.com/2016/11/29/china-bans-korean-hallyu-kpop/.

Santos, Kristine Michelle L. "The Bitches of Boys Love Comics: The Pornographic Response of Japan's Rotten Women." *Porn Studies* 7, no. 3 (2020): 279–90, https://doi.org/10.1080/23268743.2020.1726204.

Sarkar, Ishani. "6 Idols who are the descendants of the Royal Yangban clans from the Joseon Dynasty." *Pink Villa*, December 3, 2020, https://www.pinkvilla.com/entertainment/6-idols-who-are-descendants-royal-yangban-clans-joseon-dynasty-579114.

Schmitt, Bernd Herbert. "Experiential Marketing." *Journal of Marketing Management* 15, nos. 1–3 (1999): 53–67.

Seno, Diana and Bryan A. Lukas. "The Equity Effect of Product Endorsement by Celebrities: A Conceptual Framework from a Co-branding Perspective." *European Journal of Marketing* 41, nos. 1–2 (2007): 121–34.

Sercombe, Peter, Tony Young, Ming Dong, and Lin Lin. "The Adoption of Non-heritage Names Among Chinese Mainlanders." *Names: A Journal of Onomastics* 62, no. 2 (2014): 65–75.

She, Chase. "Wang Yibo and Tan Songyun Cut Ties with Nike, Chinese Celebs Show Support for Xinjiang Cotton as More Brands Face Backlash." *DramaPanda*, March 25, 2021, https://dramapanda.com/2021/03/wang-yibo-and-tan-songyun-cut-ties-with-nike-chinese-celebs-show-support-for-xinjiang-cotton-as-more-brands-face-backlash.html.

"SHINee singer Jonghyun's final message before suicide: 'the depression finally engulfed me entirely.'" *South China Morning Post*, December 19, 2017, https://www.scmp.com/news/asia/east-asia/article/2124871/shinee-singer-jonghyuns-final-message-suicide-becoming-famous.

Sikarskie, Amanda. "Idols as Brand Ambassadors in China: The Rise and Fall and Rise of Xiao Zhan: Crisis Management at Estée Lauder and Olay." In *Bloomsbury Fashion Business Cases*. London: Bloomsbury, 2022.

Silvera, David H., and Benedikte Austad. "Factors Predicting the Effectiveness of Celebrity Endorsement Advertisements." *European Journal of Marketing* 38, no. 11/12 (2004): 1509–1526.

Singh, Ramendra Pratap and Neelotpaul Banerjee, "Exploring the Influence of Celebrity Worship on Brand Attitude, Advertisement Attitude, and Purchase Intention." *Journal of Promotion Management* 25, no. 2 (2019): 225–51, DOI: 10.1080/10496491.2018.1443311.

Skinner, Katie. "Big Bang's Taeyang Teases Photos Of New Fendi Collection (Ready To Spend $9K?)" *Billboard*, June 22, 2017, https://www.billboard.com/articles/news/lifestyle/7841808/big-bangs-taeyang-teases-photos-of-new-fendi-collection-ready-to.

Smilansky, Shaz. *Experiential Marketing: A Practical Guide to Interactive Brand Experiences*. Philadelphia: Kogan Page, 2009.

Socha, Miles. "Lessons from Fendi's Fashion Show on the Great Wall of China." *WWD*, September 24, 2020.

Solano, Steffi. "K-R&B Artist WOODZ Opens Up About Mental Health and Developing His Identity As a Soloist." *Status Magazine*, March 27, 2019.

Sontag, Susan. *On Photography*. New York: Farrar, Straus and Giroux, 1977.

Staff. "Over 50 Chinese stars show support for Xinjiang cotton products as H&M finds itself mired in controversy." *Global Times*, March 25, 2021, https://www.globaltimes.cn/page/202103/1219474.shtml.

Standaert, Michael. "Nike and H&M face backlash in China over Xinjiang statements: Chinese social media condemns statements by the companies as celebrities cancel contracts with brands." *Guardian*, March 25, 2021, https://www.theguardian.com/world/2021/mar/25/nike-and-hm-face-backlash-in-china-over-xinjiang-statements.

Suen, Zoe. "Luxury's Bigger-Than-Ever K-Drama Opportunity." *The Business of Fashion*, January 21, 2021, https://www.businessoffashion.com/articles/global-markets/luxurys-bigger-than-ever-k-drama-opportunity.

Suen, Zoe. "Where Global Brands Are Moving Their Asia-Pacific Headquarters." *Business of Fashion*, May 11, 2021, https://www.businessoffashion.com/briefings/china/why-are-brands-moving-their-asia-headquarters.

Suen, Zoe. "Why Chinese Brands Say Yes to the Dress." *Business of Fashion*, July 13, 2021, https://www.businessoffashion.com/briefings/china/why-chinese-brides-say-yes-to-the-dress.

Sung, Youngjun and Jooyoung Kim. "Effects of Brand Personality on Brand Trust and Brand Affect." *Psychology and Marketing* 27, no. 7 (2010): 639–61.

Suzuki, K. "What Can We Learn from Japanese Professional BL Writers?: A Sociological Analysis of Yaoi/BL Terminology and Classifications." In Mark McLelland, Kazumi Nagaike, Katsuhiko Suganuma, and James Welker, eds., *Boys Love Manga and Beyond: History, Culture, and Community in Japan*, 93–118. Jackson: University Press of Mississippi, 2015.

Sweeney, Jillian C. and Carol Brandon. "Brand Personality: Exploring the Potential to Move from Factor Analytical to Circumplex Models." *Psychology and Marketing* 23, no. 8 (2006): 639–63.

Tamaki, Saito. *Hikikomori: Adolescence Without End*. Translated by Jeffrey Angles. Minneapolis: University of Minnesota Press, 2013.

Teixeira, Lauren. "K-Pop's Big China Problem." Foreignpolicy.com, July 30, 2019, https://foreignpolicy.com/2019/07/30/k-pops-big-china-problem/.

Tétart-Vittu, Françoise. "Shops Versus Department Stores." In Gloria Groom, ed., *Impressionism, Fashion and Modernity*. New Haven, CT: Yale University Press, 2012.

Tétart-Vittu, Françoise. "Who Creates Fashion?" In Gloria Groom, ed., *Impressionism, Fashion and Modernity*. New Haven, CT: Yale University Press, 2012.

TFL. "Louis Vuitton is Betting Big on the Korean Market and the Global Fame of K-Pop Royalty BTS." *The Fashion Law*, April 23, 2021, https://www.thefashionlaw.com/louis-vuitton-is-betting-big-on-the-korean-market-and-the-global-fame-of-k-pop-royalty-bts/.

Thomas, Bronwen. "What is Fanfiction and Why are People Saying Such Nice Things About It?" *Storyworlds: A Journal of Narrative Studies* 3 (2011): 1–24.

Thomson, Matthew. "Human Brands: Investigating Antecedents to Consumers' Strong Attachments to Celebrities." *Journal of Marketing* 70, no. 3 (2006): 104–19.

Thorn, Rachel. "Girls And Women Getting Out Of Hand: The Pleasure And Politics Of Japan's Amateur Comics Community." In William W. Kelly, ed., *Fanning the Flames: Fans and Consumer Culture in Contemporary Japan*, 169–86. Albany: State University of New York Press, 2004.

Tortora, Phyllis and Keith Eubank. *Survey of Historic Costume*. 3rd edn. New York: Fairchild Publications, 1998.

Trestain, Eileen Jahnke. *Dating Fabrics: A Color Guide*. Paducah, KY: American Quilter's Society, 1998.

Tsiotsou, Rodoula. "Developing a Scale for Measuring the Personality of Sport Teams." *Journal of Services Marketing* 26, no. 4 (2012): 238–52.

Turner, Simon. "Interdisciplinary Approaches to Yaoi Manga: A Review." *Journal of Graphic Novels and Comics* 9, no. 5 (2018): 458–72.

Turra, Alessandra. "Giuseppe Zanotti, G-Dragon Collaborate on Footwear Capsule." *WWD*, September 3, 2015, https://wwd.com/fashion-news/fashion-scoops/giuseppe-zanotti-g-dragon-footwear-limited-edition-10210286/.

Ueno, Chizuko. 厭女：日本的女性嫌惡．翻譯：王嵐. 上海三聯書店, 2015. (*Mistry: Hate of Japanese Women*. Translated by Lan Wang. Shanghai: Shanghai SDX Joint Publishing Company).

Vänskä, Annamari. *Fashionable Childhood: Children in Advertising*. Translated by Eva Malkki. London: Bloomsbury Academic, 2017.

Velthuis, Olav. "Damien's Dangerous Idea: Valuing Contemporary Art at Auction." In Jens Beckert and Patrick Aspers, eds., *The Worth of Goods: Valuation and Pricing in the Economy*. Oxford: Oxford University Press, 2011.

Walker, Mary, Lynn Langmeyer and Daniel Langmeyer. "Celebrity Endorsers: Do You Get What You Pay For?" *Journal of Services Marketing* 6, no. 4 (1992): 35–42.

Wang, Hao and Mingfa Yao. "The Discursive Construction of English Naming Practice in Mainland China: A Nationalism and Authenticity Perspective." *English Today* 34, no. 2 (2018): 39–45.

Wang, Jingxin, "The Future of Fashion Magazines in China: From Print to Douyin," Master's thesis defense, Parsons Paris, May 12, 2021.

Wang, Peggy. "19 Awesome Eye Makeup Ideas for Asians." *Buzzfeed*, August 15, 2013, https://www.buzzfeed.com/peggy/awesome-makeup-ideas-for-asian-eyes.

Wang-Ngai, Siu. *Chinese Opera: The Actor's Craft*. Hong Kong: Hong Kong University Press, 2014.

Wei, John. "Queer Encounters Between Iron Man and Chinese Boys' Love Fandom." *Transformative Works and Cultures* 17 (2014).

Weiss, Zachary. "The Non-Profit Cotton Company Used by Gucci, Prada and Dior." *Observer*, July 13, 2016, https://observer.com/2016/07/the-non-profit-cotton-company-used-by-gucci-prada-and-dior/.

Welker, James. "Beautiful, Borrowed, and Bent: 'Boys' Love' as Girls' Love in Shôjo Manga." *Signs: Journal of Women in Culture and Society* 31, no. 3 (2006): 841–70.

Welker, James. "Lilies of the Margin: Beautiful Boys and Queer Female Identities in Japan." In Fran Martin, Peter A. Jackson, Mark McLelland, and Audrey Yue, eds., *AsiapacifiQUEER: Rethinking Genders and Sexualities*, 46–66. Chicago: University of Illinois Press, 2008.

Welker, James. "A Brief History of Shōnen'ai, Yaoi, and Boys Love." In Mark McLelland, Kazumi Nagaike, Katsuhiko Suganuma, and James Welker, eds., *Boys Love Manga and Beyond: History, Culture, and Community in Japan*, 42–75. Jackson: University Press of Mississippi, 2015.

Winterich, Karen Page, Manish Gangwar, and Rajdeep Grewal. "When Celebrities Count: Power Distance Beliefs and Celebrity Endorsements." *Journal of Marketing* 82 (2018): 70–86.

Wintour, Patrick. "US and Canada follow EU and UK in sanctioning Chinese officials over Xinjiang." *Guardian*, March 22, 2021, https://www.theguardian.com/world/2021/mar/22/china-responds-to-eu-uk-sanctions-over-uighurs-human-rights.

Wong, Alvin K. "Towards a Queer Affective Economy of Boys' Love in Contemporary Chinese Media." *Continuum* 34, no. 4 (2020): 500–13.

Wood, Andrea. "'Straight' Women, Queer Texts: Boy-Love Manga and the Rise of a Global Counterpublic," *Women's Studies Quarterly* 34, nos. 1–2 (2006): 394–414.

Wood, Andrea. "Boy's Love anime and queer desires in convergence culture: transnational fandom, censorship and resistance." *Journal of Graphic Novels and Comics* 4, no. 1 (2013): 44–63.

Wu, JuanJuan. *Chinese Fashion from Mao to Now*. New York: Berg, 2009.

Wu, Wenzhuo. "Is Celebrity Endorsement Enough For Brands To Elevate Their China Approach?" *Jing Daily*, October 23, 2020, https://jingdaily.com/celebrity-endorsement-brands-china-approach-wang-yibo/.

"Xinjiang Cotton Boycott Issue: Celebrities Busy Terminating Endorsement Contracts, Li Ning and Xiao Zhan's Collaboration Steals The Show." *Sip of Tea*, March 30, 2021, https://sipoftea.net/2021/03/30/xinjiang-cotton-boycott-issue-celebrities-are-busy-terminating-endorsement-contracts-li-ning-and-xiao-zhans-collaboration-steals-the-show/.

Xu, Kaibin and Yan Tan. "The Chinese Female Spectatorship: A Study of the Network Community of the 'Boys Love' Movie 'Call Me by Your Name.'" *Feminist Media Studies* 21, no. 1 (2019): 35–50, https://doi.org/10.1080/14680777.2019.1597752.

Xu, Yanrui and Ling Yang. "Forbidden Love: Incest, Generational Conflict, and the Erotics of Power in Chinese BL Fiction." *Journal of Graphic Novels and Comics* 4, no. 1 (2013): 30–43.

Xue, Faith. "Eye Makeup Tips for Asian Women." *Byrdie*, December 18, 2019, https://www.byrdie.com/makeup-tips-for-asian-women-346645.

Yann. "Cho Seung Youn is Out to Dominate the Modeling Industry as He Becomes the First Male Personality to Represent the Beauty Brand Cledbel!" *Hello Kpop*, March 13, 2020, https://www.hellokpop.com/news/cho-seung-youn-model-beauty-brand-cledbel/.

Yeung, Audrey. Qtd. in Hall, Amalissa. "Top 10: If you could swap lives with someone for a day, who would you choose and what would you do?" *South China Morning Post*, January 26, 2021, https://www.scmp.com/yp/discover/your-voice/article/3119309/top-10-if-you-could-swap-lives-someone-day-who-would-you.

Yi, David. *Pretty Boys*. Boston: Houghton Mifflin Harcourt, 2021.

Yi, Erika Junhui. "Reflection on Chinese Boys' Love Fans: An Insider's View." *Transformative Works and Culture* 12 (2013), http://dx.doi.org/10.3983/twc.2013.0424.

Yoon, Tae-Jin, and Dal Yong Jin, eds. *The Korean Wave: Evolution, Fandom, and Transnationality*. Lanham, MD: Lexington Books, 2017.

Zanghellini, Aleardo. "'Boys Love' in Anime and Manga: Japanese Subcultural Production and Its End Users." *Continuum: Journal of Media & Cultural Studies* 23, no. 3 (2009): 279–94.

Zanghellini, Aleardo. "Underage Sex and Romance in Japanese Homoerotic Manga and Anime." *Social and Legal Studies* 18 (2009): 159–77.

Zhang, Chunyu. "Loving Boys Twice as Much: Chinese Women's Paradoxical Fandom of 'Boy's Love' Fiction." *Women's Studies in Communication* 39, no. 3 (2016): 249–67.

Zhang, Tianwei and Tiffany Ap. "Xinjiang Cotton: Li Ning, Anta Shares Surge While Nike, Adidas, Burberry Hit With Backlash." *WWD*, March 25, 2021, https://wwd.com/business-news/retail/xinjiang-cotton-ban-china-nike-uniqlo-hm-1234787090/.

Zhao, Ma. "China's Last War." Talk given via Zoom at the Asian Studies Center, Michigan State University, March 18, 2021.

Zhou, Marrian. "When China's Massive Fan Economy Goes Wrong." *Nikkei Asia*, May 6, 2020, https://asia.nikkei.com/Business/Media-Entertainment/When-China-s-massive-fan-economy-goes-wrong.

Zhou, Shiliang, Zou Xinhui, Zhou Zhiqin, Liu Jing, Xu Chao, Yu Jing, Wang Qiang, Zhang Daming, Wang Xiaoquan, Ge Song, Sang Tao, Pan Kaiyu, and Hong Deyuan. "Multiple Species of Wild Tree Peonies Gave Rise to the 'King of Flowers,' Paeonia suffruticosa Andrews." *Proceedings of the Royal Society B*, Royal Society Publishing, 281 (1797): 2014.

Zsila, Agnes, Dru Pagliassotti, Robert Urban, Gabor Orosz, Orsolya Kiraly, and Zsolt Demetrovics. "Loving the Love of Boys: Motives for Consuming Yaoi Media." *PLoS One* 13, no. 6 (2018): e0198895, https://doi.org/10.1371/journal.pone.0198895.

Index

Note: Chinese and Korean names in this index appear in the traditional format "Family Name Given Name," without a comma.